Digital
Image
Restoration

PRENTICE-HALL SIGNAL PROCESSING SERIES

Alan V. Oppenheim, *Editor*

ANDREWS AND HUNT   *Digital Image Restoration*

BRIGHAM   *The Fast Fourier Transform*

OPPENHEIM AND SCHAFER   *Digital Signal Processing*

RABINER AND GOLD   *Theory and Application of Digital Signal Processing*

Digital
Image
Restoration

H. C. Andrews

*Departments of Electrical Engineering
and Computer Science
Image Processing Institute
University of Southern California*

B. R. Hunt

*Department of Systems Engineering
and Optical Sciences Center
University of Arizona*

PRENTICE-HALL, INC., Englewood Cliffs, New Jersey 07632

Library of Congress Cataloging in Publication Data

Andrews, Harry C (date)
　　Digital image restoration.

　　(Prentice-Hall signal processing series)
　　Bibliography: p.
　　Includes indexes.
　　1. Optical data processing.　2. Imaging systems.
I. Hunt, Bobby Ray (date), joint author.　II. Title.
TA1632.A5　　　001.6′443　　　76-25965
ISBN　0-13-214213-9

10　9　8　7　6　5　4　3　2

Printed in the United States of America

PRENTICE-HALL INTERNATIONAL, INC., *London*
PRENTICE-HALL OF AUSTRALIA PTY. LIMITED, *Sydney*
PRENTICE-HALL OF CANADA, LTD., *Toronto*
PRENTICE-HALL OF INDIA PRIVATE LIMITED, *New Delhi*
PRENTICE-HALL OF JAPAN, INC., *Tokyo*
PRENTICE-HALL OF SOUTHEAST ASIA PTE. LTD., *Singapore*
WHITEHALL BOOKS LIMITED, *Wellington, New Zealand*

To all those colleagues and friends who have encouraged my technical development and to my wife and mother who have encouraged my human development.

H.C.A.

To my parents, who gave me a desire for knowledge, and to my wife, who sustains me in that one thing which is more precious than knowledge.

B.R.H.

Contents

Part I
INTRODUCTION

Part II
DEGRADATIONS

Part III
RESTORATION

APPENDICES

Preface

How and why does a book come to be written? Every book represents a different chain of events. The chain of events behind the writing of this book tells much about the authors' motivation in writing it and what we hope the reader will benefit from in the reading of it.

This book really began in August of 1972, when one author (H.C.A.) spent three weeks at Los Alamos Scientific Laboratory as an invited scientist/consultant. There he met the other author (B.R.H.). During the course of the three weeks, two things happened: First, a friendship was struck; and, second, both individuals found themselves viewing the image restoration problem through very similar and (at that period) very unconventional eyes. At that time the image restoration problem was most commonly viewed as a problem in designing a linear restoration filter, for implementation by Fourier computation. Los Alamos Scientific Laboratory, with one of the most powerful computer centers in the world, tempted both authors to think of the image restoration problem in terms of linear algebra, a viewpoint that results in the mammoth calculations that computers such as those at Los Alamos are presumably suited to. Further, the problems of a specific radiographic image system at Los Alamos led to consideration of nonlinear problems in restoration. Nothing came of those three weeks but viewpoints; but the viewpoints served to guide much of the research of both authors during the next two years. One author (H.C.A.) began to exploit some of the concepts associated with linear algebra and generalized inverses; while the other author (B.R.H.) began to consider various nonlinear phenomena. Both authors began to make increasing use of relations between matrix theory formulation and the concept of eigenspace analysis. H.C.A. approached The Aerospace Corporation concerning the possibility of using their very fine computing facilities to experimentally verify some of these concepts. Since those early discussions in 1972–1973 with Aerospace management concerning this endeavor, a rich and valuable relationship has developed around the use of large digital computers for image restoration. It is sufficient to say that, without the facilities at Aerospace and Los Alamos, many aspects of this book would be sorely lacking if not completely absent.

By the summer of 1974 both authors had come far from the three weeks of 1972. The concepts that had been initiated in 1972 had been tested, refined, and strengthened. Although each looked at the problem from a specific frame of reference, there was a common ground into which the viewpoints could meet and be merged. The decision was made to attempt the construction of the common ground, and to write the book that the reader now holds.

In the sense of chronology, the latter chapters came first; this was the material developed in the individual research pursuits of both authors in the period from 1972 to the present. The material in these chapters, however, grew from a number of separate research projects. Further, a great flurry of activity in image restoration and enhancement resulted in many worthy techniques being published by other authors. Thus, the challenge became to relate the different efforts of *all* the workers in the field. To do so, the material in the earlier chapters was prepared. It is an attempt, the authors believe, for the first time to form a consistent set of models and concepts for the reader to use in surveying the methods of image restoration. In doing such, the authors found themselves posing a new framework for restoration—that of optimization theory— and then exploiting it in subsequent chapters. Of course, the optimization problem approach was already present—in least squares, minimum mean-square error, etc.— but the emphasis the authors gave it made the approach of intuitive appeal, given the basic ill-conditioned, nonunique properties of restoration. We hope, in addition, that the material in this book becomes part of the "working capital" of other workers as they tackle—from their own viewpoints—the image restoration problem.

Thus, we can see in this chronology the wish of the authors for the readers of this book:

1. To describe image formation and degradation processes in a realistic and meaningful way.
2. To relate image formation and degradation processes to specific concepts in linear algebra and matrix theory (e.g., linear operators, eigenspaces, fast transformation computations, etc.), given the motivation of digital computer implementation.
3. To give structure to the diversity of surveyed techniques by emphasizing the fundamental nature of optimization methods in developing a restoration scheme.
4. To provide a frame of reference in which new schemes may be compared and/or developed.

This book is, in a final sense, incomplete. New schemes for image restoration are being created continuously, and several have been noted by the authors in the space of time following assembly of the final manuscript. This is always the unfortunate truth in any field of active research; it is also what makes an active field of research so exciting intellectually. The authors will be satisfied if they have met, to the readers' satisfaction, the objectives listed above, and if they have also satisfied to some degree any other needs the reader had in mind when selecting this book. To that end we have strived.

The authors believe this book can be utilized by scientists and engineers actively working in image processing research and development and by graduate students and teachers in fields of electrical engineering, computer science, information processing, and optics. Much of the material has been successfully taught to graduate students at the University of Southern California, to students at the Los Alamos graduate center of the University of New Mexico, and to students in the intensive summer short courses at the University of Southern California. Except for the omission of teaching-type problems, the book is virtually a self-contained text; the inclusion of many references is particularly useful in graduate courses, in order to give the student an appreciation of the sources and workers to be found in the technical literature. This latter feature will also make it useful, we hope, to the worker active in the field, either experienced or just beginning a career in some form of image processing.

Both authors have the support and friendship of many individuals to acknowledge. Probably the individual most directly concerned with this book is Mr. Claude Patterson III, of The Aerospace Corporation, who so generously provided his motivation and time to read, reread, and rewrite the manuscript to a far higher level of intelligibility than its initial phases.

Of course, such a book would not have evolved without the encouragement and support of the authors' individual sponsors. H.C.A. wishes to thank the University of Southern California for providing both an intellectual environment and sabbatical leave for preparation of the manuscript. Particular thanks are due Professors Zorhab Kaprielian, Nasser Nahi, and William Pratt who, through their university offices as Vice-President, Department Chairman, and Image Processing Institute Director, respectively, have always encourage his endeavors. Funding for much of the research presented herein was provided by the Defense Advanced Research Projects Agency (ARPA) for which this author is heavily indebted and thankful. Considerable additional support, however, both in computer time and consulting contact, was furnished through The Aerospace Corporation, whose computer and image processing facility this author all too frequently took advantage of. The patience of Mr. Allan Boardman, Mr. John Schroeder, Mr. Claude Patterson III, and The Aerospace Corporation IR and D fee sponsor research funds are eternally acknowledged.

B.R.H. wishes to thank particularly D. H. Janney, R. K. Ziegler, and the staff and management of the Los Alamos Scientific Laboratory for their enduring support of this author's endeavors.

Finally, both authors wish to acknowledge the typing task that was distributed throughout the Electronic Sciences Laboratory technical typing pool at the University of Southern California. The precise and accurate results of their work is especially valued, and the final manuscript was expertly prepared by Mrs. Kristin Pendleton, without whose nimble fingers this manuscript would have remained a dream.

Abbreviations and Significant Notation

Abbreviations

CIE	a standard color coordinate system
CIR	color infrared (imagery)
CRT	cathode-ray tube
DFT	discrete Fourier transform
DOF	degrees of freedom
FFT	fast Fourier transform
H–D	Hurter–Driffield (curve)
MAP	maximum *a posteriori* (estimator)
ML	maximum likelihood (estimator)
MMSE	minimum mean-square error
MTF	modulation transfer function
NSIPSF	nonseparable space-invariant point-spread function
NSVPSF	nonseparable space-variant point-spread function
OTF	optical transfer function
PCM	pulse code modulation
PDF	probability density function
PSF	point-spread function
PSWF	prolate spheroidal wave functions
ROM	read only memory
SIPSF	space-invariant point-spread function
SNR	signal-to-noise ratio
SSIPSF	separable space-invariant point-spread function
SSVPSF	separable space-variant point-spread function
SVD	singular value decomposition
SVPSF	space-variant point-spread function
TV	television

Significant Notation

Chapter 2

$f(\xi, \eta)$	object energy distribution
(ξ, η)	coordinates of object plane
(x, y)	coordinates of image plane
$g(x, y)$	image energy distribution—also data available to the user for subsequent attempted restoration
$h(x, y, \xi, \eta, f(\xi, \eta))$	nonlinear point-spread function
$h(x, y, \xi, \eta)$	linear point-spread function
$h(x - \xi, y - \eta)$	space-invariant point-spread function
$h_1(x, \xi)h_2(y, \eta)$	separable point-spread function
$n(x, y)$	random noise field
$s\{\cdot\}$	a nonlinear memoryless operator usually modeling film or electronic response curves

Chapter 3

(w_x, w_y)	coordinates of two-dimensional spatial frequency plane
$G(w_x, w_y)$	Fourier representation of $g(x, y)$
$[G]$	sampled and quantized image in matrix representation
$[U], [V]$	unitary matrices used to transform a matrix to other linear domains (representations)
$\mathbf{u}_i, \mathbf{v}_i$	the ith column vectors of $[U]$ and $[V]$
N	the dimension or number of samples in either axis of an image
$[I]$	the identity matrix
$[\mathscr{F}]$	the Fourier matrix with entries $\exp\{2\pi i w_x x/N\}$
$[\Lambda]$	a diagonal matrix whose diagonal entries are usually eigenvalues
λ_i	the ith eigenvalue (often the singular value in a singular value decomposition)
$C([G])$	the condition number of a matrix, proportional to the ratio of the largest to the smallest eigenvalues
$[\phi_x], [\phi_y]$	covariance matrices associated with the x and y coordinates, respectively
$[C_x], [C_y]$	circulant matrix approximation to Toeplitz versions of $[\phi_x]$ and $[\phi_y]$; circulants are diagonalized by the Fourier matrix $[\mathscr{F}]$
$\otimes$	a Kronecker or direct matrix product operator
$\mathbf{g}$	stacked (lexicographic) vector form of the matrix $[G]$ representing the image or data available for restoration
$[\phi_g]$	the covariance matrix describing the second-order statistics of the signal $\mathbf{g}$

$\mathcal{E}\{\cdot\}$ the expectation operator, equivalent to integrating its argument over a probability density function

$[Q]$ linear operator usually designed to provide a constraint on the restored object

R rank of a matrix, i.e., the number of linearly independent rows (or columns of a matrix)

Chapter 4

f   the stacked vector form of the discrete version of the matrix $[F]$ representing the object

$\mathcal{R}$ correlation function of the PSF; its nonzero eigenvalues give an indication of the number of degrees of freedom in the imaging system

$[F]$ sampled version of the object (used in discrete–discrete models)

$[A], [B]^t$ vertical and horizontal distortion matrices for separable imaging models, respectively

$H(w_x, w_y)$ the OTF (Fourier transform of a space-invariant point-spread function)

$F(w_x, w_y)$ the Fourier transform of the object $f(\xi, \eta)$

$\psi(x, y)$ eigenfunctions of imaging systems

$[H]$ PSF matrix $N^2 \times N^2$

$p(n(x, y))$ probability density function of the noise random process

$\mathcal{R}_{nn}(\epsilon_x, \epsilon_y)$ stationary autocorrelation function of noise

$\mathcal{R}_{gf}(\epsilon_x, \epsilon_y)$ stationary crosscorrelation function of image with object

$W(w_x, w_y)$ Wiener filter for stationary noise and SIPSF imaging (in the Fourier domain)

$P_{nn}(w_x, w_y)$ noise power spectrum

$P_{gg}(w_x, w_y)$ image power spectrum

$P_{ff}(w_x, w_y)$ object power spectrum

Chapter 5

$J_1(a, \rho)$ first-order Bessel function

$H(\rho, \theta)$ OTF in polar spatial frequency coordinates

$\hat{P}_{\ln (g)}(w_x, w_y)$ estimated power spectrum of the log of a segmented image

$R([H])$ rank of the matrix $[H]$

Chapter 6

$\{ \ \}$ in this and other chapters $\{\cdot\}$ implies an operator notation

$s\{\cdot\}$ the nonlinear memoryless response of the image sensor

Chapter 7

$[H_{BT}]$	block Toeplitz PSF matrix resulting from SIPSF systems
$[H_{BC}]$	block circulant PSF matrix approximation $[H_{BC}]$
$[\mathcal{F}_{N^2}]$	$[\mathcal{F}] \otimes [\mathcal{F}]$ is the Kronecker product of two $N \times N$ Fourier matrices, operating on a lexicographically ordered vector; $N^2 \times 1$ is equal to a two-dimensional Fourier transform and diagonalizes block circulants
n	a noise vector
$\hat{\mathbf{f}}$	vector estimate of the object **f**
$Tr\{\cdot\}$	trace operator of a matrix
$[R]$	autocorrelation matrices

Chapter 8

$[A][B]$	column and row blurs, respectively, for a separable PSF
$W(f)$	objective function used for optimization in linear algebraic filter derivation
$[Q]$	linear operator on **f** to provide smoothing, eye model, etc.
$[\hat{F}]$	estimated matrix of $[F]$
$[H]^+$	the $[\ ]^+$ notation refers to the pseudo-inverse
$\mathbf{h}(\xi)$	the PSF in the continuous–discrete model
d	vector of *B*-spline expansion coefficients

Chapter 9

$p(\mathbf{f}\,|\,\mathbf{g})$	probability of the object, given the image
$p(\mathbf{g}\,|\,\mathbf{f})$	probability of the image, given the object
$p(\mathbf{f})$	probability of the object
$p(\mathbf{g})$	probability of the image
$p(\mathbf{n})$	probability of the noise
$\boldsymbol{\nabla}$	multidimensional gradient (partial derivative) vector

Part I

INTRODUCTION

Chapter 1

Imaging

1.0 Introduction

Separate events, connected by a common thread:

The radiologist stands in his office, viewing a woman's breast X ray. He thinks he sees a small nodule in the breast, but the X ray is low in contrast and not sharp, and the small nodule is ill-defined. He must decide if surgery is called for on the basis of this X-ray image.

A physicist has just received the first image from photographing a plasma shock tube. The physicist believes he sees instabilities in the plasma confinement that have been theoretically predicted. The image is poor, due to experimental conditions, and the physicist wishes he could improve it; the shock experiments are part of research in controlled thermonuclear fusion and important to energy resources in the future.

An analyst is looking at an image of pollution from mine tailings drifting from a river into a lake. The pollution is subtle, and the analyst is wondering how the image can be manipulated so that the barely visible pollution traces in the lake will stand out vividly for presentation to a legislative body.

The remote spacecraft flies by the planet Jupiter and sends back pictures. The pictures are miraculous in themselves; yet an astronomer wonders if they suffer any degradations that can be removed for improved images.

The common thread that ties together these, and many other separate events, is the capture, storage, and interpretation of information in the form of an image and the necessity to improve images that are not of optimum utility for the purposes at hand. Millions of images are created every day. Most of them are of very fine quality. Some of them are of lesser quality; and of these that are of lesser quality a certain subset are of such importance, or are so unique, that it is feasible to consider the techniques by which the image quality may be enhanced or the techniques by which the degrading phenomena may be removed and the undegraded image restored.

The areas of space imagery, biomedical imagery, industrial radiographs, photoreconnaissance images, television, forward looking infrared, side looking radar, and several multispectral or other esoteric forms of mapping scenes or objects onto a two-dimensional format, are all likely candidates for digital image processing. Yet many nonnatural images are also subject to digital processing techniques. By nonnatural images one might refer to two-dimensional formats for general data presentation for more efficient human consumption. Thus range, range–rate planes, range–time planes, voiceprints, sonargrams, etc., may also find themselves subject to general two-dimensional enhancement and restoration techniques.

The concepts of digital restoration and enhancement are relatively recent in origin due to the need for usually large-scale computing facilities.

Restoration techniques require some form of knowledge concerning the degradation phenomenon if an attempt at inversion of that phenomenon is to be made. This knowledge may come in the form of analytic models, or other a priori information, coupled with the knowledge (or assumption) of some physical system that provided the imaging process in the first place. Thus considerable emphasis must be placed on sources and their models of degradation—the subject of the discussions that follow.

Digital computer techniques in image restoration and enhancement had their first fruitful application at the Jet Propulsion Laboratory of the California Institute of Technology. As part of the program to land a man on the moon, it was decided to land unmanned spacecraft initially, which would televise back images of the moon's surface and test the soil for later manned landings. Unfortunately, the limitations on weight and power supply made it impossible to launch a "perfect" TV camera system on the unmanned craft. Consequently, JPL measured the degradation properties of the cameras before they were launched and then used computer processing to remove, as well as possible, the degradations from the received moon images.

Since that beginning the interest in digital image restoration has continued to grow. JPL's first work was conducted in the early 1960's. Today in the mid-1970's, digital image restoration is being applied in a number of areas, most of them bearing no relation at all to JPL's original work, except for the common desire to improve or remove degradations from an image. The authors of this book have been fortunate to have observed and participated in a number of these efforts and have seen the number of different applications and groups interested in different applications grow beyond the authors' ability to keep track of them. It is probably safe to say that there is virtually no field where images are acquired (which means virtually every branch of science) that does not have active or potential work, going on or being planned, in digital image restoration. As examples from current literature, consider medicine (diagnostic X rays, cell biology, anatomy, physiology); physics (plasma diagnostics, ultrahigh-pressure shockwaves, solid-state phenomena); nondestructive testing (visual quality control inspection, radiographic inspection, acoustic holography); weather forecasting (observation of visible cloud features from weather satellites); resource exploration (two-dimensional time/reverberation seismic signal processing). And so the list can go on.

Although the number of applications of digital image restoration may be large and diverse, the problem of restoration itself is not so nebulous. Image restorations can be understood in terms of the specific type of problem, that of finding the inverse to a mapping, using the terminology of functional analysis from mathematics. Furthermore, the physics and physical processes that govern image processing make it possible to describe the mapping in a compact and specific manner. Thus, all image restoration processes, whether applied to images from medicine or aerial reconnaissance, can be encompassed with a straightforward emphasis on mathematics and not upon specific applications. Such will be the theme and purpose of this book: to examine the mathematical and physical bases of image restoration, with a viewpoint of implementing the mathematics so derived by means of the digital computer. Consequently, the reader of this book who is versed in the mathematics associated with physics and image formation should find something of interest to his specific problem, no matter what it is.

1.1 Digital Versus Optical Processing

As will be seen later, the mathematics of the image restoration problem can be posed in either discrete or continuous variable form. Thus, many image restoration schemes can be implemented either by digital computers or by analog (optical) computers. This duality in applications being noted, two obvious questions arise: First, since an image by nature is usually an analog (optical) quantity, why should there be such a growth in interest in digital implementation? Second, which is the preferable means to implement an image restoration scheme, by digital or optical means?

Several facts lie at the heart of the answer to the first question. In particular we note the following:

1. Increasingly, the natural form in which an image is formed and acquired is not analog but a discrete or digital form. A number of electronic image sensors, such as channel-plate photomultipliers, are wholly discrete [Biberman (1971)]. Further, digital data transmission is increasingly popular so that even if the original image is not discrete, there are genuine bonuses to be gained in sampling and conversion to discrete form, particularly for bandwidth reduction, noise immunity, etc.

2. The past 10 years have seen a dramatic increase in the price/performance capabilities of digital hardware. Computers that are considered medium scale by today's measures would have been considered large- or super-scale computers 10 years ago, and today's super-scale computers (e.g., the CDC 7600; the Illiac IV) are capable of performing in seconds image processing operations that would have taken hours 10 years ago.

3. Equally dramatic have been the innovations in processing algorithms. The discovery of fast transform and fast convolution algorithms has resulted in

several orders of magnitude improvement in the computation times required in many image restoration and enhancement processes.

4. Increasing sophistication in digital image input/output systems has resulted in eliminating what used to be a major source of headaches in digital image processing. Modern scanners, digitizers, and displays are accurate, reliable, and increasingly less expensive. The usage of interactive, on-line video displays is increasing; there are several installations combining interactive video displays with time-shared or multiprogrammed computers, giving a flexibility in processing and problem turnaround that cannot be equaled even in the most well-organized optical systems.

5. The digital computer is inherently more flexible and is more readily used in operations that involve nonlinearities and/or decision-making processes. As we shall see in later chapters, some of the most exciting recent work in image restoration involves the use of basis functions, functional decompositions, and nonlinear and/or iterative techniques; only with great difficulty can these operations be done optically, if at all.

Concerning the second question, whether digital or optical restoration of images is preferable, there is much less objective fact (and considerably more personal prejudice) involved in the answer than in the first question. The following point seems agreed upon by both parties in the dispute. Once an algorithm for image restoration has been selected, if the algorithm is one that can be implemented by optical means and if the system point-spread function is constant so that optical filter masks may be prepared and reused, then the optical method offers greater throughput at lower cost. This throughput/cost factor in optical systems is often overemphasized, however. Optical sytems configured for the best image quality are usually considerably more expensive than the simple systems used in demonstrating optical methods. There is difficulty in deriving clear-cut cost comparisons in digital and optical processing because of the different methods of expense and accounting that are usually involved. It is the authors' belief that most categorical attempts to claim the superiority of digital or optical processing for restoration and enhancement are futile. Some things are clearly suited to digital processing; some are suited for optical processing. Hopefully, the reader will be able to draw the conclusions for himself, given the information in this book, some knowledge of modern optical processing [Goodman (1968)], and a knowledge of the particular applied problem that must be solved.

Finally, one must not rule out future developments in hybrid digital/optical systems. Recent developments in programmable light modulators [Casasent (1975)] may make it feasible to build systems with optical computational speed controlled by minicomputers for flexibility and nonlinear processing. Such developments may create a new look at the process of solving image restoration problems as well.

1.2   Concepts, Definitions, Notation, References

Since this book has been written in the hope that it will be used by a number of different individuals with different backgrounds, training, and application interests, the authors have tried to avoid using the highly structured (and often frightening) mathematical language of definition–theorem–proof. Instead the authors have tried to communicate to the reader in a narrative fashion that emphasizes the intuitive and/or "commonsense" meaning of the ideas under discussion.

In the development of notation for the mathematics employed in this book we have tried to use generic equivalents in a consistent fashion. Thus, integer indices are usually quantities such as $i, j, k, \ldots$. Likewise, quantities such as $\mathbf{g}$ and $[G]$ are related by a transforming operation of some type, e.g., lexicographic ordering. Some symbols have been reserved in their meaning, such as h for point-spread function, and others have been chosen to allow for easy mnemonic references, such as the symbol n for noise. A symbol and notation glossary has been provided for ready reference. Unfortunately, in any large work such as this the number of symbols proliferated uncomfortably, and the temptation is great to "reuse" some symbols. We have tried to avoid doing such unless it can be made very clear to the reader from the context of the discussion that a "reused" symbol is different and distinct and not to be confused with its earlier usage.

The authors have used the name and date referencing system, believing that the recentness of much image restoration work makes it useful for the reader to be able to follow the chronological flow of concepts through the referenced work. We have tried to cite the most important works in image restoration or in topics that support same. But many fine papers have had to be omitted, particularly those that deal more heavily with applications of image restoration than with basic concepts or mathematics.

Chapter 2

Image Formation
and Recording

2.0 Introduction

Every visual scene is an image; specifically, the image forms upon the human retina by the iris–lens portion of the human eye, and thus the eye embodies image formation systems (iris–lens) and image sensor or recording systems (retina). The eye is an image formation/recording system that functions for images conveyed by wavelengths of electromagnetic radiation in the visible spectrum. Images may be formed and recorded for other wavelengths and by devices other than the human eye, including the shortest wavelengths associated with penetrating radiations. Fortunately, the great variety of image formation processes can be described with a small number of equivalent physical concepts and an associated set of equations.

Describing the processes and equations of image formation is motivated by the desire to provide image restoration. Awareness of the processes by which an image was formed before undertaking improvement in the image by restoration is fundamental. The motivation for understanding image recording processes is equally compelling. One cannot process an image without a system to sense and record the image. The effects of the sensing device upon the image must therefore be understood and calibrated. Finally, the complete image formation/image recording system has properties, as a system, that must be understood.

2.1 Image Formation

The definition of the word image is "a reproduction or imitation of the form of a person or thing" [Webster's (1968)]. This dictionary definition is useful in conceptualizing an image formation system. As seen in Figure 2.1 there is assumed to be an *object*, $f(\xi, \eta)$, in the coordinate system (ξ, η), that is referred to as the *object* plane. Either the object is illuminated by a source of radiant energy or the object is itself a source of radiant energy. The radiant energy reflected, transmitted, or emitted by the object propagates through space. An image formation system, the rectangular box in Figure 2.1, intercepts the propagating radiant energy and transforms it in such a manner that in the coordinate system (x, y), which is referred to as the *image plane*, an image is formed. It should be evident that *images are representations of objects that are indirectly sensed and that various forms of radiant energy transport are the mechanisms by which the sensing is carried out*.

There are three general principles upon which image formation is based, and the embodiment of these principles in mathematics is required as a point of origin.

Neighborhood Processes

Consider a point (ξ, η), in the object plane, and the image of that point (x, y), in the image plane, which is created by the image formation system. The image formation system creates the image point (x, y) by acting upon the radiant energy propagating from the object. However, the image formation system receives radiant energy components not only from the object point (ξ, η) but from all other points in the object. It is logical to expect that as the distance from the object (ξ, η) to other points in the object plane increases, the effect of these other points on forming the image point will decrease. We must be prepared, however, to recognize the image formation process to be a *neighborhood process*; i.e., the image of an object point may be dependent on the object point and on points in a (possibly infinite) neighborhood surrounding the object point. If the neighborhood contains only the object point, it is said to be a *point process* of image formation.

Nonnegativity

The image is formed by the transport of radiant energy. Radiant energy is assumed to propagate from object to image, and the smallest possible amount of radiant energy

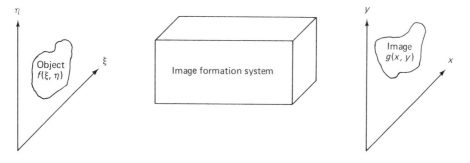

Figure 2.1   Schematic of image formation system.

transport is zero. Thus, the radiant energy distributions for both object and image must be positive or zero; i.e.,

$$f(\xi, \eta) \geqq 0,$$
$$g(x, y) \geqq 0 \tag{2.1}$$

are nonnegative.

Superposition

Consider two points in the object plane and the associated radiant energy distributions: $f_1(\xi, \eta)$ and $f_2(\xi, \eta)$. If only point 1 was emitting radiant energy, then the energy at the image plane may be measured as the quantity $g_1(x, y)$. Likewise, if only point 2 was emitting energy, we would measure energy $g_2(x, y)$ in the image plane. Since the image formation system is responsible for the distribution of energy in the object plane, let us postulate a function that describes the transformation of energy from object plane to image plane. The function must be referenced to both coordinates (ξ, η) and (x, y), to account for the change in distribution of energy in the different planes. Calling this function h, we describe the energy in the image plane in terms of h and the object radiant energy distribution, f as:

$$g(x, y) = h(x, y, \xi, \eta, f(\xi, \eta)). \tag{2.2}$$

The superposition of energy distributions from two points is represented in terms of this function. It is the nature of many transport processes that radiant energy is *additive*. Therefore, in both object and image plane the radiant energy distributions add; however, the behavior of the image formation system need not relate additive components in the object plane to additive components in the image plane. Such a system is said to be *nonlinear*, and

$$g_1(x, y) + g_2(x, y) = h(x, y, \xi, \eta, f_1(\xi, \eta)) + h(x, y, \xi, \eta, f_2(\xi, \eta))$$
$$\neq h(x, y, \xi, \eta, f_1(\xi, \eta) + f_2(\xi, \eta)). \tag{2.3}$$

If equality holds in the last relation of (2.3), then the image formation system is said to be *linear* and obeys the principle of superposition under addition. It is trivial to show that if

$$h(x, y, \xi, \eta, f(\xi, \eta)) = h(x, y, \xi, \eta) f(\xi, \eta), \tag{2.4}$$

then the image formation system is linear.

Whether linear or nonlinear image formation, the additivity of radiant energy distributions at the image plane makes it possible to describe the image formation process by extending from a single point to an object made up of a continuum. Summing the infinitesimal contributions in the image plane due to all object point contributions in the object plane gives the general image formation equation:

$$g(x, y) = \int_{-\infty}^{\infty} \int_{-\infty}^{\infty} h(x, y, \xi, \eta, f(\xi, \eta)) \, d\xi \, d\eta \tag{2.5}$$

For the case in which the image formation system is linear, then

$$g(x, y) = \int_{-\infty}^{\infty} \int_{-\infty}^{\infty} h(x, y, \xi, \eta) f(\xi, \eta) \, d\xi d\eta. \tag{2.6}$$

The function h is termed the *point-spread function* (PSF) of the image formation system. It is evident that it determines the radiant energy distribution in the image plane due to a point source of radiant energy located in the object plane.

The description of the PSF with all four coordinate variables (x, y, ξ, η) is the most general possible description. Since it allows the point-spread function to vary with the position in both image and object plane, the description in either (2.5) or (2.6) is of a *space-variant point-spread function* (SVPSF). On the other hand, it is possible to envision an image formation system that acts uniformly across image and object planes; hence the point-spread function is independent of position. Such an image formation system is said to possess a *space-invariant point-spread function* (SIPSF). The output is then a function only of the difference in variables in the coordinate systems, and the corresponding equations for space-invariant image formation are, for the nonlinear case,

$$g(x, y) = \int_{-\infty}^{\infty} \int_{-\infty}^{\infty} h(x - \xi, y - \eta, f(\xi, \eta)) \, d\xi \, d\eta, \tag{2.7}$$

and, for the linear case, we have the familiar *convolution*

$$g(x, y) = \int_{-\infty}^{\infty} \int_{-\infty}^{\infty} h(x - \xi, y - \eta) f(\xi, \eta) \, d\xi \, d\eta. \tag{2.8}$$

The final simplification possible in the image formation process is that of *separability*. The PSF is said to be separable if it can be decomposed in the fashion

$$h(x, y, \xi, \eta) = h_1(x, \xi) h_2(y, \eta)$$

or

$$h(x - \xi, y - \eta) = h_1(x - \xi) h_2(y - \eta).$$

If the PSF is separable, then the integrations can be sequentially performed and

$$g(x, y) = \int_{-\infty}^{\infty} h_1(x, \xi) \left[\int_{-\infty}^{\infty} h_2(y, \eta) f(\xi, \eta) \, d\eta \right] d\xi$$

$$= \int_{-\infty}^{\infty} h_2(y, \eta) \left[\int_{-\infty}^{\infty} h_1(x, \xi) f(\xi, \eta) \, d\xi \right] d\eta \tag{2.9a}$$

or

$$g(x, y) = \int_{-\infty}^{\infty} h_1(x - \xi) \left[\int_{-\infty}^{\infty} h_2(y - \eta) f(\xi, \eta) \, d\eta \right] d\xi$$

$$= \int_{-\infty}^{\infty} h_2(y - \eta) \left[\int_{-\infty}^{\infty} h_1(x - \xi) f(\xi, \eta) \, d\xi \right] d\eta. \tag{2.9b}$$

Equation (2.9) shows the image formation process in terms of independent horizontal and vertical image formation.

The preceding equations are the fundamental mathematical descriptions of the image formation processes. To illustrate image formation in terms of these equations,

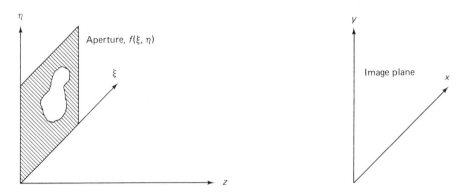

Figure 2.2   Optical diffraction imaging.

we shall discuss the nature of the image formation process for several systems that are in common use.

2.2   Optical Systems

In Figure 2.2 we have idealized the simplest possible optical system. The object plane is an opaque sheet except for an opening $f(\xi, \eta)$, which is termed the *aperture*. This plane is illuminated from the left by a uniform plane electromagnetic wave. Only the aperture passes the wave, which propagates to the image plane. The problem is to determine $g(x, y)$, the distribution of the radiated electromagnetic field energy in the image.

In this example the mechanism of radiant energy transport is the propagation of electromagnetic waves in free space; its solution is applicable to all such waves, including longer wavelengths associated with radio, radar, etc., as well as optical wavelengths. The wave equation in free space must be used to determine the image distribution $g(x, y)$, given the boundary conditions imposed by the aperture. Solutions of the wave equation are not simple. There are two solutions, however, that can be derived by approximation, and we shall state the meanings of these solutions.

These solutions result in what has come to be known as *diffraction theory*. Diffraction theory is based upon the scalar theory of light in which phasor notation, similar to that of electrical theory [Goodman (1968), Van Bladel (1964)], is used. Under the assumption of coherent illumination, the complex field distribution in the image plane is given by

$$g(x, y) = K_1 \int_{-\infty}^{\infty} \int_{-\infty}^{\infty} f(\xi, \eta) \exp\left\{ i \frac{\pi}{\lambda z} [(x - \xi)^2 + (y - \eta)^2] \right\} d\xi \, d\eta, \quad (2.10)$$

where K_1 is a complex constant, λ is the wavelength, and z is the distance from object plane to image plane. If the image plane is removed even farther from the object plane (Fraunhofer assumption), then a new approximation formula becomes valid. In this case the coherent image $g(x, y)$ is given by

$$g(x, y) = K_2 \int_{-\infty}^{\infty} \int_{-\infty}^{\infty} f(\xi, \eta) \exp\left[-i\frac{2\pi}{\lambda z}(x\xi + y\eta) \right] d\xi d\eta, \qquad (2.11)$$

where K_2 is a different complex constant. Equations (2.10) and (2.11) are based on scalar wave theory; i.e., interdependence between electric and magnetic fields is neglected. The conditions associated with Equation (2.10) are referred to as *Fresnel* diffraction theory, and Equation (2.11) describes *Fraunhofer* diffraction.

Diffraction image formation systems are so simple that the reader may have difficulty in associating them with image processes. More realistic image formation systems, such as Figure 2.3, will contain entrance and exit apertures and a lens (or lenses). Further, the coherence assumptions are seldom satisfied in optical image formation systems that are encountered in daily life. Detailed analysis of the behavior of lenses, however, shows many similarities between elementary diffraction theory and images formed by lenses.

It is possible to show [Goodman (1968)] that the resulting incoherent image formation process is given by

$$g(x, y) = \int_{-\infty}^{\infty} \int_{-\infty}^{\infty} f(\xi, \eta) |h(x, \xi, y, \eta)|^2 \, d\xi d\eta; \qquad (2.12)$$

i.e., the system is still linear but the incoherent PSF is the squared magnitude of the coherent PSF. In (2.12) $f(\xi, \eta)$ is no longer a complex field distribution but is an intensity distribution; $g(x, y)$ is the resulting intensity distribution in the image plane.

Our treatment of optical image formation has been cursory and has been centered on the correspondence between physical processes (electromagnetic wave propagation) and the equations developed in Section 2.1. More detailed models of optical systems will be developed in subsequent chapters.

2.3 Penetrating Radiation Systems

The diffraction phenomena associated with optical image formation, as just discussed, occur because of the nonpenetrating nature of radiation in the visible spectrum

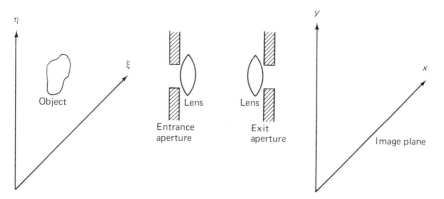

Figure 2.3 Typical optical image formation system.

and the consequent opaque qualities of aperture boundaries in optical systems. There are mechanisms of radiant energy transport that are able to penetrate through matter opaque to light. Very short wavelength electromagnetic waves (X rays, gamma rays), ionized high-energy particles (protons, electrons, alpha particles), and neutral particles (neutrons) have all been used in imaging.

Image formation by penetrating radiation is different from image formation by optical systems. First, the penetrating nature of the radiation, as well as the extremely short wavelengths, eliminates diffraction effects in images of common macroscopic scale.[1] Second, one does not make coherent–incoherent distinctions.

An important distinction for penetrating radiation systems is that of objects which are passive, i.e., emit no radiation, and objects which are active, i.e., emit radiations of the type used in the image formation process. In active objects it is usually the distribution of active radiation emitting substance that is of interest in the image formation, e.g., radionucleide imaging of the brain for tumor identification. In passive objects an active source of radiation is used to penetrate into a region of interest.

A typical scheme for imaging with active penetrating radiation is shown in Figure 2.4. The object is a source of radiation (neutrons, X rays, etc.) and is imaged into the image plane by means of a *pinhole*; the principle is the same as the pinhole camera. Due to the penetrating nature of the radiation, however, it is difficult to create a true pinhole. If the stop plate is too thin, a high background penetrates and floods the image plane. Making the plate very thick can cut the background to zero; however, the resulting hole through a thick plate possesses some of the properties of a beam collimator and as a result the pinhole imaging properties are poor. The resulting compromise in plate thickness yields an image formation system that is linear (additivity

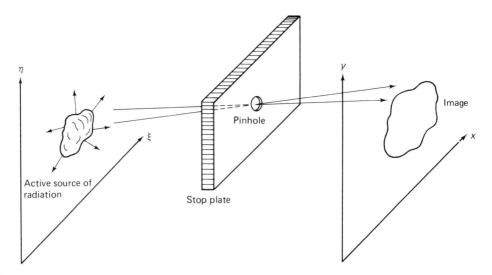

Figure 2.4   Pinhole imaging in penetrating radiation images.

[1]Diffraction imagery is encountered at the atomic level instead and is exploited in fields such as X-ray diffraction analysis to determine crystal structure.

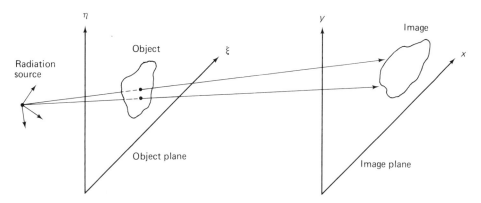

Figure 2.5   Image formation in passive objects by penetrating radiation.

of energies occurs in both object and image planes) and thus expressible in the simplest form as

$$g(x, y) = \int_{-\infty}^{\infty} \int_{-\infty}^{\infty} f(\xi, \eta) h(x - \xi, y - \eta) \, d\xi d\eta, \qquad (2.13)$$

i.e., the convolution of $f(\xi, \eta)$, the object plane distribution of active radiation, with a space-invariant aperture function. Due to the problems discussed above, it is usually quite difficult to calculate analytically the aperture point-spread function; it must usually be measured or calculated by Monte Carlo methods [Tomnovec and Mather (1957)].

Image formation of passive objects is achieved by the geometry of Figure 2.5. A point source of radiation penetrates the object and is intercepted in the image plane. The image is a *shadow projection* of the interior of the object. Such images are usually referred to by the generic term of *radiographs*, and the process is known as *radiography*.

There are three separate processes that are readily identified as distinctly different in image formation by radiography. We discuss the three effects separately, in order of increasing complexity.

Finite Source Size

To resolve fine detail in a radiograph requires an infinitesimally small source of radiation. A finite-size radiation source spreads the projection image, as seen in Figure 2.6(a). The technique of modeling these effects in image formation is via a linear space-invariant PSF, $h(x - \xi, y - \eta)$, where h, the PSF, is the radiation source distribution function and must usually be determined by experimental methods.

Parallax and Geometry Effects

Consider the geometry in Figure 2.6(b) where two parallel edges are projected, one lying on a radius to the source and the other not. The edge on the radius projects

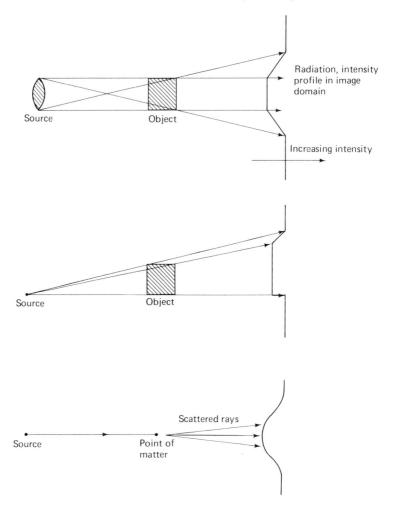

Figure 2.6   Sources of error in radiographic image formation.

a sharp image, while the other edge is spread out. Such effects are obviously dependent on object shapes, source-to-object geometry, and image plane orientation. If the object is of small thickness, compared to distances between source and image plane, however, then it is possible to approximate the geometric effects in a space-variant point-spread function, $h(x, y, \xi, \eta)$.

Radiation Scatter

Penetrating radiation images show details by the varying amounts of radiation absorbed in the object being radiographed. The strength of the radiation quanta is attenuated by interaction, but the quanta are also scattered from their incident paths, resulting in a distribution of radiation about the point. The scattering process is dependent on energy of the quanta, their type, the thickness and atomic number of the object, the scattering cross section of the object atoms, the probability of secondary interactions, etc. For objects of approximately the same atomic composition and density, illuminated by quanta with a narrow energy spectrum, the scattering effects can be approximated with a space-invariant PSF. For thick objects containing materials with a wide variety of atomic numbers, illuminated by radiation quanta with a broad energy spectrum, however, the PSF becomes nonlinear (the underlying scattering equations are nonlinear) and object-dependent. Thus, object scattering is described by a PSF, $h(x, y, \xi, \eta, f(\xi, \eta))$. [See Hunt, Janney, and Zeigler (1970) for detailed aspects of scatter in radiographic image formation.]

We have described these effects separately. In a real radiographic image formation system all effects are present simultaneously and may be combined to create a PSF that has an approximately Gaussian shape, due to the central-limit effects in convolution of several positive functions. The alternative is to examine the physics and geometry of the radiographic image formation system to determine if a single effect, e.g., finite source size, is dominant. Suffice it to say that radiographic image formation systems are sufficiently complex to result in image formation processes describable by any (or none!) of Equations (2.5)–(2.8).

It is assumed that the discussions in these previous sections have been sufficient to convince the reader of the role of radiant energy transport and the analysis of underlying physical processes in image formation. We have not exhausted the possible image formation systems or their application, of course. Other systems of interest can be found in synthetic aperture radar; acoustical holography; radio astronomy; as well as image-like data from applications in seismology, sonar, geophysics, etc.

2.4 Image Detectors and Recorders

Image detection and recording is divided into two major technologies: photochemical and photoelectronic. Photochemical technology is exemplified by photographic film; photoelectronic technology is exemplified by the television camera. Both technologies are widespread in digital image processing. Photochemical methods have the advantage of combining image detection and recording into a single compact entity: the film. Photoelectronic systems, on the other hand, usually require separation of the image detection process from the image recording process; however, photoelectronic systems sense images in a fashion that makes them ideally suited for conversion to digital computer processing.

Image detection and recording by photographic film relies upon the properties of halide salts of silver. Silver halides (e.g., AgCl and AgBr) are changed by exposure to light (the exact nature of the change is still not definitely known) so that the action of mild reducing agents results in the precipitation and deposition of grains of free silver [Mees (1954)]. The reducing agents that precipitate silver are known as *developers*, hence the terminology of *developing* a photographic image. It has been found experimentally that the mass of silver deposited is linearly proportional to the logarithm of the *total exposure E*, where

$$E = \int_{t_1}^{t_2} i(t)\, dt \qquad (2.14)$$

and $i(t)$ is the optical intensity incident on the film. There is, in addition, a region of *saturation*, where all available silver is deposited due to intense light, and a region of *fog*, where some small amount of silver is deposited even in the absence of any light exposure. This behavior of film is usually displayed in a curve of D–log E, where D is the *optical density*, and is defined as

$$D = \log_{10}\left(\frac{I_1}{I_2}\right), \qquad (2.15)$$

where I_1 is the intensity of a reference source of light and I_2 is the intensity of light transmitted through (or reflected from) a photographic film when illuminated by the reference source I_1; thus $I_1 \geq I_2$ always. A typical D–log E curve appears in Figure 2.7 and is sometimes called the *characteristic curve* of a film or the H–D curve, after Hurter and Driffield who discovered it [Mees (1954)].

To analyze the recording properties of film, let an incident intensity of I_0 illuminate the film for an interval of time such that the total exposure E falls in the linear region of the curve in Figure 2.7. The film is then developed into a transparency and examined by illuminating it with light. The light transmitted through the film is governed by a form of Bouger's law, which defines the attenuation of light passing through a mixture of particles in suspension:

$$I_2 = I_1 \exp(-k_1 M_{Ag}), \qquad (2.16)$$

where I_1 and I_2 are defined in a fashion similar to Equation (2.15), k_1 is a constant, and M_{Ag} is the mass of silver per unit area deposited after development. Hurter and Driffield showed that, for a suitable choice of k_1,

$$D = k_1 M_{Ag}, \qquad (2.17)$$

where D is the measured density from Equation (2.15); thus,

$$I_2 = I_1 \exp(-D). \qquad (2.18)$$

But in the linear region of Figure 2.7,

$$D = \gamma \log_{10} E - D_0, \qquad (2.19)$$

where γ is the slope of the linear region (referred to as the gamma of the film) and D_0 is the offset (the linear portion does not pass through the origin).

If it is assumed that the exposure was constant during the time interval, so that $E = I_0 t$, and if we let $t = 1$, then by substituting (2.19) into (2.18) we have

$$I_2 = I_1 \exp(-\gamma \log_{10} I_0 + D_0) = K_2 (I_0)^{-\gamma}. \qquad (2.20)$$

Equation (2.20) is the basic equation of film behavior as a device that records image intensities. It is noted that

1. The intensity I_2 observed through the transparency is, in general, a highly nonlinear mapping of the intensity that originally exposed the film.
2. If γ is positive, the intensity observed is the reciprocal of the γ power of the incident intensity. A film with positive γ is known as a *negative* material.
3. If γ is negative, the intensity observed is the γ power of the incident intensity.

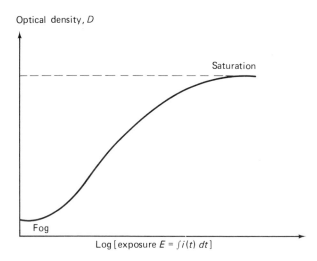

Figure 2.7   Typical D–log E curve of a film.

A film with negative γ is known as a *positive* material; $\gamma = -1$ yields a linear mapping of incident intensity.

4. The slope of the curve γ determines the *contrast* characteristics of the photographic material. High-contrast materials are associated with large slope; low-contrast materials, with a small slope (for fixed total exposure range).

Only in the case of a positive film of unit slope do we find linear mapping of incident intensity to observed intensity transmitted through film. Thus, film is a nonlinear element in the process of detecting and recording images. The nonlinearity should be emphasized, for the effects will arise in later discussions on image restoration.

Photoelectronic image detecting devices usually consist of three principal subsystems: *optics* to form the image, the *photoactive surface* to detect the image, and *scanning electronics*, to read out the electronic image formed on the photoactive surface. [See the two volumes by Biberman and Nudelman (1971) for detailed analysis of different devices.]

Viewed as a system, the input or stimulus variable of a photoelectronic image detector is radiant energy (light, X-ray photons, etc.). The output or response variable is an electrical quantity, typically current in an electron beam scanning the electronic image. Response over a wide range of input and output variables is common, so it is conventional to plot the logarithm of the output (response) variable as a function of the logarithm of the input (stimulus) variable. A typical plot of input and output is seen in Figure 2.8. As in the case of film, there is a saturation response at high intensities; at low intensities there is a limit response, usually referred to as the *dark current* (response of the detector with no incident radiation). There exists a linear region in which the log of response is proportional to the log of stimulus. This is analogous to film also, and it is conventional practice to refer to the slope of the linear portion of the curve as the *gamma* of the detector, as in film.

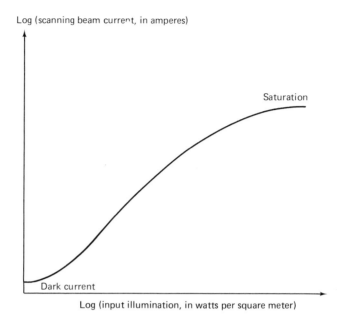

Figure 2.8 Transfer characteristic of typical photoelectronic image detector.

Given the behavior exemplified in Figure 2.8, we can express the behavior in the linear region in a form similar to Equation (2.19):

$$\log i_b = \gamma \log I_0 + C_1 \tag{2.21}$$

where i_b is the scanning beam current, I_0 is the incident illumination intensity, γ is the linear slope, and C_1 is the offset. Thus, we have the relation

$$i_b = C_2(I_0)^\gamma, \tag{2.22}$$

which governs the transfer characteristics between input light intensity and measured electron beam current.

There are two practical differences between the responses represented by Equations (2.20) and (2.22). First, the photoelectronic detector produces a response proportional to the incident light quanta; whereas photographic film has the negative exponent behavior (which is seen in the photographic negative image). Second, there are many photoelectronic systems for which the input–output characteristics are linear over a wide range; i.e., $\gamma = 1$, and deviations from linearity are not too severe even in the nonlinear systems; e.g., $\gamma \cong 0.7$ to $\gamma \cong 0.8$ in commercial TV orthicons.

2.5 Detector/Recorder Noise

In photographic film the noise that is introduced is a function of the detection/recording mechanism, i.e., the grains of silver that compose the developed image.

The image is formed by the masses of silver deposited after development, but there is a fundamental randomness inherent in the grain deposition. First, the silver grains are randomly distributed with respect to their size and shape. Second, they are randomly located in distance from one another in the film emulsion. Third, they behave randomly under conditions of exposure and development; two grains of silver halide that look identical can be subjected to the same conditions of exposure and development and yet result in deposition of different masses of free silver. This randomness results in a type of noise referred to as *film–grain noise*.

Film–grain noise is a complicated type of noise, as the surveyed work of the number of researchers in the area indicates [Mees (1954)]. There are, however, a few simple objective facts that can be stated about film–grain noise:

1. Film–grain noise is a Poisson process that in the limit is approximated by a Gaussian process. If the mean optical density in a region of the film is μ_D, then the distribution of optical densities d about μ_D is given by the Gaussian probability density function (PDF):

$$p(d) = \frac{1}{\sigma_D \sqrt{2\pi}} \exp\left\{-\frac{1}{2}\left(\frac{d - \mu_D}{\sigma_D}\right)^2\right\}, \qquad (2.23)$$

   where σ_D is the standard deviation of the noise about the mean density μ_D.

2. The standard deviation σ_D is not a constant but varies with the mean density. Simple physical arguments show that [Falconer (1970)]

$$\sigma_D = \alpha(\mu_D)^\beta, \qquad (2.24)$$

   where $\alpha = 0.66(a/A)^{1/2}$, $\beta = \frac{1}{2}$, a is the average film grain area, and A is the area of the microscopic region being examined.

3. If optical density measurements are taken in different spatial positions in a photographic film, the statistical correlations between samples are zero when the samples are spaced farther apart than the grain size of the film or the aperture diameter, whichever is larger. Grain noise is thus a *white-noise* random process under these sampling conditions. In most practical situations these conditions are met.

The most troublesome property of film–grain noise is embodied in Equation (2.24). The noise is *signal-dependent*. If we conceive of the density in a microscopic region of film as being the local mean density, then the variation of this local mean density with position (x, y) in the film defines a *density image* $d(x, y)$. If we let $n(x, y)$ be a random process, whose amplitude fluctuations are Gaussian distributed with zero mean and with standard deviation of unity, then the noisy density values recorded on film can be described as

$$d_r(x, y) = d(x, y) + \alpha(d(x, y))^\beta n(x, y), \qquad (2.25)$$

where d_r is the noise-corrupted density image recorded on film and d is the noise-free density image. The model of Equation (2.25) was basically proposed by Huang (1966), who suggested $\beta = \frac{1}{3}$ was a more realistic value than $\beta = \frac{1}{2}$.

A simple approximation is to assume signal-independent noise. In this case $d(x, y)$

in the second term of (2.25) is replaced by $\overline{d(x, y)}$, the mean density over the entire density image. Then

$$d_r(x, y) = d(x, y) + \alpha(\overline{d(x, y)})^\beta n(x, y)$$
$$= d(x, y) + n_1(x, y), \tag{2.26}$$

where n_1 is a Gaussian random process with zero mean and standard deviation $\sigma_D = \alpha(\bar{d})^\beta$. In this latter case we see that the equivalent noise effects are multiplicative if film characteristics are used to convert density units back to intensity. If Equation (2.20) is used, then the *intensity image* $i(x, y)$ corresponding to the recorded density image is

$$i_r(x, y) = k_2(i(x, y))^\gamma \cdot (10)^{n_1(x,y)}$$
$$= k_2(i(x, y))^\gamma \cdot n_2(x, y), \tag{2.27}$$

where i_r is the recorded intensity image and $i(x, y)$ is the intensity image that would be observed in the absence of noise. The effect of film–grain noise, under signal-independent assumptions, is to generate a multiplicative noise process. In fact, under the Gaussian assumptions for $n_1(x, y)$, the process $n_2(x, y)$ has to obey log-normal statistics [Johnson and Leone (1965)].

In the case of photoelectronic systems for image detection and recording, the noise problem is not so simple. Two separate processes are likely to contribute to noise in the detected image: (1) random fluctuations in the number of photons and photoelectrons on the photoactive surface of the detector; (2) random thermal noise sources in the circuits that sense, acquire, and process the signal from the detector's photoactive surface. The second process has a behavior that is well-known; random thermal noise is usually described by a zero-mean Gaussian process with a uniform ("white") power spectrum [Davenport and Root (1958)]. The first process, photoelectron fluctuations, is more complex to describe. The noise emissions should be independent of spatial position on the photoactive surface, which results in the noise process being spatially uncorrelated with a uniform ("white") power spectrum. The amplitude statistics of photoelectron noise can be described in two limiting cases [Mandel (1959)]:

Case 1:   For low light levels on the photoactive surface, the number of photoelectrons emitted is governed by Bose–Einstein statistics, often approximated by the Poisson PDF; thus, the standard deviation of the noise is equal to the square root of the mean.

Case 2:   For high light levels, the number of photoelectrons emitted is governed by the Gaussian PDF with a standard deviation equal to the square root of the mean.

In case 2 the relation between the standard deviation and the mean is a property of Poisson PDF convergence to the Gaussian PDF at high event rates. In either case, the result is a signal-dependent noise when we interpret the mean electron emission rate as a local property $e(x, y)$ that varies with position (x, y) as was the case for film–grain noise. Let n be a zero-mean Gaussian variable with unity standard deviation; then the noisy electron image that the detector perceives is

$$e_r(x, y) = e(x, y) + (e(x, y))^{1/2}n(x, y), \tag{2.28}$$

where e_r is the noisy electron image recorded on the detector's photoactive surface and e is the image that would have been recorded in the absence of noise. As in the case of film–grain noise, we can make a signal-independent assumption. Let $\overline{e(x, y)}$ be the average electron image. Then

$$e_r(x, y) = e(x, y) + (\overline{e(x, y)})^{1/2} n(x, y) \tag{2.29}$$

is the signal-independent noise approximation to (2.28).

   If then the detector uses a readout beam to sense the electron emissions, the current in the beam is the number of electron emissions during the readout time. The introduction of a readout interval makes it possible to describe Equation (2.28) in an equivalent current form:

$$i_b(x, y) = i(x, y) + (i(x, y))^{1/2} n(x, y), \tag{2.30}$$

where i_b is the current image in the readout beam and i is the image that would have been recorded in the absence of noise. The signal-independent approximation is

$$i_b(x, y) = i(x, y) + (\overline{i(x, y)})^{1/2} n(x, y). \tag{2.31}$$

The quantity $i(x, y)$ is known from Equation (2.22), however. Substituting into (2.30) from (2.22) and adding a zero-mean Gaussian process to describe thermal fluctuations yields

$$i_b(x, y) = C_2(I_0(x, y))^\gamma + (C_2(I_0(x, y))^\gamma)^{1/2} n(x, y) + n_t(x, y) \tag{2.32}$$

as the description of noisy current perceived by the detector system and its relation to the original intensity distribution $I_0(x, y)$ in the image plane.

2.6   Canonic Model for Image Formation, Detection, Recording

   We can now summarize the discussion in the preceding five sections by a canonic model that embodies the processes of image formation, detection, and recording, including the existence of noise. Figure 2.9 shows the canonic model in block diagram form. The symbolism shown will be used in the remainder of the book.

   The description of the elements in the canonic model is as follows:

$f(\xi, \eta)$ Object plane radiant energy distribution.

h The image formation systems' point-spread function; used in formation of images via equations such as (2.5)–(2.8).

$b(x, y)$ Image plane radiant energy distribution.

s Detector response function; transforms image plane radiant energies into a response variable (usually nonlinear).

$r(x, y)$ Response variable of detector; i.e., $r(x, y) = s\{b(x, y)\}$.

ϵ_1, ϵ_2 Gain parameters: $\epsilon_1 = 0$ or 1, $\epsilon_2 = 0$ or 1.

ψ Feed-forward function to account for signal-dependent noise.

n_1, n_2 Noise processes.

n_3 Resulting signal-dependent noise.

$g(x, y)$ Response plus noises $= r_1(x, y) + n_3(x, y) + \epsilon_2 n_2(x, y)$.

24

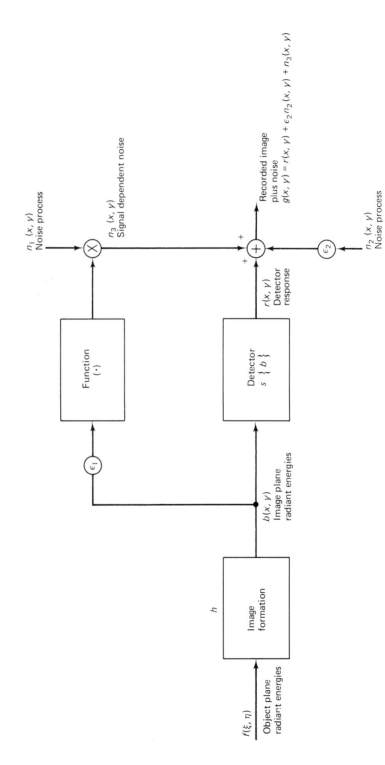

Figure 2.9 Canonic model of image formation, detection, and recording.

The advantage of the signal symbolism in Figure 2.9 is that it concentrates upon the *structure* of the image formation and detection process, without undue concern about variables and their physical representations and dimensions. Thus, $f(\xi, \eta)$ is a radiant energy distribution from the object, regardless of whether the energy is visible light or X rays. Likewise, $r(x, y)$ is the detector response whether the detector is film (where r would be optical density) or a photoelectronic camera (where r would be output current). Finally, $g(x, y)$ is the output image available to the user for subsequent attempted restoration.

The whole discussion of this chapter is embodied in Figure 2.9, and we shall rely upon it and the common nomenclature it establishes in defining and examining the problem of image restoration.

Chapter 3

Image Representations and Models

3.0 Introduction

While Chapter 2 concentrated on the physical process involved in image formation and model definition, this chapter is devoted to the image representation aspects necessary for restoration. Because this book is motivated by *digital* restoration techniques, image representation must necessarily be described by mathematical and numerical principles consistent with discrete processes. Thus the purpose of this chapter is to develop a frame of reference for both notation and operators to be used in various aspects of the material presented in the remaining portion of this book. Because many imaging models can be approximated by linear techniques, one can utilize the notation of linear algebra (tensor, matrix, and vector operators) in the formulation of material in this chapter.

Thus, the chapter will begin with a discussion of the sampling theorem in two dimensions. Once the image is represented by a finite set of numbers, we shall investigate other representations of the image in arbitrary orthogonal basis spaces. To illustrate such image (or matrix) representations in other basis spaces, pictorial examples will be shown. In addition the chapter will include a description of the concept of separability, Kronecker product, and stacking operators, three aspects of linear algebra that become particularly significant in our image restoration and enhancement models.

3.1 Sampled Pictures

As discussed in Chapter 2, a basic premise throughout this book is that the object of interest $f(\xi, \eta)$ is described in two-dimensional notation on a domain of continuous

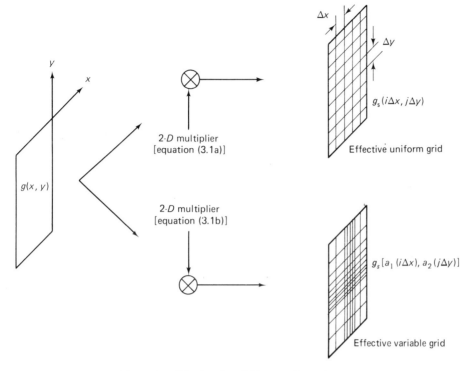

Figure 3.1   Fixed and variable sampling schemes.

support, or plane, indexed with variables (ξ, η). The image $g(x, y)$ is described in a similar continuous plane with variables (x, y). In order that this image, or any other continuous function, be represented in a discrete space, it is necessary to investigate a two-dimensional sampling theorem. We shall see that the uniform grid sampler can be likened to the uniform fixed knot problem of applied mathematics and the variable knot or variable sample problem will be relegated to subsequent chapters. The reader should be aware, however, that variable knot sampling systems in two dimensions may, in fact, provide a larger number of degrees of freedom in an imaging system than uniform sampling. Figure 3.1 shows a schematic representation of the possible differences between the variable and fixed sampling rates.

Returning to the fixed or uniform sampling, it may be shown that for a band-limited image $g(x, y)$ with spatial frequency cutoffs of w_{xc} and w_{yc}, respectively, we are able to sample the image with a two-dimensional infinite number of Dirac delta functions such that

$$g_s(i\,\Delta x, j\,\Delta y) = \sum_i^\infty \sum_j^\infty g(x, y)\,\delta(x - i\,\Delta x, y - j\,\Delta y), \qquad (3.1a)$$

where $\Delta x \leq 1/2w_{xc}$ and $\Delta y \leq 1/2w_{yc}$. For a variable sampling rate we would have

$$g_s(i\,\Delta x, j\,\Delta y) = \sum \sum g(x, y)\,\delta(x - a_1(i\,\Delta x), y - a_2(j\,\Delta y)). \qquad (3.1b)$$

Returning to the uniform sampling of Equation (3.1a), we see that such a sampling rate guarantees the possibility of perfect reconstruction according to the two-dimensional sampling theorem [Goodman (1968)]. Taking the Fourier transform of the image yields

$$G(w_x, w_y) = \int_{-\infty}^{\infty} \int_{-\infty}^{\infty} g(x, y) \exp\left\{-2\pi\sqrt{-1}(w_x x + w_y y)\right\} dx dy \qquad (3.2)$$

$$= 0 \qquad\qquad\qquad |w_x, w_y| \geqq w_{xc}, w_{yc},$$

where w_x and w_y refer to the Fourier domain, and the Fourier transform of the infinite array of Dirac delta function samples becomes

$$S(w_x w_y) = \int_{-\infty}^{\infty} \int_{-\infty}^{\infty} \sum_{i} \sum_{j} \delta(x - i\,\Delta x, y - j\,\Delta y) \exp\left\{-2\pi\sqrt{-1}(w_x x + w_y y)\right\} dx dy$$
$$\qquad (3.3a)$$

$$= \frac{4\pi^2}{\Delta x\,\Delta y} \sum_{i} \sum_{j} \delta\left(w_x - \frac{2\pi i}{\Delta x}, w_y - \frac{2\pi j}{\Delta y}\right). \qquad (3.3b)$$

Using the Fourier multiplication–convolution relationship, it is easily shown that

$$G_s(w_x, w_y) = G(w_x, w_y) \circledast S(w_x, w_y) \qquad (3.4a)$$

$$= \frac{4\pi^2}{\Delta x\,\Delta y} \sum_{i}^{\infty} \sum_{j}^{\infty} G\left(w_x - \frac{2\pi i}{\Delta x}, w_y - \frac{2\pi j}{\Delta y}\right). \qquad (3.4b)$$

The Fourier transform of the sampled image is then replicated in a two-dimensional array. One must have a sampling rate to avoid aliasing (Fourier frequency overlap) such that

$$\frac{1}{\Delta x} \geqq 2w_{xc}$$

or equivalently in two dimensions $w_{xc} \leqq 1/2\,\Delta x$, $w_{yc} \leqq 1/2\,\Delta y$ (see Figure 3.2). In order to obtain a reconstruction of the original image from its sampled version, we pick a zero–one function that selects the principal Fourier transform ($i = j = 0$) and rejects all others in the frequency domain. Consequently,

$$g(x, y) = h(x, y) \circledast g_s(i\,\Delta x, j\,\Delta y), \qquad (3.5)$$

where $h(x, y)$ is the impulse response to the zero–one filter used to select the zeroth-order replication in the Fourier domain. If a rectangle is used, then $h(x, y)$ is a two-dimensional sinc function and

$$g(x, y) = \sum_{i}^{\infty} \sum_{j}^{\infty} g_s(i\,\Delta x, j\,\Delta y) \, \text{sinc}\,(2w_{xc}(x - i\,\Delta x))\, \text{sinc}\,(2w_{yc}(y - j\,\Delta y)). \qquad (3.6)$$

Of course, different zero–one sampling functions (other than rectangles) result in different reconstruction functions.

There are real-world practical limits to the image sampling and reconstruction process. The effect of practical limits can be summarized as follows [Hunt and Breed-love (1974)]:

1. The sampling system is never a Dirac function sampler; consequently, the spectrum of the sampled image is degraded by the transfer function of the sample spot.
2. The reconstruction and display system cannot be a true sinc function response since this implies negative light and a display spot of infinite extent, due to

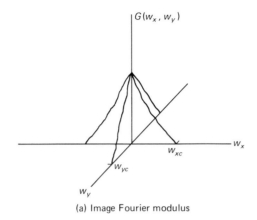

(a) Image Fourier modulus

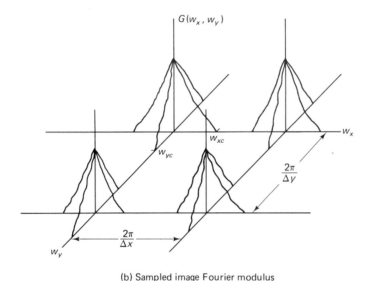

(b) Sampled image Fourier modulus

Figure 3.2   Pictorial illustration of the uniform sampling theorem.

the negative lobes and infinite extent of the sinc function. Realistic display systems use positive light and finite spots; consequently, there is never perfect separation of the zero-order alias from higher-ordered aliases of the data.

3. The effects of spectrum degradation due to finite sampling and display spots can be computed and corrected for by an image restoration process. The result is a displayed digital image that has better resolution and fine structure detail.

4. The lack of perfect separation of the zero-order alias from higher aliases is seldom a problem in displays; it is usually visible only in special cases, i.e., periodic structures with frequencies near the Nyquist sampling limit.

Once the image $g(x, y)$ has been sampled, $g_s(i\,\Delta x, j\,\Delta y)$, we then must quantize these samples for storage in digital form. This means that the continuum range of values possible for $g_s(i\,\Delta x, j\,\Delta y)$ to take on must be divided into discrete bins or regions that then become represented by a particular number in the computer. The placement of the decision regions on the g_s axis is often dictated by a desire to minimize quantization noise based on various fidelity measures. The interested reader is referred to the literature for discussions on the optimum quantizer [Max (1960)], a good mean-square approximation [Panter and Dite (1951)], and more practical companding and uniform quantization [Habibi (1974), Andrews (1970)]. For purposes of this book, however, sufficient quantization accuracy will be assumed such that quantization effects are not noticeable. Once the image has been quantized, each sample point then becomes known as a *pixel* (for *picture element*, also referred to as a *pel*). Thus an image made up of 1000×1000 samples becomes a million-pixel image. The logarithm base 2 of the number of brightness values g_s is quantized into defines the number of bits required to describe each pixel. Nominally 8 bits will cover 0.5% dynamic range resolution, which, when converted properly to visual response units, matches the sensitivity of the human eye. Consequently a properly sampled and quantized image may have 1000×1000 pixels, which at 8 bits per pixel provide an image described by 8 million bits. This is often referred to as the PCM (pulse code modulation) representation of the image.

3.2 Image Representations in Orthogonal Bases

Consider the matrix $[G]$ as an image that has been sampled and quantized in space, where the ith row and the jth column correspond to the x and y spatial coordinates of a scene $g(x, y)$. Hence

$$[G] = SQ\{g(x, y)\}, \tag{3.7}$$

where the nonlinear operator $SQ\{\cdot\}$ represents the sampler and quantizer. Assume that $[G]$ has the dimensions $N \times N$. Techniques involving nonsquare image matrices have been explored in much of the literature; however, no discussion will be offered herein, as it does not significantly contribute to the philosophy of this book. A general *separable linear transformation* on an image matrix $[G]$ may be written in the form

$$[\alpha] = [U]^t[G][V], \tag{3.8}$$

where $[\alpha]$ is termed the *unitary transform* domain of the image, $[U]$ and $[V]$ are unitary operators, and the superscript t denotes the matrix transpose. The unitary nature of $[U]$ and $[V]$ implies the following relations:

$$[U][U]^t = [I], \tag{3.9}$$

$$[V][V]^t = [I]. \tag{3.10}$$

Hence the "inverse" transform of (3.8) may be written in the form

$$[G] = [U][\alpha][V]^t. \tag{3.11}$$

If the quantities $[U]$ and $[V]$ are written in the form

$$[U] = [\mathbf{u}_1\mathbf{u}_2 \ldots \mathbf{u}_N], \tag{3.12}$$

$$[V] = [\mathbf{v}_1\mathbf{v}_2 \ldots \mathbf{v}_N], \tag{3.13}$$

where the terms $\mathbf{u}_i$ and $\mathbf{v}_i$ are the vectors made up from the columns of $[U]$ and $[V]$, respectively, then

$$[G] = [\mathbf{u}_1\mathbf{u}_2 \ldots \mathbf{u}_N][\alpha] \begin{bmatrix} \mathbf{v}_1^t \\ \mathbf{v}_2^t \\ \cdot \\ \cdot \\ \cdot \\ \mathbf{v}_N^t \end{bmatrix}. \tag{3.14}$$

If the matrix $[\alpha]$ is written as a sum of the following form,

$$[\alpha] = \begin{bmatrix} \alpha_{11} & 0 & 0 & \cdots & 0 \\ & 0 & 0 & & \cdot \\ \cdot & & & & \cdot \\ \cdot & & & & \cdot \\ 0 & \cdot & \cdot & \cdot & 0 \end{bmatrix} + \begin{bmatrix} 0 & \alpha_{12} & 0 & \cdots & 0 \\ & 0 & 0 & & \cdot \\ \cdot & & & & \cdot \\ \cdot & & & & \cdot \\ 0 & \cdots & 0 & \cdot & 0 \end{bmatrix} + \cdots, \tag{3.15}$$

then it follows that

$$[G] = \sum_{i=1}^{N} \sum_{j=1}^{N} \alpha_{ij}\mathbf{u}_i\mathbf{v}_j^t. \tag{3.16}$$

The outer product $\mathbf{u}_i\mathbf{v}_j^t$ may be interpreted as an "image" so that the sum over all combinations of the outer products, appropriately weighted by the α_{ij} regenerates the original image $[G]$.

In terms of a *degrees of freedom* analysis, Equation (3.16) suggests that the image matrix $[G]$ has a total maximum number of degrees of freedom equal to N^2. These correspond to the $N \times N$ pixels comprising the image. Those independent degrees of freedom are converted to N^2 coefficients α_{ij} by Equation (3.16). The vectors $\mathbf{u}_i$ and $\mathbf{v}_j^t$ are deterministic, however, and therefore have no additional degrees of freedom, as one would expect, considering the expansion of Equation (3.16) neither adds nor subtracts information from the image but simply rearranges it.

As a graphical illustration of this process, consider the example of Figure 3.3(a). Here we see that the image $[G]$ is decomposed into a sum of N^2 rank 1 matrices each weighted by the appropriate coefficient $\alpha_{i,j}$. The rank 1 matrices will represent two-dimensional *basis images*, examples of which are trigonometric waveforms for Fourier expansions or binary waveforms for Walsh expansions. By rank 1 matrices we mean the number of linearly independent rows of the matrix equals one.

Selection of the transforms represented by matrix quantities $[U]$ and $[V]$ is essentially arbitrary. The quantities $[U]$ and $[V]$ may be selected from the same or different orthogonal basis functions.

While it may not be readily evident from Equation (3.16), the expansion may be interpreted as a *singular value decomposition* (SVD) of the image into its singular

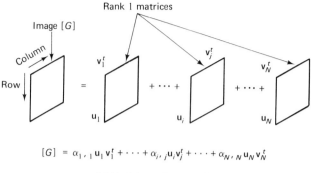

$$[G] = \alpha_{1,1} \mathbf{u}_1 \mathbf{v}_1^t + \cdots + \alpha_{i,j} \mathbf{u}_j \mathbf{v}_j^t + \cdots + \alpha_{N,N} \mathbf{u}_N \mathbf{v}_N^t$$

(a) Rank I matrix expansions

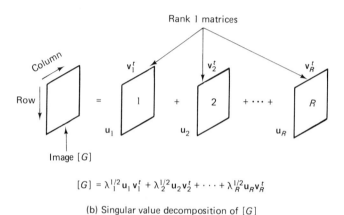

$$[G] = \lambda_1^{1/2} \mathbf{u}_1 \mathbf{v}_1^t + \lambda_2^{1/2} \mathbf{u}_2 \mathbf{v}_2^t + \cdots + \lambda_R^{1/2} \mathbf{u}_R \mathbf{v}_R^t$$

(b) Singular value decomposition of $[G]$

Figure 3.3   Image expansion into outer products.

vectors under certain circumstances [Golub and Reinsch (1970), Albert (1972)]. If the $[\alpha]$ matrix is *diagonal of rank* R {i.e., if only R finite positive diagonal terms exist in $[\alpha]$}, then

$$[G] = \sum_i^R \alpha_i \mathbf{u}_i \mathbf{v}_i^t. \tag{3.17}$$

The α_i become the square root of the singular values of $[G]$ (i.e., $\alpha_i = \lambda_i^{1/2}$), and $\mathbf{u}_i$ and $\mathbf{v}_i$ are the singular vectors. The more traditional approach would be the following definitions.

$$[G] = [U][\Lambda]^{1/2}[V]^t \tag{3.18a}$$

and

$$[G][G]^t = [U][\Lambda][U]^t, \tag{3.18b}$$

$$[G]^t[G] = [V][\Lambda][V]^t, \tag{3.18c}$$

where $[\Lambda]$ is the diagonal matrix of eigenvalues of $[G][G]^t$, the columns of $[U]$ are the eigenvectors of $[G][G]^t$, and the columns of $[V]$ are the eigenvectors of $[G]^t[G]$. Because $[G][G]^t$ and $[G]^t[G]$ are symmetric and square, the λ_i are real and the eigenvector sets $\{\mathbf{u}_i\}$ and $\{\mathbf{v}_i\}$ are self-orthogonal. From (3.17) it is evident that the smaller R, the fewer the independent rows (columns) required to define the image $[G]$. Ordering the eigen-values in monotonic decreasing order yields the most efficient least-square represen-tation of the image in the fewest (truncated) set of retained components: $\{\lambda_i^{1/2}, \mathbf{u}_i \mathbf{v}_i^t\}$.

Referring back to the SVD expansion of Equation (3.17) one might initially be concerned that we have lost some of the possible N^2 degrees of freedom inherent in an $N \times N$ image. If the rank R of the image is full, then $R = N$ and we have a total of N degrees of freedom associated with the diagonal entries $\{\alpha_i\}$. In previous expan-sions, Equation (3.16), the basis vectors $\mathbf{u}_i$ and $\mathbf{v}_j^t$ were deterministic and offered no further number of independent parameters or degrees of freedom. In this SVD approach, however, the matrices $[U]$ and $[V]$ are determined by the original image $[G]$. Because $[U]$ and $[V]$ are orthonormal, the set of basis vectors $\{\mathbf{u}_i\}$ represent $(N^2 - N)/2$ degrees of freedom. In other words, there are $N - 1$ degrees of freedom in the first vector (one degree is fixed by normalization), $N - 2$ degrees of freedom in the second vector, etc., until $N - N = 0$ degrees of freedom in the Nth vector. This sums to

$$\sum_{i=1}^{N} (N - i) = \frac{N^2 - N}{2}.$$

The same number holds for the set $\{\mathbf{v}_i\}$. Thus the total of N^2 degrees of freedom in the original image is broken into the following partitions:

$$\{\alpha_i\} + \{\mathbf{u}_i\} + \{\mathbf{v}_i\}$$

$$N + \frac{N^2 - N}{2} + \frac{N^2 - N}{2} = N^2.$$

Therefore the singular value decomposition technique also preserves N^2 degrees of freedom (as it must, being an orthogonal decomposition). Here the SVD approach does not put all N^2 degrees into N^2 coefficients, however, but distributes them into N coefficients $\{\alpha_i\}$ and $N^2 - N$ parameters defining the orthonormal matrices $[U]$ and $[V]$. Of course if not all N^2 degrees of freedom are required in describing an image $[G]$ (which is highly likely due to the correlation in an image), then the rank R may be considerably smaller than N.

Referring to Figure 3.3(b), it is noted that the SVD expansion of $[G]$ consists of only R terms, each weighted by the square root of the appropriate singular value. These rank 1 matrices also represent orthogonal basis images and are directly "tuned" to the specific image at hand representing a unique and optimal image-dependent basis expansion.

3.3   Examples of Image Representations

For digital image representation in image processing, an efficient means is sought to minimize truncation errors for storage savings [Wintz (1972), Huang (1971)]. The methods of transform coding use the matrix $[\alpha]$ defined by (3.8) and introduce trunca-tion by setting certain α_{ij} to zero. Thus

$$[G_K] = \sum_{i,j \in \{K\}}^{N} \sum^{N} \alpha_{ij} \mathbf{u}_i \mathbf{v}_j^t, \qquad (3.19a)$$

where $\{K\} = \{i, j : |\alpha_{ij}| > T_K\}$ and T_K is a threshold selected such that a total of K terms remain above that threshold.

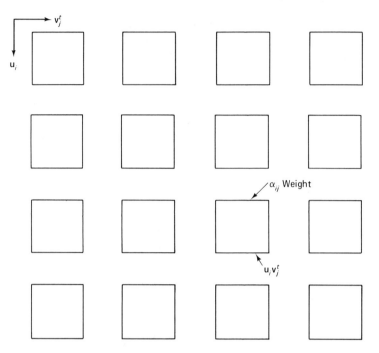

Figure 3.4   General outer product separable kernel orthogonal expansion format.

Examples of expansions into general orthogonal separable kernel transformations might best be displayed as in Figure 3.4. The outer product images are displayed in an array showing that the image $[G]$ can be decomposed into the α_{ij} weighting of the $\mathbf{u}_i \mathbf{v}_j^t$ squares in the figure. The possible set of orthogonal systems for decomposition of images is infinite; only a few of the simplest ones will be discussed. In all these cases, $[U] = [V]$ (i.e., the row and column transformations are the same), and the $[U]$ matrices become

1.   Identity:

$$[U] = \begin{bmatrix} 1 & 0 & 0 & 0 & 0 & 0 & 0 & 0 \\ 0 & 1 & 0 & 0 & 0 & 0 & 0 & 0 \\ 0 & 0 & 1 & 0 & 0 & 0 & 0 & 0 \\ 0 & 0 & 0 & 1 & 0 & 0 & 0 & 0 \\ 0 & 0 & 0 & 0 & 1 & 0 & 0 & 0 \\ 0 & 0 & 0 & 0 & 0 & 1 & 0 & 0 \\ 0 & 0 & 0 & 0 & 0 & 0 & 1 & 0 \\ 0 & 0 & 0 & 0 & 0 & 0 & 0 & 1 \end{bmatrix} = [I]$$

2. Haar:

$$[U] = \begin{bmatrix} 1 & -1 & \sqrt{2} & 0 & 2 & 0 & 0 & 0 \\ 1 & -1 & \sqrt{2} & 0 & -2 & 0 & 0 & 0 \\ 1 & -1 & -\sqrt{2} & 0 & 0 & 2 & 0 & 0 \\ 1 & -1 & -\sqrt{2} & 0 & 0 & -2 & 0 & 0 \\ 1 & 1 & 0 & \sqrt{2} & 0 & 0 & 2 & 0 \\ 1 & 1 & 0 & \sqrt{2} & 0 & 0 & -2 & 0 \\ 1 & 1 & 0 & -\sqrt{2} & 0 & 0 & 0 & 2 \\ 1 & 1 & 0 & -\sqrt{2} & 0 & 0 & 0 & -2 \end{bmatrix}$$

or

$$[U] = [HAAR].$$

3. Hadamard/Walsh:

$$[U] = \begin{bmatrix} 1 & -1 & -1 & 1 & 1 & -1 & -1 & 1 \\ 1 & -1 & -1 & 1 & -1 & 1 & 1 & -1 \\ 1 & -1 & 1 & -1 & -1 & 1 & -1 & 1 \\ 1 & -1 & 1 & -1 & 1 & -1 & 1 & -1 \\ 1 & 1 & 1 & 1 & 1 & 1 & 1 & 1 \\ 1 & 1 & 1 & 1 & -1 & -1 & -1 & -1 \\ 1 & 1 & -1 & -1 & -1 & -1 & 1 & 1 \\ 1 & 1 & -1 & -1 & 1 & 1 & -1 & -1 \end{bmatrix}$$

or

$$[U] = [W].$$

4. Hadamard/Other:

$$[U] = \begin{bmatrix} 1 & 1 & 1 & -1 & -1 & 1 & 1 & 1 \\ 1 & 1 & 1 & -1 & 1 & -1 & -1 & -1 \\ 1 & 1 & -1 & 1 & 1 & -1 & 1 & 1 \\ 1 & 1 & -1 & 1 & -1 & 1 & -1 & -1 \\ 1 & -1 & 1 & 1 & 1 & 1 & -1 & 1 \\ 1 & -1 & 1 & 1 & -1 & -1 & 1 & -1 \\ -1 & 1 & 1 & 1 & 1 & 1 & 1 & -1 \\ -1 & 1 & 1 & 1 & -1 & -1 & -1 & 1 \end{bmatrix}$$

5. Fourier:

$$[U] = \overset{\overset{x \rightarrow}{w_z\downarrow}}{\left[\exp \frac{2\pi i w_x x}{N} \right]} = \exp \left\{ \frac{2\pi i}{8} \begin{bmatrix} 0 & 0 & 0 & 0 & 0 & 0 & 0 & 0 \\ 0 & 1 & 2 & 3 & 4 & 5 & 6 & 7 \\ 0 & 2 & 4 & 6 & 0 & 2 & 4 & 6 \\ 0 & 3 & 6 & 1 & 4 & 7 & 2 & 5 \\ 0 & 4 & 0 & 4 & 0 & 4 & 0 & 4 \\ 0 & 5 & 2 & 7 & 4 & 1 & 6 & 3 \\ 0 & 6 & 4 & 2 & 0 & 6 & 4 & 2 \\ 0 & 7 & 6 & 5 & 4 & 3 & 2 & 1 \end{bmatrix} \right\}$$

or

$$[U] = [\mathfrak{F}].$$

See Harmuth (1972) for pictorial examples of these orthogonal bases.

Mixes between orthogonal sets are possible such that $[U] \neq [V]$; due to space limitations, they are not presented here.

As an illustration of the application of such expansions, consider larger dimensional arrays that represent true images. Figure 3.5 presents the α matrices corresponding to the expansions in the identity, Fourier, Walsh, and Haar outer products for two different images. The transform planes are displayed as a componentwise logarithm of the magnitude of the α_{ij}, allowing the small dynamic range of film for display purposes to be accommodated. The viewer sees the matrix $[\alpha']$ where $\alpha'_{ij} = \log(|\alpha_{ij}| + 1)$.

As evident from Figure 3.5, image energy tends to be concentrated in a few select coefficients α_{ij}, and only a small number of terms are required for good representation of the original imagery. Since the expansions under discussion are unitary, image energy is preserved so that a few large α_{ij} coefficients may represent a large fraction of the total image energy. The selection of appropriate outer product expansions and the transmission of selected coefficients are the subjects of digital transform image coding research in which storage reductions of approximately 10 : 1 have been achieved [Wintz (1972), Habibi and Wintz (1971), Pratt (1971)].

The off-diagonal coefficients, α_{ij} for the SVD case, are zero for $i \neq j$. Therefore, Figure 3.6 illustrates the orthogonal system of functions utilized in the image expansion in this case. Using the SVD as a means of representation (retaining only R such outer products) we find that

$$[G] = \sum_{i=1}^{R} \lambda_i^{1/2} \mathbf{u}_i \mathbf{v}_i^t, \tag{3.19b}$$

where $\mathbf{u}_i$, $\mathbf{v}_i$, and λ_i are the column vectors of $[U]$, $[V]$, and diagonal terms of $[\Lambda]$, respectively. The limit of the summation R represents the rank (number of nonzero singular values) of $[G]$. The outer product $\mathbf{u}_i \mathbf{v}_i^t$ is termed herein as an *eigenimage*. Naturally if $[G]$ is nonsingular, R will equal N. The outer product notation of Equation (3.17) can be interpreted as a summation of R matrices of eigenimages of rank 1, each weighted by the square root of the respective singular value.

In Figures 3.7, 3.8, and 3.9, the SVD's of images are illustrated. Selected individual singular vector outer product images are presented (in componentwise magnitude

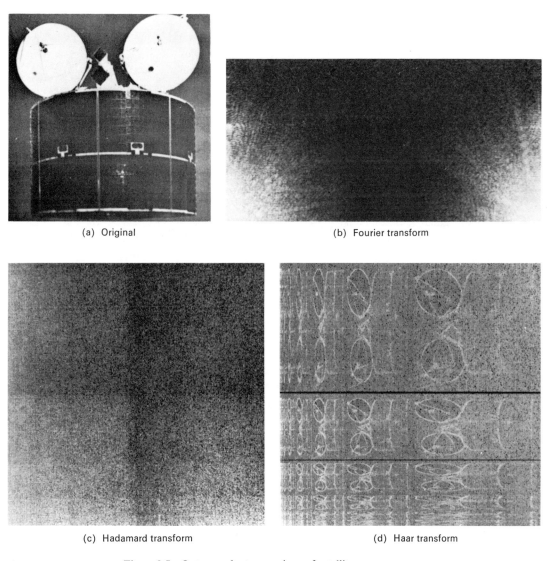

(a) Original   (b) Fourier transform

(c) Hadamard transform   (d) Haar transform

Figure 3.5   Outer product expansions of satellite.

form) to illustrate the decomposition of imagery into its basic two-dimensional components. It should be noted that the basis set of eigenimages (of which three are
presented in the figures) are matched to their particular images and contain both high
and low spatial frequencies. In theory the expansion of an image in terms of its eigenimages is a straightforward process, however, computationally the task is not simple.
Specifically it is difficult to determine R, the rank of $[G]$ when the computer provides
singular values that are not zero but are quite small (i.e., 10^{-11}). If an approximate
representation of the matrix $[G]$ is formed by truncation, then

$$[G_K] = \sum_{i=1}^{R} \lambda_i^{1/2} \mathbf{u}_i \mathbf{v}_i^t \tag{3.20}$$

and the squared norm between $[G]$ and $[G_K]$ becomes

$$\|[G] - [G_K]\|^2 = \sum_{i=K+1}^{R} \lambda_i, \tag{3.21}$$

where the matrix norm is the Euclidean measure, $Tr[G]^t[G] = \|G\|^2$. The motivation for utilizing the SVD expansion is that, hopefully, small K provides a good representation of $[G]$ and storage requirements drop from N^2 to $K(2N + 1)$ computer words (i.e., $2N$ words for two eigenvectors and one word for the eigenvalue). The truncation error of Equation (3.21) is minimized by the monotonic ordering of the singular values. In addition, the expansion of $[G]$ into its eigenimages implies there is no other orthonormal expansion with as efficient an energy representation in as few a number of coefficients. In order to understand the effect of the lower energy eigenimages more fully, the condition number $C([G])$ of the matrix $[G]$ becomes useful, where

$$C([G]) = \frac{\lambda_{\max}^{1/2}}{\lambda_{\min}^{1/2}} = \frac{\lambda_1^{1/2}}{\lambda_N^{1/2}}. \tag{3.22}$$

The condition number for the image in Figure 3.9 (the mandrill baboon) is $C([G]) \cong 10^4$, representing a reasonably stable and nonsingular matrix. The eigenvalue map (a plot of eigenvalue versus index in monotonic decreasing order) provides an intuitive feel for the effective possible bandwidth reduction. Figure 3.10 presents two extreme cases for possible image representations. The smaller the rank with concentrated energy in lower indexed eigenvalues implies a better potential savings. To illustrate the concentration of image energy in the first few eigenimages, Figures 3.11, 3.12, and 3.13 are presented. Various partial summations of the individual singular eigenimage matrices are included to demonstrate the cumulative effect of the individual outer products on the reconstruction of the entire image. Obviously, only a small number of terms are required for retention of significant image information.

In concluding this section a summary of various transform techniques will be presented to attempt to put into perspective the variety of techniques that have been discussed in the literature. The major objective in transform image processing is to manipulate the image into an invertible form more amenable to coding, storage, and restoration techniques. Table 3.1 presents a list of the more commonly discussed transforms. In all cases the domain (matrix or plane of data) used for coding, storage, and restoration is described by the $[\alpha]$ matrix, previously defined. The table should not be interpreted as an exhaustive listing. It should be obvious that many combinations of the transforms listed are all possible candidates depending on storage, hardware, and timing configurations and constraints.

3.4   Separability, Kronecker Products, and Stacking Operators

The discussion presented so far has made use of the assumption of rectangular separability. This is equivalent to separate operations on the columns and rows of

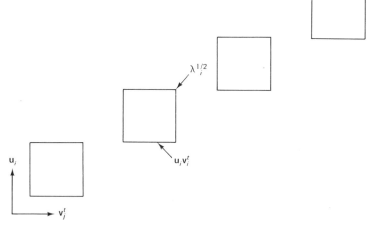

Figure 3.6 General singular value decomposition format.

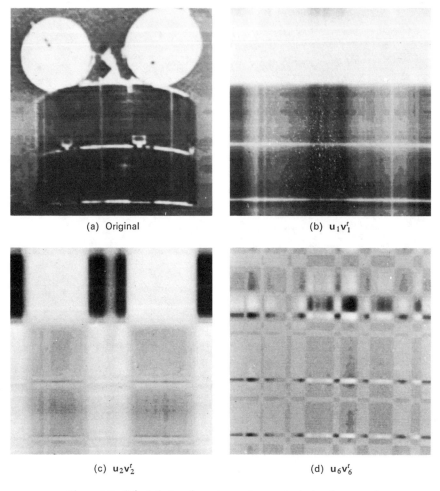

(a) Original

(b) $u_1 v_1^t$

(c) $u_2 v_2^t$

(d) $u_6 v_6^t$

Figure 3.7 Selected singular value outer product eigenimages of satellite.

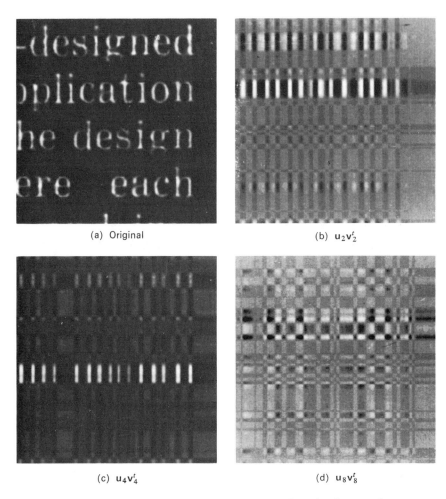

(a) Original   (b) $u_2 v_2^t$

(c) $u_4 v_4^t$ (d) $u_8 v_8^t$

Figure 3.8   Selected singular value outer product eigenimages of text.

a matrix image in order to form the matrix $[\alpha]$ as

$$[G] = [U][\alpha][V]^t. \tag{3.11}$$

In order not to be limited to row–column operations but to allow diagonal and non-rectangular separable manipulations on our imagery, we may resort to a *lexico-graphic* [Hunt (1973)] or *stacked notation*. This operation essentially raster scans and strings out the image $[G]$ and transforms $[\alpha]$ into $N^2 \times 1$ vectors, $\mathbf{g}$, α, respectively. The stacking operator [Ekstrom (1973)] allows the most general linear system relating α and $\mathbf{g}$ to be given by

$$\mathbf{g} = [H]\alpha. \tag{3.23}$$

In this case $[H]$ has dimension $N^2 \times N^2$, implying N^4 entires or possible degrees of freedom, whereas the separable case of Equation (3.11) allows only $2N^2$ possible

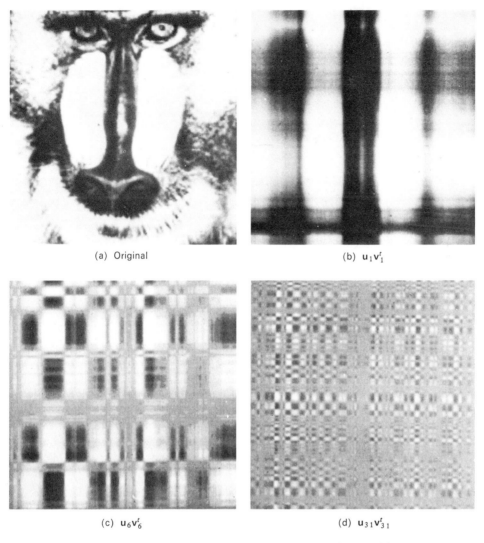

(a) Original

(b) $\mathbf{u}_1\mathbf{v}_1^t$

(c) $\mathbf{u}_6\mathbf{v}_6^t$

(d) $\mathbf{u}_{31}\mathbf{v}_{31}^t$

Figure 3.9 Selected singular value outer product eigenimages of the mandrill baboon.

degrees of freedom. If $[H]$ is used to represent the operations of the separable case of Equation (3.11), however, then $[H]$ becomes a *Kronecker* or *direct product* of matrices [Bellman (1960)],

$$[H] = [U] \otimes [V], \qquad (3.24a)$$

and takes on a block structured form. Thus

$$[H] = \begin{bmatrix} u_{11}[V] & u_{12}[V] & \cdots & u_{1N}[V] \\ u_{21}[V] & & & \\ \vdots & & & \\ u_{N1}[V] & \cdots & & u_{NN}[V] \end{bmatrix}. \qquad (3.24b)$$

41

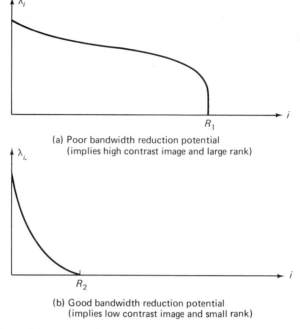

(a) Poor bandwidth reduction potential
(implies high contrast image and large rank)

(b) Good bandwidth reduction potential
(implies low contrast image and small rank)

Figure 3.10   Eigenvalue map for image representation ($R_1 \gg R_2$).

It will be shown that the separability assumption will allow computational advantages but will be restricted to a set of a priori assumptions that may not be intuitively satisfying. The important conclusion to be emphasized is that the stacking operator allows a more general description of linear relationships between $[\alpha]$ and $[G]$ planes than allowed in the separable case. The relationship given by Equations (3.11) and (3.24) in the more general context of separable image restoration will be discussed later. In addition, even when faced with nonseparable space-variant point-spread functions, it will be found that the lexicographic and/or stacked notation will simplify the tensor notation of a four-variable point-spread function to the more familiar two-variable matrix notation. Additional properties associated with the separable notation for restoration lie in the fact that the eigenspace (diagonalization) of the $N^2 \times N^2$ point-spread function matrix $[H]$ is accomplished by simply diagonalizing two $N \times N$ column and row matrices. These facts will be heavily utilized in subsequent chapters.

In the next sections we turn from image representations to a topic that is closely related: image models. The distinction, as we shall see, between these two is that an image representation, such as SVD, is usually an information preserving transformation of an image; whereas a model is an abstraction of the structure or nature of an image or whole class of images. Thus, a model may not preserve information about a particular image but it is usually a more powerful or general description for many images.

3.5   Parametric Statistical Models

The first class of models discussed is the class of parametric statistical models. A statistician will often make a model of the problem in the form of an underlying

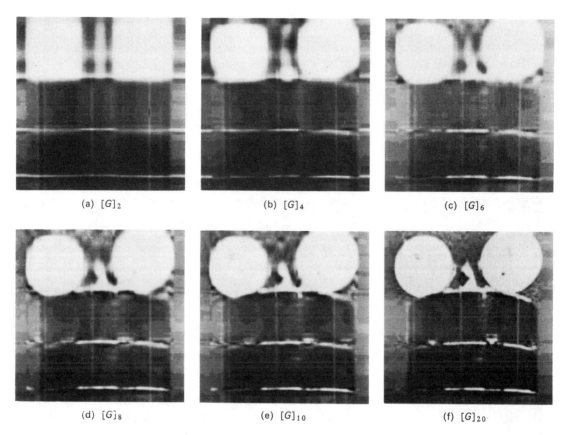

(a) $[G]_2$ (b) $[G]_4$ (c) $[G]_6$

(d) $[G]_8$ (e) $[G]_{10}$ (f) $[G]_{20}$

Figure 3.11 Selected partial sums of SVD expansions of satellite.

probability density function (PDF). Since the PDF is a specific function, and is assumed to govern the problem's behavior, it is only the parameters that describe the PDF that are available to the modeler, hence the term *parametric statistical model*.

Let $g(x, y)$ be the $N \times N$ matrix of samples from the image. Here (x, y) take on only integer values. As discussed above, the matrix $g(x, y)$ can be converted to an $N^2 \times 1$ column vector by lexicographic ordering or by using the stacking operator. Let this column vector be $\mathbf{g}$:

$$\mathbf{g} = \begin{bmatrix} g(1, 1) \\ g(1, 2) \\ \cdot \\ \cdot \\ \cdot \\ g(1, N) \\ \cdot \\ \cdot \\ \cdot \\ g(N, N) \end{bmatrix}. \tag{3.25}$$

Since the image is now described as a vector in N^2-dimensional space, then the parametric statistical models relevant to vector (multivariate) data are the models to be applied to descriptions of $\mathbf{g}$.

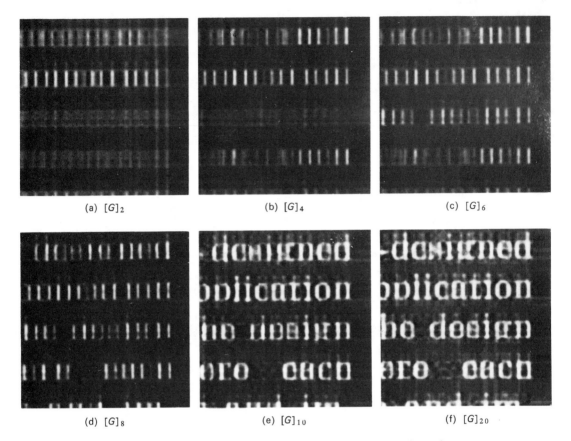

(a) $[G]_2$ (b) $[G]_4$ (c) $[G]_6$

(d) $[G]_8$ (e) $[G]_{10}$ (f) $[G]_{20}$

Figure 3.12   Selected partial sums of SVD expansions of text.

If all N^2 components of **g** in (3.25) were statistically independent of each other, then it would be possible to choose N^2 different PDF's to describe each component, and by independence the joint PDF of the entire vector would be the product of the N_2 component PDF's. Images (and most other real data sources) exhibit varying amounts of statistical dependence, however (i.e., the ith and jth component of the vector **g** are not statistically independent). The multivariate Gaussian allows a simple and compact description of the joint PDF of a vector that explicitly includes the correlation between any and all individual components of the PDF, hence the popularity of the multivariate Gaussian PDF. It is virtually the only tool for which analytical techniques exist and is frequently used even in cases where the assumed multivariate Gaussian behavior may not be borne out by the data or physical reality of the problem.[1]

In making a parametric statistical model, we are actually modeling not a specific image **g** but a class of images. Given the specific image **g**, we are asserting by the

[1]See the work by Johnson and Kotz (1972) for more discussion of multivariate PDF's.

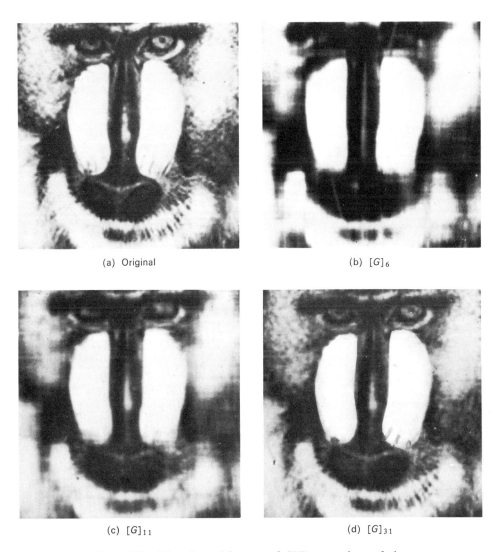

(a) Original   (b) $[G]_6$

(c) $[G]_{11}$ (d) $[G]_{31}$

Figure 3.13 Selected partial sums of SVD expansions of the mandrill baboon.

model that **g** is a sample from a multivariate class of random data that is governed by a Gaussian joint PDF:

$$p(\mathbf{g}) = ((2\pi)^{N^2/2} |\phi_g|^{1/2})^{-1} \exp\{-\tfrac{1}{2}(\mathbf{g} - \bar{\mathbf{g}})^t [\phi_g]^{-1} (\mathbf{g} - \bar{\mathbf{g}})\}, \qquad (3.26)$$

where $[\phi_g]$ is the covariance matrix and $\bar{\mathbf{g}}$ is the mean-value vector.

For more insight, consider the structure of $[\phi_g]$, the covariance matrix. By definition,

$$[\phi_g] = \mathcal{E}\{(\mathbf{g} - \bar{\mathbf{g}})(\mathbf{g} - \bar{\mathbf{g}})^t\}, \qquad (3.27)$$

TABLE 3.1 Transform Domains for Image Representations

Entry	Transform Name	Representation	Unknown Parameters (to be computed)	Algorithmic Implementation (on the order of:)	Reference	Footnote
1	Singular value decomposition	$[G][G]^t = [U][\Lambda][U]^t$ $[G]^t[G] = [V][\Lambda][V]^t$ $[\alpha] = [\Lambda^{1/2}] = [U]^t[G][V]$	Basis vectors and singular values	$\left.\begin{array}{l}N^3\\N^3\\2N^3\end{array}\right\}$ computed for each image	Golub (1970) Albert (1972)	1
2	Karhunen-Loève, Hotelling, principal components, factor analysis	$[\phi_x] = [E_x][\Lambda_x][E_x]^t$ $[\phi_y] = [E_y][\Lambda_y][E_y]^t$ $[\alpha] = [E_x]^t[G][E_y]$	Transform coefficients	$\left.\begin{array}{l}N^3\\N^3\\2N^3\end{array}\right\}$ computed only once	Wintz (1972) Huang (1971)	1
3	Cosine	$[\alpha] = [\cos]^t[G][\cos]$	Transform coefficients	$4N^2 \log_2 2N$	Ahmed (1974)	1, 2
4	Fourier	$[\alpha] = [\mathcal{F}][G][\mathcal{F}]$	Transform coefficients	$2N^2 \log_2 N$ (complex)	Andrews (1970)	1, 2
5	Slant	$[\alpha] = [\text{Slant}]^t[G][\text{Slant}]$	Transform coefficients	$2N^2 \log_2 N$	Pratt (1974)	1
6	DLB	$[\alpha] = [DLB]^t[G][DLB]$	Transform coefficients	$2N^2 \log_2 N$ (integer arith.)	Haralick (1974)	1, 2
7	Walsh	$[\alpha] = [W][G][W]$	Transform coefficients	$2N^2 \log_2 N$ (additions)	Pratt (1969)	1
8	Haar	$[\alpha] = [HAAR]^t [G] [HAAR]$	Transform coefficients	$2(N - 1)$	Andrews (1970)	1

[1]N is proportional to the size of the image.
[2]When $N \neq 2^k$, the computations increase.

where $\mathcal{E}$ is the expectation over the ensemble of all possible samples from the PDF in Equation (3.26). The vector $\mathbf{g}$ is a lexicographic order or stacking of the rows of the original sampled image matrix $g(x, y)$. Thus, $[\phi_g]$ is an $N^2 \times N^2$ matrix made of partitions. Each partition is $N \times N$. If $\mathbf{g}_j$ signifies the column vector made up of the jth row of $g(x, y)$, i.e.,

$$\mathbf{g}_j = \begin{bmatrix} g(j, 1) \\ g(j, 2) \\ \cdot \\ \cdot \\ \cdot \\ g(j, N) \end{bmatrix}, \tag{3.28}$$

then the m, nth partition of $[\phi_g]$ is

$$[\phi_{mn}] = \mathcal{E}[(\mathbf{g}_m - \bar{\mathbf{g}}_m)(\mathbf{g}_n - \bar{\mathbf{g}}_n)^t]. \tag{3.29}$$

It follows directly that each partition $[\phi_{mn}]$ is symmetric,

$$[\phi_{mn}] = [\phi_{mn}^t], \tag{3.30}$$

and further the entire matrix $[\phi_g]$ is symmetric since

$$[\phi_{mn}] = [\phi_{nm}]. \tag{3.31}$$

The matrix $[\phi_g]$ is said to be a *block covariance matrix* since the blocks or partitions $[\phi_{mn}]$ carry the information about the covariance between individual rows m, n.

The initial reaction may be that the assumed model of (3.26) is inefficient since the original image $g(x, y)$ possessed at most only N^2 degrees of freedom; yet the PDF in (3.26) requires $N^4 + N^2$ parameters to be specified (a covariance matrix $N^2 \times N^2$ and a mean vector $N^2 \times 1$). The modeling is really quite powerful, however, because the $N^4 + N^2$ parameters in $[\phi_g]$ and $\bar{g}$ specify an infinite class of images, and the vector $\mathbf{g}$ is only one sample from this infinite class.

The following points can be made about the philosophy of using a description such as (3.26) for modeling a class of images.

1.   The value of the model in describing images in a class is related to our ability to a priori describe the conditions. The covariance matrix and mean-value vector play entirely different roles. For example, suppose that the a priori limit of knowledge was that the image possessed a constant mean value; i.e., the mean-value vector was a constant in each position:

$$\bar{\mathbf{g}} = \mathcal{E}\{\mathbf{g}\} = \boldsymbol{\mu}, \tag{3.32}$$

where

$$\boldsymbol{\mu} = \mu \begin{bmatrix} 1 \\ 1 \\ \cdot \\ \cdot \\ \cdot \\ 1 \end{bmatrix}.$$

Since $\bar{\mathbf{g}}$ is a vector constant, then the covariance matrix $[\phi_g]$ must be used to represent the structure of the image in the model; however, covariance is a *gross* or *global* constraint in image models. Images contain much more structure than can be represented only by covariance parameters.

2. On the other hand, the mean-value vector can convey this extra structure. Suppose that the mean-value vector $\bar{\mathbf{g}}$ is not a constant but represents the underlying structure in an image; e.g., if an image of a face is involved, the $\bar{\mathbf{g}}$ might be a vector giving a crude representation of a face: an oval with implanted features for eyes, nose, mouth, etc. Then a model in the form of (3.26) can be used to describe images that possess random fluctuations about the underlying structure $\bar{\mathbf{g}}$. In fact, it is possible to make the PDF of (3.26) model *any* specific image $\mathbf{g}'$. For the mean value in (3.26) we use the specific image, i.e., $\bar{\mathbf{g}} \leftarrow \mathbf{g}'$, and then let all elements of the covariance matrix $[\phi_g]$ approach zero at the same rate. The result is a multivariate density (or zero width) that is centered on the specific image $\mathbf{g}'$. Thus, the mean value has very specific parameter properties that can be used to represent specific structures in an image. Only a change in viewpoint is required.

3. Images modeled by Equation (3.26) can also be dichotomized as *stationary* or *nonstationary* models. A one-dimensional stationary[2] model has the properties that

$$\mathcal{E}\{\mathbf{g}\} = \boldsymbol{\mu} \qquad \text{(a constant vector)}$$

and

$$\mathcal{E}\{[(\mathbf{g} - \bar{\mathbf{g}})(\mathbf{g} - \bar{\mathbf{g}})']\} = [\phi_g],$$

where $[\phi_g]$ has the property that elements on diagonals are the same; i.e., if $j - k = m - n$, then

$$\{\phi_g\}_{jk} = \{\phi_g\}_{mn}. \tag{3.33}$$

For two-dimensional stacked vectors of the kind used herein, the equivalent form of the matrix relation in (3.33) for stationarity is that if $j - k = m - n$ and $p - q = r - s$, then

$$[\phi_{pq}] = [\phi_{rs}] \tag{3.34a}$$

and

$$\{[\phi_{pq}]\}_{jk} = \{[\phi_{pq}]\}_{mn}, \tag{3.34b}$$

where the partition matrices are as described in (3.29) and where $\{\ \}$ and subscript denote elements of a matrix or vector. Matrices with properties described by (3.33) are known as *Toeplitz matrices* or *Toeplitz forms*, after the mathematician who discovered them. A matrix with properties of (3.34) is a *block Toeplitz matrix*. If the covariance matrix is not Toeplitz, the model is said to be *nonstationary*. If the mean vector is not a constant but is known, however, it can be subtracted, leaving the possibility of a stationary process. It should be evident from the discussions in points 1 and 2 that a stationary image model can be expected to model only the more gross properties of a

---

[2]Stationarity defined via mean and covariance is more specifically referred to as *wide sense* stationarity [Papoulis (1965)].

class of images; whereas nonstationary models can be expected to be more adaptive to the specific structure of an image.

4.   Aspects of ergodicity are involved in the discussion above. In an ergodic random process, spatial averages and ensemble averages are equal. Thus, in a stationary, ergodic process model, one could estimate the ensemble mean value by the spatial average:

$$\langle \hat{\mu} \rangle = \frac{1}{N^2} \sum_{x=1}^{N} \sum_{y=1}^{N} g(x, y). \tag{3.35}$$

To assume that the mean-value vector $\bar{\mathbf{g}}$ is not a constant, but conveys structure that is representative of the underlying structure in the class of images being modeled, however, is equivalent to assuming that the image model is not ergodic. It is the ensemble average

$$\mathcal{E}\{\mathbf{g}\} = \bar{\mathbf{g}} \tag{3.36}$$

that becomes of interest, precisely because the use of a spatial average, as in (3.36), is too gross a representation of the important structure. Thus, the representation of image models with specific structure, through the use of a particularly desired choice of $\bar{\mathbf{g}}$, is associated with nonstationary models and with the failure of the ergodic hypothesis.

These points of philosophy aside, there are some important practical considerations to be borne in mind when modeling images by the multivariate normal PDF. First, the image may not be well-represented by a Gaussian distribution on the samples $g(x, y)$. An image that was basically black and white, say the image of a blackbird standing in snow, would not seem likely to possess Gaussian amplitude statistics. Second, the Gaussian PDF can generate negative values in the components of the sample vector. Light intensities are always positive, however, as we emphasized in Chapter 2, and a Gaussian model is therefore subject to violations of physical reality.

The negativity conflict for a Gaussian image model can be resolved, or at least alleviated, in two different ways. First, if the multivariate variance about the mean-value $\bar{\mathbf{g}}$ is small compared to $\bar{\mathbf{g}}$ itself ($\bar{\mathbf{g}}$ assumed to be positive in every component), then the density function is concentrated sufficiently about $\bar{\mathbf{g}}$ so that negative values are very infrequent and can be neglected. If this condition cannot be satisfied, then the *truncated Gaussian* may be used. Finally, if the truncated Gaussian is not appropriate, then the homomorphic model may be useful. This has intuitive appeal and leads to interesting nonlinear processes in image restoration. Stockham (1972) has argued that image formation is a multiplicative process and that an image $g(x, y)$ can be considered the product of two components: an illumination component and a reflectance component, denoted as $g_i(x, y)$ and $g_r(x, y)$, respectively. Thus

$$g(x, y) = g_i(x, y) g_r(x, y). \tag{3.37}$$

The illumination component usually carries background variations in the "brightness" of an image (i.e., slowly varying mean vector information); whereas the reflectance component is generally more specular, carrying information of small details that reflect and/or break up the illumination variations. This also corresponds to intuition about images and is consistent with nonstationary models such as discussed above.

Now by using a logarithm operation we can separate the multiplicative effects of Equation (3.37) into additive processes such that

$$\log (g(x, y)) = \log (g_i(x, y)) + \log (g_r(x, y)). \tag{3.38}$$

Now the assumption of Gaussian statistics in the logarithm domain is consistent, implying that g is log normal where

$$g = e^z \tag{3.39}$$

and z is Gaussian (normally distributed). Thus the exponentiation of the Gaussian random variable $\log (g(x, y))$ guarantees a positive density function for g [Lindgren (1970), Johnson and Leone (1964), Aitchison and Brown (1957)].

A third alternative in dealing with the problem of positive light which is inherent in light intensities is to use a statistical model which is always positive in the joint PDF. There are many PDF's for always positive random variables; unfortunately, the generalizations of these PDF's to multivariate data are complicated. The multivariate Gaussian remains our basic model and will be used in succeeding chapters, particularly in Bayesian analysis.

3.6 Nonparametric Statistical Models

What about the case where we feel neither justified in adopting a specific PDF model nor constrained by the failure to do so? In such cases the mean value and covariance matrix are still important to use in modeling a class of images; however, they are only *descriptive statistics* for modeling the class and are not parameters of a specific PDF. We refer to the resulting models as *nonparametric* statistical models. It is evident that not specifying the amplitude statistics of the image class, and the joint PDF of the amplitude statistics, results in a much more general class of models.

The arguments made in Section 3.5 are still valid for interpreting $\bar{g}$ and $[\phi_g]$ as descriptive statistics. That is, the global properties of the covariance matrix are still valid; but as a descriptive statistic it is very crude. Likewise the mean value of the ensemble can convey much specific structure as a descriptive statistic. The properties of stationarity and ergodic behavior (or lack thereof) also apply from the discussion in Section 3.5. By analogy to one dimension, similar models are used in the analysis of time series [Jenkins and Watts (1968)], and the mean and covariance are used to describe a statistical phenomenon with unknown joint PDF.

More specific properties may be imposed upon the descriptive statistics. For example, it may be assumed that the covariance matrix is *separable*, i.e.,

$$[\phi_g] = [\phi_y] \otimes [\phi_x], \tag{3.40}$$

where $[\phi_x]$ and $[\phi_y]$ are the covariance matrices in the x and y directions. This is equivalent to stating that the variability in the x direction is unrelated to the variability in the y direction. Thus, $[\phi_x]$ and $[\phi_y]$ are $N \times N$ matrices and

$$[\phi_x] = \mathcal{E}_x\{(\mathbf{g}_x - \bar{\mathbf{g}}_x)(\mathbf{g}_x - \bar{\mathbf{g}}_x)'\},$$
$$[\phi_y] = \mathcal{E}_y\{(\mathbf{g}_y - \bar{\mathbf{g}}_y)(\mathbf{g}_y - \bar{\mathbf{g}}_y)'\},$$

(3.41)

where $\mathcal{E}_x$ and $\mathcal{E}_y$ are ensemble averages in the x and y directions separately, i.e., averages over all possible rows and columns of the ensemble of images. $\mathbf{g}_x$ and $\mathbf{g}_y$ are column vectors indicating x and y directions (rows and columns) in the image matrices, and

$$\mathcal{E}_x\{\mathbf{g}_x\} = \bar{\mathbf{g}}_x,$$
$$\mathcal{E}_y\{\mathbf{g}_y\} = \bar{\mathbf{g}}_y.$$

(3.42)

It is straightforward to show that the separable covariance matrix has the block structure

$$[\phi_g] = \begin{bmatrix} \phi_{11}^y[\phi_x] & \phi_{12}^y[\phi_x] & \cdots & \phi_{1N}^y[\phi_x] \\ & & & \\ \vdots & & & \\ & & & \\ \phi_{N1}^y[\phi_x] & \phi_{N2}^y[\phi_x] & \cdots & \phi_{NN}^y[\phi_x] \end{bmatrix},$$

(3.43)

where ϕ_{ij}^y is the ijth element of $[\phi_y]$ and there are only $2N^2$ possible degrees of freedom, as opposed to the N^4 degrees of freedom possible in the definition of Equation (3.27). Finally, if the process model is stationary as well as separable, then $[\phi_x]$ and $[\phi_y]$ are both Toeplitz matrices, where

$$[\phi_x] = \begin{bmatrix} \phi_{1x} & \phi_{2x} & \cdots & \phi_{Nx} \\ \phi_{2x} & \phi_{1x} & & \cdot \\ \cdot & & \cdot & \cdot \\ \cdot & & & \cdot \\ \cdot & & & \cdot \\ \phi_{Nx} & & & \phi_{1x} \end{bmatrix}$$

(3.44)

and likewise for $[\phi_y]$. There are only $2N$ total degrees of freedom as a result.

Because digital computers inherently operate on a rectangular coordinate system for rectangularly scanned imagery, separability initially implies rectangular separation of statistical parameters. Because of an inherent circular or polar coordinate symmetry of lens and many optical components, however, imaging systems are often separable in polar rather than rectangular systems. This implies the need for a coordinate transformation in the computer from rectangular to polar form prior to utilizing the separability assumptions mentioned above.

The use of separable statistics can be further qualified on the nonparametric model by assuming a *Markov process*. In time-series analysis, the Markov process is defined on an ordered sequence of random variables, $g_1, g_2, g_3, \ldots, g_j, \ldots$. A process that generates the ordered sequence of random variables is Markov if the conditional density function of g_j depends only on a finite number of g's prior to j. As an example,

$$p(g_j | g_{j-1}, g_{j-2}, \ldots, g_1) = p(g_j | g_{j-1})$$

(3.45)

is the requirement for a process to be *first-order* Markov. *n*th-order Markov processes are described by extension. It is easy to show that the first-order Markov process has an autocovariance function of the form

$$\phi(j) = \sigma_g^2(\rho)^j \qquad \text{for } j = 0, 1, 2, 3, \dots, \tag{3.46}$$

where ρ is the adjacent element correlation [Jenkins and Watts (1968)]. If an image is assumed to be modeled by separable Markov processes, then $[\phi_g]$ is defined by Equation (3.40) and

$$[\phi_x] = \sigma_x^2 \begin{bmatrix} 1 & \rho_x^1 & \rho_x^2 & \cdots & \rho_x^{N-1} \\ \rho_x^1 & 1 & & & \cdot \\ \cdot & & & & \cdot \\ \cdot & & & & \cdot \\ \cdot & & & \cdot & \rho_x^1 \\ \rho_x^{N-1} & \cdot & \cdot & \cdot & \rho_x^1 & 1 \end{bmatrix},$$

$$[\phi_y] = \sigma_y^2 \begin{bmatrix} 1 & \rho_y^1 & \rho_y^2 & \cdots & \rho_y^{N-1} \\ \rho_y^1 & 1 & & & \cdot \\ \cdot & & & & \cdot \\ \cdot & & & & \cdot \\ \cdot & & & \cdot & \rho_y^1 \\ \rho_y^{N-1} & \cdot & \cdot & \rho_y^1 & 1 \end{bmatrix} \tag{3.47}$$

where σ_x^2 and σ_y^2 are the *x*- and *y*-direction variances and ρ_x and ρ_y are the adjacent element correlations in the *x* and *y* directions. There are only two degrees of freedom in this model, making it most restrictive. Since a Markov process with an autocovariance function such as (3.46) is stationary about the mean value, then only $\bar{g}$, the mean-value vector; σ_x, σ_y; and ρ_x, ρ_y must be specified for the descriptive statistics. This is, obviously, the simplest image model for the nonparametric case. Similar comments are applicable to the parametric case and Equation (3.25).

Since the mean and covariance are descriptive statistics in the nonparametric case, what other descriptive statistics are useful? Two other commonly employed *scene statistics* or *image statistics* are the *histogram* and the *entropy*. As before, we let the digital image be the matrix $g(x, y)$. As discussed above, the sampling of the image will be followed by a quantization of the sample into a finite number of bits. This quantization defines a natural choice for the number of bins in a histogram; e.g., eight-bit quantization results in a histogram with 256 bins, where each bin is one of the integer sample values $0, 1, 2, \dots, 255$. The histogram on the bins is a function $h(j)$, for $j = 1, 2, 3, \dots, B$, where B is the number of bins. Then $h(j)$ is defined as

$$h(j) = \sum_{x=1}^{N} \sum_{y=1}^{N} \chi_j[g(x, y)], \tag{3.48}$$

where χ_j is the characteristic or indicator function of the *j*th bin; i.e.,

$$\begin{aligned} \chi_j(g) &= 1 \qquad \text{if } b_{j-1} \leq g < b_j \\ \chi_j(g) &= 0 \qquad \text{otherwise,} \end{aligned} \tag{3.49}$$

where b_{j-1} and b_j are the lower and upper boundaries of the jth bin. The total number of counts in the histogram is

$$N^2 = \sum_{j=1}^{B} h(j). \tag{3.50}$$

The normalized histogram is

$$p_h(j) = \frac{h(j)}{N^2} \tag{3.51}$$

and $p_h(j)$ is an approximation to the PDF of the original image. Each element $p_h(j)$ can be taken as an estimate of the probability of an image sample lying within the interval $[b_{j-1}, b_j]$. This approximation is best applied for finely quantized imagery over the appropriate transmission dynamic range.

The *entropy* statistic is defined in terms of the information capacity of a single element of the "message," where for scene statistics the message is the given image $g(x, y)$. The *information* is defined [Harman (1963)] as

$$I(p_h(j)) = -\log_2 (p_h(j)), \tag{3.52}$$

and I is measured in units of bits. The entropy scene statistic based on the normalized histogram p_h is

$$H(p_h) = \sum_{j=1}^{B} p_h(j) I(p_h(j))$$

$$= -\sum_{j=1}^{B} p_h(j) \log_2 (p_h(j)). \tag{3.53}$$

The entropy scene statistic is seen as the average over the assumed PDF $p_h(j)$ of the information I. It represents the average information in bits per picture element of the sampled image $g(x, y)$. As with other uses of the entropy function in information theory, the entropy scene statistic has a maximum value of $\log_2 B$, where B is the number of bins in the original histogram. Thus, for an eight-bit quantization, the maximum entropy is eight bits per picture sample. This is achieved only when all bins are equally populated; i.e., the amplitude statistics of $g(x, y)$ are governed by the uniform PDF.

The histogram and entropy models discussed so far refer to only zero-order statistics, i.e., the statistics associated only with individual pixels as if they were uncorrelated with their neighbors. This is obviously only a rough approximation to the real world, better models being first- and higher-order histograms and entropies. Naturally the higher the order of statistical knowledge, the better the description of the class of images and the lower the uncertainty or entropy in a given image. Unfortunately, computing higher-order joint histograms requires on the order of B^{q+1} core locations where q is the order of statistic desired. Thus for an eight-bit image and first-order density functions, $(256)^2$ storage locations are necessary to develop the histogram alone. Consequently such higher-order statistics are often left undeveloped.

Finally, it is important to note a class of statistical models developed in the work of Frieden (1971) and Hershel (1971), which require a simultaneous discussion of the

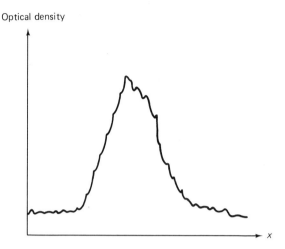

Figure 3.14   Fuel rod density profile.

role of image formation in the generation of the random-grain allocations. Hence, we shall postpone detailed discussion of the methods of Frieden and Hershel until a later chapter.

3.7 Parametric Deterministic Models

We now turn to image models which are deterministic and which assume the fundamental nature of the deterministic image can be specified by means of a set of parameters. The principal difficulty is the definition of the parameters and the choice of a minimum set of parameters in the representation.

As an example illustrating the point, consider a bundle of fuel rods in a nuclear reactor test program that is radiographed as part of the routine inspection processes. Of interest is the spacing between the wall of the fuel-rod bundle container and the rods themselves. Due to the image formation properties of radiography, as discussed in Chapter 2, however, the gap image is blurred by the effects of X-ray scatter and finite source size. A typical gap profile in optical density on the X-ray film is shown in Figure 3.14.

The dimension of interest is the width of the gap. As seen in Figure 3.15, a trace through the fuel bundle geometry gives the shape of the ideal density profile, in the absence of X-ray scatter and source size effects. This ideal profile can be described in a small number of parameters. Let $f(x, p_1, p_2, \ldots, p_m)$ be a function (polynomial, spline, etc.) of these parameters across the gap dimension x. Then the image on film is a convolution of this function with the point-spread-function effects due to X-ray scatter and source size:

$$g(x, p_1, p_2, \ldots, p_m) = \int_{-\infty}^{\infty} h(x - x_1) f(x_1, p_1, p_2, \ldots, p_m)\, dx_1. \qquad (3.54)$$

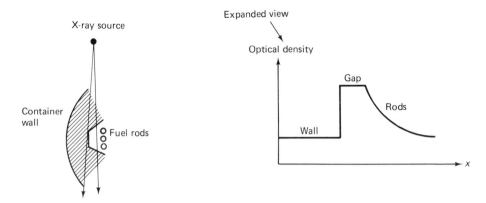

Figure 3.15   Ideal gap profile.

The function g is thus the model of the image. It is obscured partially by film–grain noise. The parameters p can be fitted from the data recorded on film, however. The result is a deterministic model specified by a set of parameters, even though there is randomness introduced by noise. It is the sensor noise which is ignored in developing a model of the image which would be observed in the absence of noise [Demuth (1974)].

It is apparent that the one-dimensional modeling discussion presented above is applicable to two-dimensional modeling of imagery. For example, the model of a rocket image could be made from the surface-of-revolution parameters for a cylinder with conical subsurfaces. The point is that making models in functional parametric form is limited only by the skill of the analyst in perceiving the underlying structure and then encompassing that structure in a compact, analytic form.

The functional parametric form discussed above might be likened to structural or linguistic methods of "primitive" definition used by the artificial intelligence community. In these techniques an image is segmented or "parsed" into regions known as *primitives*. These primitives then are used as a linguistic or structural description of the image from whence greater image understanding develops. Unfortunately, the proper parameterization to define the best primitives is not an easy task. In addition, noise tends to dominate such segmenting algorithms, rendering them less useful in real-world imagery.

The functional methods discussed above are not the only means by which a parametric and deterministic model of an image can be made, however. It should be obvious from the discussion earlier in this chapter that the general topic of *image representations* presented there is pertinent to the image modeling question. Indeed, given the two perspectives, image representations and image modeling, one can state the following general points.

1.   Image representations can be treated as modeling problems in which the model parameters are linear with respect to a set of basis functions or basis images. Conceptually, however, a model of an image is not an exact representation;

a model preserves the important overall structure of an image but not all fine details. In terms of an equation in the form of (3.16), a model may be derived from a representation equivalent to summing selective values in the expansion. Or

$$[G_K] = \sum_{i,j \in \{K\}} \alpha_{ij} \mathbf{u}_i \mathbf{v}_j^t, \tag{3.55}$$

where $i, j \in \{K\}$ and $\{K\}$ is a set of integers imposing suitable model constraints.

2. Given this viewpoint of linearity in a set of basis functions or basis images, the question of parsimony arises: What is the smallest number of parameters that must be specified to model the image or class of images? As also discussed earlier, the singular value decomposition is an image representation in which

$$\alpha_{ij} = 0 \qquad (\text{if } i \neq j).$$

Thus

$$[G] = \sum_{i=1}^{R} \alpha_i \mathbf{u}_i \mathbf{v}_i^t \tag{3.17}$$

as presented above, where R is the rank of the sampled image matrix $[G]$. If $[G]$ is of rank $R < N$, then inherently the image can be specified proportional to R parameters. Similar comments apply with respect to image models, even though (3.17) was originally posed for image representations. Suppose that a specific class of images is to be modeled, for example, the oval shape of a face, as discussed previously. Let the model image be $[G]$. Then the image $[G]$ could be singular value decomposed into basis images $\mathbf{u}_i \mathbf{v}_i^t$ and

$$[G] = \sum_{i=1}^{R} \alpha_i \mathbf{u}_i \mathbf{v}_i^t \tag{3.56}$$

would represent the model image in a set of R basis images. Presumably, if the model is a good one, then given any other image, say $[G']$ in the class modeled by $[G]$, then the expansion,

$$[G'] = \sum_{i=1}^{N} \sum_{j=1}^{N} \alpha'_{ij} \mathbf{u}_i \mathbf{v}_j^t, \tag{3.57}$$

of $[G']$ in the basis images of the model should be nearly optimal in the sense of the SVD. That is, one need not expand $[G']$ in its own SVD vectors but use the SVD vectors of the model and then determine the corresponding coefficients α'_{ij} by means of

$$\alpha'_{ij} = \mathbf{u}_i^t [G'] \mathbf{v}_j. \tag{3.58}$$

This use of the SVD also conforms to the intuitive ideal of what a model should do, i.e., represent a class of images. Thus, the SVD may be used to represent a single image, as above, or to represent the model image of a class of images. In either case, the representation is parsimonious.

3. In the case of image representations, the basis functions either are determined without relation to the image (Fourier, Walsh, etc.) or are determined by orthogonal eigenproperties of the image (singular value decomposition). It is possible to make representations, and hence models, in orthogonal sets that depend solely on the image (SVD). Finally for a class of images given in class

{{[G]}}, its vector representation is {g}. By the Gram–Schmidt orthogonalization process an orthogonal set of basis vectors can be constructed from a set of images {g}. The complete and direct dependence of this basis set on {g} seems to offer great potential in image modeling; no applications are yet known, however.

Finally, image models, such as discussed above in the nuclear reactor fuel-rod problem, are characterized by either nonlinear parameter relations and/or the human imposition of order into the modeling process. For example, the general functional relation in (3.54) admits the potential for nonlinear behavior of functions **f** and **g** with respect to the parameters.

3.8   Nonparametric Deterministic Models

Given the discussion of the previous three sections, it is logical to consider the other half of the dichotomy for deterministic models, i.e., nonparametric. As we shall see, they are more appropriately considered as *constraints* upon the general class of matrices, $[G]$ or $g(x, y)$, that represent a sampled image.

The first important nonparametric constraint we place upon an image is that of *nonnegativity*. As discussed in Chapter 2, an image is formed by radiant energy transport, which is restricted to unsigned quantities and hence nonnegative. Thus

$$g(x, y) \geqq 0 \qquad \text{for } x, y = 1, 2, \ldots, N. \tag{3.59}$$

The matrix $[G]$ is thus a so-called nonnegative matrix, in the sense used by Gantmacher (1959). Such matrices have a number of interesting properties but the relevance of these properties to image processing problems has not yet been demonstrated.

A second constraint to be used in modeling is that of *boundedness*. Since the image is formed by radiant energy transport, clearly the image must be finite due to the finiteness of the transported energy. Thus, we can postulate the existence of an upper bound M, such that

$$g(x, y) \leqq M \qquad \text{for } x, y = 1, 2, \ldots, N. \tag{3.60}$$

The use of bounded, positive matrices results in a very general class of image models.

Additional constraints upon the class of matrices $g(x, y)$ can be imposed as a function of the specific knowledge at hand. For example, the knowledge of the total radiant energy transport involved in image formation can be utilized. If the image was formed by a system emitting a total of E units of some form of radiant energy, then

$$\sum_{y=1}^{N} \sum_{x=1}^{N} g(x, y) \leqq E \leqq N^2 M, \tag{3.61}$$

where the first equality holds only if the image formation system intercepts all the emitted radiant energy.

As another example, consider an image formed by an off-axis radiographic system. Then, as discussed in Chapter 2, the penumbra effect of off-axis geometry will result in all step discontinuities being blurred into ramp or ramp-like functions. Here the image is restricted to contain no step-function discontinuities. If $[Q]$ is the operator matrix of size $N \times N$,

$$[Q_1] = \begin{bmatrix} 1 & & & & & & \\ 1 & -1 & & & & & \\ & 1 & -1 & & & \text{\Large 0} & \\ & & 1 & -1 & & & \\ & & & & \cdot & & \\ & \text{\Large 0} & & & \cdot & & \\ & & & & 1 & -1 & \\ & & & & & 1 & \end{bmatrix}, \qquad (3.62)$$

then the Kronecker product of $[Q_1]$ with itself,

$$[Q] = [Q_1] \otimes [Q_1], \qquad (3.63)$$

generates an $N^2 \times N^2$ matrix $[Q]$ such that the operation of $[Q]$ on a lexicographically ordered image vector $\mathbf{g}$,

$$\mathbf{g}' = [Q]\mathbf{g}, \qquad (3.64)$$

generates an image that is the separable [rows and columns of $g(x, y)$ operated on independently] first difference of the original image. Thus, we can express discontinuity constraints on an image in terms of the operator $[Q]$. The penumbra example considered above can be expressed as the constraint that $\mathbf{g}'$ can contain only step discontinuities of the first kind.

The difference constraint formulated in terms of the operator leads to immediate generalization. Any useful or meaningful operator acting on the image vector $\mathbf{g}$ can be used as a constraining relation, the actual nature of the operator imposed by the a priori knowledge at hand. Thus, one might impose generalized norm constraints, i.e., $\|[Q]\mathbf{g}\|$ is minimized, or boundedness of operators on the image,

$$[Q]\mathbf{g} \leq \mathbf{c}, \qquad (3.65)$$

where $\mathbf{c}$ is a vector of constraints, etc. We shall see the employment of these general constraints in several formulations of image restoration in later chapters.

Part II

DEGRADATIONS

Chapter 4

Sources and Models
of Degradations

4.0 Introduction

In order that a more successful attempt at image restoration be undertaken, a variety of models will be postulated as reasonable examples of traditional imaging systems. The sources and models of degradation that contribute to the recording of a poor rendition of an object of interest can be lumped into two general categories: deterministic processes and stochastic processes.

This chapter will first introduce models for nonlinear imaging systems and suggest application areas where such systems do occur. All deterministic models will be based upon the concept of a point-spread function (PSF), i.e., the effect on the recorded image of a point source of light in the object of interest. In the nonlinear model it will be shown that the point-spread function itself becomes a function of the object of interest, and, as with many nonlinear analyses, progress in this restoration area is quite slow and painful.

Consequently, we shall resort to more traditional linear models to illustrate the mapping of object information to the image at hand. Such linear models will then allow us the luxury of borrowing from the field of linear systems theory, Fourier optics, linear algebra, numerical analysis, and many other disciplines for clues as to useful inversion techniques.

4.1 Nonlinear Systems

Many imaging systems, in which the thickness of an object is of interest, result in object-dependent point-spread functions. Such systems superficially appear to be linear but in fact are not. Consider imaging systems in which the information-carrying phenomenon passes through the object of interest, specifically X-ray, temperature profile, or three-dimensional reconstruction systems (see Figure 4.1). Such systems are characterized by forward scattering imaging systems wherein an effective point source of imaging energy is modified by the density of the object. The point-spread function becomes

$$h = h(\xi, \eta, x, y, f). \tag{4.1}$$

As the point source explores the input plane of Figure 4.1(a), the image $g(x, y)$ is simply a superposition of all the individual point sources resulting in the imaging equation

$$g(x, y) = \int_{-\infty}^{\infty} \int_{-\infty}^{\infty} h(x, y, \xi, \eta, f) f(\xi, \eta)\, d\xi\, d\eta. \tag{4.2}$$

In the low-energy X-ray example of biomedical imaging in Figure 4.1(b), the object-dependent point-spread-function phenomenon is a relatively low-order effect and as such is only used as a possible example of the phenomenon. In higher energy industrial X-ray systems, however, where objects of interest take on far greater densities, the

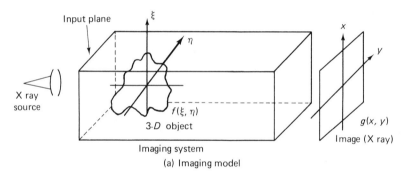

(a) Imaging model

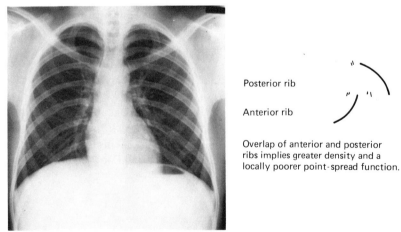

Posterior rib

Anterior rib

Overlap of anterior and posterior ribs implies greater density and a locally poorer point-spread function.

(b) Typical X-ray photograph

Figure 4.1   Forward scattering imaging systems.

Mie scattering phenomenon can become a first-order effect. Other examples in which this type of imaging might be of interest are the measurement of temperature profiles of the atmosphere or the three-dimensional reconstruction techniques of transaxial tomography in medical applications. Returning to Equation (4.2) the point-spread function can be expanded in a Taylor series around $f(\xi, \eta) = a$, obtaining

$$h(x, y, \xi, \eta, f(\xi, \eta)) = \sum_{n=0}^{\infty} \frac{(f(\xi, \eta) - a)^n}{n!} \frac{\partial^n h(x, y, \xi, \eta, f(\xi, \eta))}{\partial^n f(\xi, \eta)}\bigg|_{f(\xi, \eta) = a}. \quad (4.3)$$

As an example of such a process, assume a Gaussian point-spread function that is circularly symmetric with variance (or spread) proportional to $f^2(\xi, \eta)$. Thus

$$h(x, y, \xi, \eta, f(\xi, \eta)) = \frac{1}{2\pi f(\xi, \eta)} \exp\left\{-\frac{1}{f^2(\xi, \eta)}\left((\xi - x)^2 + (\eta - y)^2\right)\right\} \quad (4.4)$$

and

$$\frac{\partial h}{\partial f} = \frac{2\pi}{4\pi^2 f^4(\xi, \eta)}\{2[(\xi - x)^2 + (\eta - y)^2] - f^2(\xi, \eta)\}$$

$$\exp\left\{-\frac{1}{f^2(\xi, \eta)}[(\xi - x)^2 + (\eta - y)^2]\right\}. \quad (4.5)$$

Using the first two terms in the Taylor series expansion yields

$$h(x, y, \xi, \eta, f(\xi, \eta))$$

$$= \frac{1}{\pi a^4}\left\{a^3 - a[(\xi - x)^2 + (\eta - y)^2] + \left((\xi - x)^2 + (\eta - y)^2 - \frac{a^2}{2}\right)f(\xi, \eta)\right\}$$

$$\exp\left\{-\frac{1}{f^2(\xi, \eta)}[(\xi - x)^2 + (\eta - y)^2]\right\}. \quad (4.6)$$

Notice that the series consists of a constant term and a linear term in f that modulates a parabola, both of which modulate an exponential (Gaussian) point-spread function. If our object is very slowly varying or in fact becomes a constant $f(\xi, \eta) = a$, we then see that the point-spread function is no longer object-dependent and becomes

$$h(x, y, \xi, \eta) = \frac{1}{2\pi a} \exp\left\{-\frac{1}{a^2}[(\xi - x)^2 + (\eta - y)^2]\right\}. \quad (4.7)$$

The analysis holds, however, only for $f(\xi, \eta)$ constant over a region proportional to f^2. Therefore, for highly oversampled imagery, $f(\xi, \eta)$ will be slowly varying and "isoplanatic" patches result. Thus let

$$r(\alpha) = \iint\limits_{\{\alpha\}} f(\xi, \eta) \, d\xi \, d\eta, \quad (4.8)$$

where $\{\alpha\}$ is an isoplanatic patch or region of slowly varying $f(\xi, \eta)$. Then

$$h(x, y, \xi, \eta, r(\alpha)) = \frac{1}{\pi a^4}\left\{a^3 - \frac{a^2 r(\alpha)}{2} + [r(\alpha) - a]\right\}[(\xi - x)^2 + (\eta - y)^2]$$

$$\exp\left\{-\frac{1}{r^2(\alpha)}[(\xi - x)^2 + (\eta - y)^2]\right\} \quad (4.9)$$

and as $r \rightarrow 2a$, the first two terms go to zero and the second term dominates as a bimodal hump.

If a rectangular PSF is assumed, then

$$h(x, y, \xi, \eta, r(\alpha)) = \text{rect}\,(r(\xi - x), r(\eta - y))$$

$$= \begin{cases} \dfrac{1}{4r^2(\alpha)} & |\xi - x|,\ |\eta - y| < r \\ 0 & \text{otherwise.} \end{cases} \tag{4.10}$$

Then

$$\frac{\partial h}{\partial r} = \lim_{\Delta r \to 0} \frac{h(r + \Delta r/2) - h(r - \Delta r/2)}{\Delta r} \tag{4.11}$$

$$= \boxed{\begin{array}{c} \boxed{h_1} \\ h_2 \end{array}} \qquad h_1 < h_2,$$

where again we have a type of bimodal point-spread function. This type of point-spread function does appear to be a realistic model for many X-ray sources [Krusos (1974); Arnold, *et al.* (1973)]. The pictorial illustrations of Equations (4.9) and (4.11) are given in Figure 4.2.

The problem with the model above is that the nonlinear analysis does not lend itself to simple solution. In search for greater insight into the analysis of physically meaningful degradation models, consideration will be given to object-independent linear point-spread-function systems.

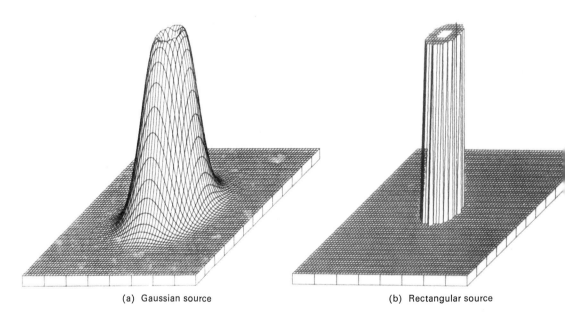

(a) Gaussian source   (b) Rectangular source

Figure 4.2 Isoplanatic (slowly varying object dependent) point-spread functions.

4.2 Linear Systems

Traditional linear systems are often developed around an operator or impulse response notation in which the output function results in the superposition of weighted input impulses passing through a system. Referring to Figure 4.3(a) we see a possible model in continuous notation of such a process. If an impulse or point source of light is placed in the object plane (ξ, η) at location (ξ_0, η_0), then the image plane (x, y) would be expected to respond with a function $g(x, y)$ equal to $h(x, y, \xi_0, \eta_0)$. If the point source of light is weighted by the value of the object at (ξ_0, η_0), then it would be expected that the output would behave as $f(\xi_0, \eta_0)h(x, y, \xi_0, \eta_0)$. In the limit of an infinite number of point sources completely illuminating the object, it would be expected that

$$g(x, y) = \int_{-\infty}^{\infty} \int_{-\infty}^{\infty} f(\xi, \eta)h(x, y, \xi, \eta)\, d\xi\, d\eta. \qquad (4.12)$$

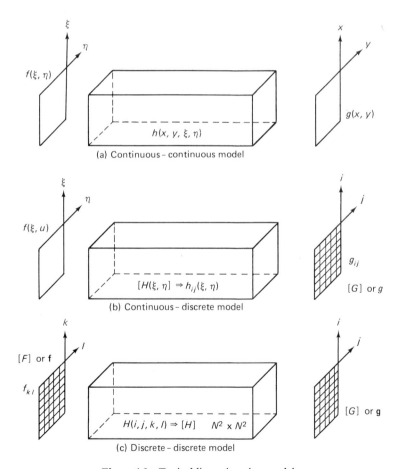

(a) Continuous – continuous model

(b) Continuous – discrete model

(c) Discrete – discrete model

Figure 4.3 Typical linear imaging models.

This equation, known as a Fredholm integral with a four-dimensional (variable) kernel, is a general description of a linear system in which the operator $H = h(x, y, \xi, \eta)$ maps an object $f(\xi, \eta)$ into an image $g(x, y)$. In other words,

$$g = H\{f\}. \tag{4.13}$$

The linearity assumption was developed in Chapter 2 at some length. If, as the point source explores the object plane, the form of the impulse or point-spread function changes shape as well as position, then a "spatially variant point-spread-function" system results (SVPSF). If, however, as the point source explores the object plane, the point-spread function changes only position but maintains the same functional form, then a "spatially invariant point-spread function" (SIPSF) is said to exist. In this case,

$$h(x, y, \xi, \eta) = h(x - \xi, y - \eta) \tag{4.14}$$

and the imaging equation becomes

$$g(x, y) = \int_{-\infty}^{\infty} \int_{-\infty}^{\infty} f(\xi, \eta) h(x - \xi, y - \eta)\, d\xi\, d\eta. \tag{4.15}$$

This equation is often referred to as a two-dimensional convolution and is related to a mathematical equivalent in Fourier transform theory.

Models described in Figure 4.3(a), and Equation (4.12), are often referred to as *continuous–continuous* systems with reference to the analysis and notation employed. Much of current image processing technology has evolved from coherent and incoherent Fourier optics [Goodman (1968)], which is best analyzed through the continuous–continuous formation.

Although the continuous–continuous model will provide insight into many imaging and restoration techniques, the more meaningful model for use with computer image processing is probably that known as the *continuous–discrete* system. The continuous–discrete model is of practical interest since the original object of interest is usually continuous but because of our sensors, sampling process, matrix operations, and discrete display processes, only discrete images result. Figure 4.3(b) indicates how such a model might be used and the Fredholm-like imaging equation [similar to that of Equation (4.12) for the continuous–continuous model] is given by

$$g_{ij} = \int_{-\infty}^{\infty} \int_{-\infty}^{\infty} h_{ij}(\xi, \eta) f(\xi, \eta)\, d\xi\, d\eta \qquad i, j = 1, \ldots, N. \tag{4.16a}$$

The representation implies that the ijth sensor or sample value is given by the integral equation above, where the point-spread function depends on the continuous object plane variables (ξ, η) and the discrete image plane variables (i, j). Thus, in matrix notation,

$$[G] = \int_{-\infty}^{\infty} \int_{-\infty}^{\infty} [H(\xi, \eta)] f(\xi, \eta)\, d\xi\, d\eta, \tag{4.16b}$$

where $[H(\xi, \eta)]$ is a matrix whose entries are two variable functions of coordinates (ξ, η). The matrix notation above, as developed, implies that the grid sampler was uniform in two dimensions. While this may be most commonly encountered in continuous–discrete systems, we shall not be restricted to uniform samples and in fact may wish to develop nonuniform samplers based on a degree of freedom argument yet to come.

In addition to the matrix representation of Equation (4.16b) for the continuous–discrete imaging model, it may be useful at times to develop a vector representation. Because [G] is just an array of scalar numbers, the array can be simply reordered into a vector such that

$$\mathbf{g} = \int_{-\infty}^{\infty} \int_{-\infty}^{\infty} \mathbf{h}(\xi, \eta) f(\xi, \eta) \, d\xi \, d\eta, \tag{4.16c}$$

where $\mathbf{g}$ and $\mathbf{h}(\xi, \eta)$ are $N^2 \times 1$ matrices (vectors) and the former has scalar entries, while the latter has entries that are functions of the object plane (ξ, η).

While the continuous–discrete model is the most realistic in both a physical and practical sense, algorithmically, it may prove a bit cumbersome. Mathematically speaking, a continuous object $f(\xi, \eta)$ can never be represented in the computer and, consequently, only approximations to that object are possible. In addition, if it is desired to use some linear algebra and numerical analysis techniques available in the literature, a possibly more useful model might be that given by a *discrete–discrete* system. Figure 4.3(c) indicates how such an imaging model might be established where the object of interest has been discretized, thereby allowing a purely tensor or matrix formulation. Using discrete scalar notation,

$$g_{ij} = \sum_{k=1}^{N} \sum_{l=1}^{N} f_{k,l} h_{i,j,k,l} \tag{4.17a}$$

and, in tensor notation,

$$[G] = [[H]] \{[F]\}, \tag{4.17b}$$

where [H] is a four-index operator working on the two-index function [F] known as a matrix. In order to keep the operation notation reasonable, lexicographic or stacking operators, introduced earlier, can be used to represent simply the image and object as vectors $\mathbf{g}$ and $\mathbf{f}$, respectively, and the point-spread-function operator as [H], which is an $N^2 \times N^2$ matrix. Thus

$$\mathbf{g} = [H]\mathbf{f}, \tag{4.17c}$$

where [H] takes on certain "block" properties reflecting the effect of the stacking (or raster scanning) operator on both [F] and [G]. The potential degrees of freedom in [H] using this notation are N^2 if, indeed, every point in [F] is mapped perfectly into a respective point in [G]. In the discussion above it has been implicitly assumed that the object was sampled in a square array with $N \times N$ points as was the image. Again for notational convenience this seems to be a reasonable assumption, although one might argue from physical intuition that [F] should have more points or samples than [G]. This of course could be accomplished by forcing some of the points in [G] to be zero. For large-size N these sampling and window effects become of second-order importance as demonstrated in the Appendices. Needless to say, the notation developed in Equation (4.17c) may be deceptive since the size of the arrays can become quite large. For instance, consider a low resolution image of 256×256 pixels represented by a matrix [G] of dimension 256×256. The point-spread-function matrix then takes on a size $65,536 \times 65,536$, which is difficult to operate upon in the computer. For high resolution imagery of 1000×1000 the point-spread-function matrices are of the order of $10^6 \times 10^6$; obviously storage alone is a monumental task. Insight, intuition, and physical constraints on imaging systems must be developed to make use of the various models presented above.

4.3 A Priori Imaging Constraints

The models developed so far have not used some additional constraints that may become quite valuable in various restoration techniques. The assumption of non-negativity must be maintained throughout our models since optical energies inherent in imaging must always be nonnegative quantities. Both the object and image being nonnegative imply that the point-spread function must also be componentwise non-negative. Thus, in the notation of the various models,

1. Continuous–continuous:

$$f(\xi, \eta) \geqq 0 \qquad \forall\ (\xi, \eta)$$
$$g(x, y) \geqq 0 \qquad \forall\ (x, y) \qquad\qquad (4.18a)$$
$$h(x, y, \xi, \eta) \geqq 0 \qquad \forall\ (x, y, \xi, \eta).$$

2. Continuous–discrete:

$$f(\xi, \eta) \geqq 0 \qquad \forall\ (\xi, \eta)$$
$$g_{ij} \geqq 0 \qquad \forall\ i, j = 1, \ldots, N \qquad\qquad (4.18b)$$
$$h_{ij}(\xi, \eta) \geqq 0 \qquad \forall\ (\xi, \eta); i, j = 1, \ldots, N.$$

3. Discrete–discrete:

$$f_j \geqq 0 \qquad \forall\ j = 1, \ldots, N^2$$
$$g_i \geqq 0 \qquad \forall\ i = 1, \ldots, N^2 \qquad\qquad (4.18c)$$
$$h_{ij} \geqq 0 \qquad \forall\ i, j = 1, \ldots, N^2.$$

The implications of the positivity property on the point-spread function have ramifications in the discrete–discrete model in which the matrix $[H]$ is known as component-wise nonnegative [Gantmacher (1959)]. The Perron and/or Froebenius theorem predicts that this class of matrices (i.e., all point-spread-function matrices) have their dominant eigenvalue associated with an eigenvector whose components all have the same sign. The implications of this property will be developed in some of the discrete–discrete restoration algorithms. In addition to $[H]$ being componentwise nonnegative, it appears that often it falls into the class of totally nonnegative matrices (a term used to refer to componentwise nonnegative matrices that have their determinants of all minors of all degree also nonnegative); and furthermore $[H]$ seems to fall often into a further subset known as *oscillatory matrices*, [Ekstrom (1974)]. Such matrices have oscillating eigenvectors associated with decreasing eigenvalues such that an increasing number of sign changes in the eigenvectors corresponds to a decreasing eigenvalue magnitude. This fact combined with the zero sign change dominant eigenvector implies that a complete system of eigenvectors results with 0 through $N^2 - 1$ sign changes. This property will become significant in various pseudo-inverse restoration attempts to be described in subsequent numerical analysis sections.

A bounded restoration argument may also be involved such that any estimates $\hat{\mathbf{f}}$ of the object $\mathbf{f}$ must not exceed some finite limit. This limit may be as large as the total intensity of the sum and as small as the maximum sampled image value. Thus, to this point, positive and bounded object restoration estimates are required.

An assumption that may be of some value occurs in lossless imaging. Somewhat similar to an energy conservation concept, lossless imaging implies that the total energy in the object is preserved in the image; that is, the lenses, etc., do not absorb or generate optical energy (i.e., a passive system). The ramifications of this assumption in our models results in

1. Continuous–continuous:

$$\iint f(\xi, \eta)\, d\xi\, d\eta = \iint g(x, y)\, dx\, dy$$

or

$$\iint h(x, y, \xi, \eta)\, dx\, dy = 1 \qquad \forall\ (\xi, \eta). \tag{4.19a}$$

2. Continuous–discrete:

$$\iint f(\xi, \eta)\, d\xi\, d\eta = \sum_{i=1}^{N} \sum_{j=1}^{N} g_{ij}$$

or

$$\sum_{i=1}^{N} \sum_{j=1}^{N} h_{ij}(\xi, \eta) = 1 \qquad \forall\ (\xi, \eta). \tag{4.19b}$$

3. Discrete–discrete:

$$\sum_{j=1}^{N^2} f_j = \sum_{i=1}^{N^2} g_i$$

or

$$\sum_{i=1}^{N^2} h_{ij} = 1 \qquad \forall\ j = 1, \ldots, N^2. \tag{4.19c}$$

The equations above can be intuitively justified on the basis that a point source of light in the object $\mathbf{f}$ of unit energy, must image into a total energy of one. In the discrete–discrete case it is noted that $[H]$ has column sums equal to unity, a property that when combined with the componentwise nonnegativity of $[H]$ makes the point-spread-function matrix stochastic or Markov in terms of Bellman (1970).

Additional constraints on the restored object $\hat{\mathbf{f}}$ such as continuity of some order should also be included. A linear operator $Q\{\hat{\mathbf{f}}\}$ may provide additional boundary conditions with which restorations may be implemented. For instance, it may be assumed that the object is continuous in the first and second derivative if it is believed that the wave function phenomena cannot induce higher-order derivatives.

In concluding this section on *a priori* imaging constraints, attention will be turned to various forms that the point-spread function might take under a variety of assumptions that then lend themselves to simplifying restoration algorithms. Using the continuous–continuous (c–c), continuous–discrete (c–d), and discrete–discrete (d–d) models, four specific assumptions concerning the impulse response are listed. The implications of each assumption will be evaluated in the context of two- dimensional transformations and the inversion of the associated degradation phenomenon. The four specific assumptions, in order of decreasing complexity, are

1. Separable space-invariant point-spread function (SSIPSF):

   c–c: $$h(x, y, \xi, \eta) = a(x - \xi)b(y - \eta) \tag{4.20a}$$
   c–d: $$h_{ij}(\xi, \eta) = a(x_i - \xi)b(y_j - \eta) \tag{4.20b}$$
   d–d: $$[H] = [A] \otimes [B], \qquad [A], [B] \text{ Toeplitz} \tag{4.20c}$$
   (*cf.* Chapter 7).

2. Nonseparable space-invariant point-spread function (NSIPSF):

   c–c: $$h(x, y, \xi, \eta) = h(x - \xi, y - \eta) \tag{4.21a}$$
   c–d: $$h_{ij}(\xi, \eta) = h(x_i - \xi, y_j - \eta) \tag{4.21b}$$
   d–d: $$[H] = \text{Block Toeplitz} \tag{4.21c}$$
   (*cf.* Chapter 7).

3. Separable space-variant point-spread function (SSVPSF):

   c–c: $$h(x, y, \xi, \eta) = a(x, \xi)b(y, \eta) \tag{4.22a}$$
   c–d: $$h_{ij}(\xi, \eta) = a_i(\xi)b_j(\eta) \tag{4.22b}$$
   d–d: $$[H] = [A] \otimes [B], \qquad [A], [B] \text{ arbitrary} \tag{4.22c}$$
   (*cf.* Chapter 8).

4. Nonseparable space-variant point-spread function (NSVPSF):

   c–c: $$h(x, y, \xi, \eta) = h(x, y, \xi, \eta) \tag{4.23a}$$
   c–d: $$h_{ij}(\xi, \eta) = h_{ij}(\xi, \eta) \tag{4.23b}$$
   d–d: $$[H] = [H]. \tag{4.23c}$$

These properties are listed in Table 4.1 and are further discussed below.

The separable space-invariant point-spread-function (SSIPSF) imaging situation is probably a good first-order approximation of well-corrected linear systems. The space-invariant point-spread function refers to the fact that the functional form of the impulse response does not depend on the position of the point source of light (impulse response) in the original object plane. The separable assumption refers to the rectangular coordinate separability of the impulse response resulting in

$$h(x, y, \xi, \eta) = a(x - \xi)b(y - \eta). \tag{4.20a}$$

In the vector notation,

$$[H] = [A] \otimes [B], \tag{4.20c}$$

where both $[A]$ and $[B]$ are Toeplitz and $\otimes$ is the direct or Kronecker product of matrices. Because of the rectangular separability of the impulse response, the unstacked matrix notation (see Chapter 3) can be used to obtain

$$[G] = [A][F][B]^t, \tag{4.24}$$

where $[A]$ blurs the columns of the object $[F]$ and $[B]^t$ blurs the rows of $[F]$. Since $[F]$ may not be square and the blur matrices may be singular, irretrievably losing some aspect of the object, then the inversion of the degradation will necessarily have to be a pseudo-inverse.

When an imaging system is nonseparable space-invariant (NSIPSF), either in rectangular or in any other coordinate system, the computational tasks increase considerably. In the NSIPSF case the stacking operator notation is required and the point-spread-function matrix $[H]$ associated with

$$h(x, y, \xi, \eta) = h(x - \xi, y - \eta) \tag{4.21a}$$

becomes "block Toeplitz" of size $N^2 \times N^2$.

$$[H] = \begin{bmatrix} [H_0] & [H_1] & \cdots & & \\ [H_{-1}] & [H_0] & [H_1] & \cdots & \\ [H_{-2}] & [H_{-1}] & [H_0] & [H_1] & \cdots \\ & \cdot & & & \\ & \cdot & & & \\ & \cdot & & & \end{bmatrix}, \tag{4.21c}$$

where the $[H_i]$ are individually Toeplitz. Unfortunately $[H]$ cannot be equated to a single Kronecker product as separability does not hold (see Chapter 7 for details). In continuous notation, however, the model above implies an imaging system which is a two-dimensional convolution, Equation (4.16), which lends itself to Fourier transform analyses. In keeping with the motive of this section in investigating the effect of assumptions on the point-spread function, it is noted that the Fourier transform of $h(x - \xi, y - \eta)$ becomes the "optical transfer function" (OTF) given by

$$H(w_x, w_y) = \int_{-\infty}^{\infty} \int_{-\infty}^{\infty} h(w, z) \exp\left[- 2\pi i(ww_x + w_y z)\right] dw\, dz. \tag{4.25}$$

where $w = x - \xi$ and $z = y - \eta$. The optical transfer function has an upper bound known as a *Lukosz bound* [Lukosz (1962), Boas and Kac (1945)] due to the positive constraints on h. Pictorially the bound may be represented as an imaginary surface, above which the OTF cannot extend (see Figure 4.4).

In the separable space-variant point-spread-function (SSVPSF) case the point-spread function changes shape as it explores the object plane although it is still separable in rectangular coordinates. Examples of such imaging systems include side looking radars and rectangular anode radiographic imaging devices.

The SVPSF can be represented in separable form as

$$h(x, y, \xi, \eta) = a(x, \xi)b(y, \eta) \tag{4.22a}$$

and we see that the discrete matrix representation again becomes

$$[H] = [A] \otimes [B], \tag{4.22c}$$

where $[H]$ is $N^2 \times N^2$ and $[A]$ and $[B]$ are both $N \times N$ but not necessarily Toeplitz as in the SSIPSF case. The advantage of representing the SVPSF as a separable phenomenon is one of computational simplicity. In matrix notation it is unnecessary to use the lexicographic or stack notation. Rather the image $[G]$ becomes

TABLE 4.1

Model	Positivity	Lossless Imaging	Local Continuity	1. SSIPSF 3. SSVPSF 2. NSIPSF 4. NSVPSF
$g(x,y) = \iint h(x,y,\xi,\eta) f(\xi,\eta)\, d\xi\, d\eta$ Continuous–continuous	$f(\xi,\eta) \geqq 0 \quad \forall\, (\xi,\eta)$ $g(x,y) \geqq 0 \quad \forall\, (x,y)$ $h(x,y,\xi,\eta) \geqq 0 \quad \forall\, (x,y,\xi,\eta)$	$\iint f(\xi,\eta)\, d\xi\, d\eta = \iint g(x,y)\, dx\, dy$ $\iint h(x,y,\xi,\eta)\, dx\, dy = 1 \quad \forall\, (\xi,\eta)$	$Q\{f(\xi,\eta)\}$	1. $h(x,y,\xi,\eta)$ $= a(x-\xi)b(y-\eta)$ 2. $h(x,y,\xi,\eta)$ $= h(x-\xi, y-\eta)$ 3. $h(x,y,\xi,\eta)$ $= a(x,\xi)b(y,\eta)$ 4. $h(x,y,\xi,\eta)$ $= h(x,y,\xi,\eta)$
$g_{ij} = \iint h_{ij}(\xi,\eta) f(\xi,\eta)\, d\xi\, d\eta$ $\qquad\qquad i,j = 1,\ldots,N$ $[G] = \iint [H(\xi,\eta)] f(\xi,\eta)\, d\xi\, d\eta$ $\mathbf{g} = \iint \mathbf{h}(\xi,\eta) f(\xi,\eta)\, d\xi\, d\eta$ Continuous–discrete	$f(\xi,\eta) \geqq 0 \quad \forall\, (\xi,\eta)$ $g_{ij} \geqq 0 \quad \forall\, i,j$ $h_{ij}(\xi,\eta) \geqq 0 \quad \forall\, (\xi,\eta), i,j$	$\iint f(\xi,\eta)\, d\xi\, d\eta = \sum_i^N \sum_j^N g_{ij}$ $\sum_i^N \sum_j^N h_{ij}(\xi,\eta) = 1 \quad \forall\, (\xi,\eta)$	$Q\{\hat{f}(\xi,\eta)\}$	1. $h_{ij}(\xi,\eta)$ $= a(x_i - \xi)b(y_j - \eta)$ 2. $h_{ij}(\xi,\eta)$ $= h(x_i - \xi, y_j - \eta)$ 3. $h_{ij}(\xi,\eta)$ $= a_i(\xi)b_j(\eta)$ 4. $h_{ij}(\xi,\eta)$ $= h_{ij}(\xi,\eta)$
$g_{ij} = \sum_k \sum_l f_{k,l} h_{i,j,k,l}$ $[G] = [[H]]\,\{[F]\}$ $\mathbf{g} = [H]\mathbf{f}$ Discrete–discrete	$f_j \geqq 0 \qquad \forall\, j = 1,\ldots,N^2$ $g_i \geqq 0 \qquad \forall\, i = 1,\ldots,N^2$ $h_{ij} \geqq 0 \quad \forall\, i,j = 1,\ldots,N^2$	$\sum_{j=1}^{N^2} f_j = \sum_{i=1}^{N^2} g_i$ $\sum_{i=1}^{N^2} h_{ij} = 1 \quad \forall\, j = 1,\ldots,N^2$	$[Q]\hat{\mathbf{f}}$	1. $[H] = [A] \otimes [B]$, $[A],[B]$ Toeplitz 2. $[H]$ = block Toeplitz 3. $[H] = [A] \otimes [B]$, $[A],[B]$ non-Toeplitz 4. $[H] = [H]$

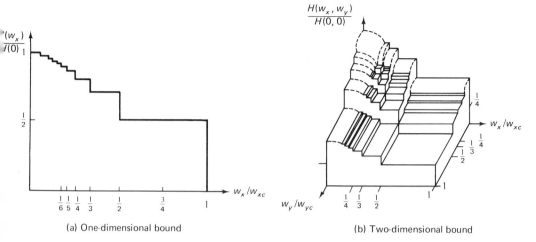

(a) One-dimensional bound

(b) Two-dimensional bound

Figure 4.4   Lukosz/Boas and Kac bounds on $H(w_x, w_y)$.

$$[G] = [A][F][B]^t \qquad (4.26)$$

and, as before, the object $[F]$ is operated upon by the column operator $[A]$ and the row operator $[B]^t$ in a separable fashion. The model of the equation above has assumed a noiseless environment and the rank of the image $[G]$ is determined by the minimum of the ranks of $[A]$, $[F]$, and $[B]$. If inversion of the space-variant blur introduced by $[A]$ and $[B]$ is desired, $[F]$ would be

$$[F] = [A]^{-1}[G][B]^{-1}, \qquad (4.27)$$

provided the inverse matrices existed. Since heuristically one might expect that irretrievable loss is equivalent to singularity, then this proviso is in fact highly unlikely as most systems irretrievably remove some portion of the object. This subject will be investigated in considerable detail in subsequent chapters. Before undertaking the inversion of such systems, however, a pictorial illustration of some SSVPSF simulations might be of interest. Figure 4.5 presents two different distortion models on a sequence of point source and photographic objects. The object comprising the bed of nails perspective of Figures 4.5(a) and (c) is passed through the SSVPSF system and the effect is demonstrated in Figure 4.5(b) and (d). It is evident that the lower left corner is in better "focus" than the more distant upper right corner. This type of imaging system might represent a quadrant of an optical system. Note that, due to the lossless imaging condition, the volume under each "hump" centered at a point source must be one (the amount of energy in each point source). The moderate distortion demonstrating a less severe blurring effect was used to blur the baboon of Figure 4.5(e) to obtain Figure 4.5(f). In this case the corner most in focus is the upper left of the photograph of Figure 4.5(f). Note that if the blur had been spatially invariant, then the "humps" in Figure 4.5(b) and (d) would have all been the same size and shape.

Finally, for the nonseparable space-variant point-spread-function (NSVPSF) system, there is very little that can be said about the point-spread function without further

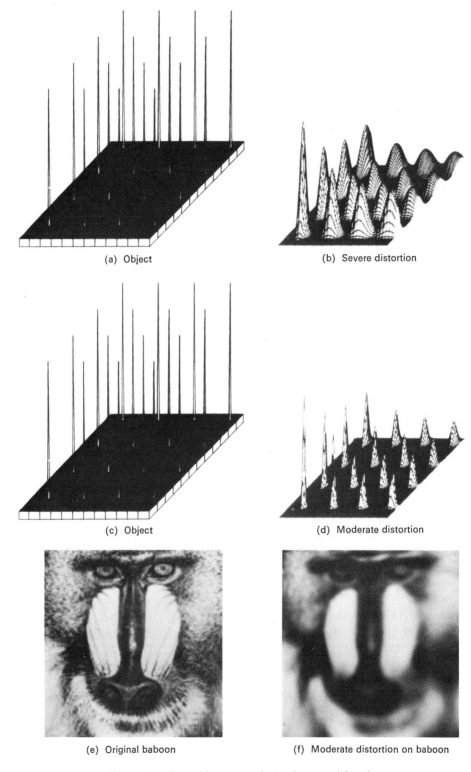

(a) Object

(b) Severe distortion

(c) Object

(d) Moderate distortion

(e) Original baboon

(f) Moderate distortion on baboon

Figure 4.5 Separable space variant point-spread functions.

analytic knowledge. The development of various approximations to this very complex case will be shown but these assumptions will be left for a later analysis.

4.4 Characterizations

There are numerous sources of degradation in imaging systems but often they can be grouped into the following general categories: (1) point degradations, (2) spatial degradations, (3) temporal degradations, (5) chromatic degradations, and (5) combinations of the above. Rigorous manipulations of the degradations above in a mathematical sense, while maintaining the assumptions of linearity, would require generalization of the continuous–continuous model to the following:

$$g(x, y, \tau, \omega) = \int\!\!\int\!\!\int\!\!\int_{-\infty}^{\infty} f(\xi, \eta, t, \lambda) h(x, \xi, y, \eta, \tau, t, \omega, \lambda)\, d\xi\, d\eta\, dt\, d\lambda. \qquad (4.28)$$

Such generalizations are useful for analysis purposes but the concern here is for spatial systems only. In passing, let it suffice to say that temporal and chromatic degradations imply time and color deterioration of their respective axes.

Returning now to Equation (4.12) it is noted that the "perfect" imaging system would have no noise and an impulse response such that

$$g(x, y) = \int_{-\infty}^{\infty} \int_{-\infty}^{\infty} f(\xi, \eta)\, \delta(x - \xi, y - \eta)\, d\xi\, d\eta \qquad (4.29a)$$

$$= f(x, y). \qquad (4.29b)$$

Possibly the first step from perfect imaging is that system that provides no spatial smearing [i.e., no (ξ, η) integration] but induces a point degradation. Thus we might have an impulse response such that

$$g(x, y) = \int_{-\infty}^{\infty} \int_{-\infty}^{\infty} f(\xi, \eta) h(x, y)\, \delta(p_1(x, y) - \xi, p_2(x, y) - \eta)\, d\xi\, d\eta \qquad (4.30a)$$

$$= h(x, y) f(p_1, p_2), \qquad (4.30b)$$

where $p_1(x, y)$ and $p_2(x, y)$ are geometrical coordinate transformations. The equation above describes imaging systems which do not blur but which introduce a distortion due to a coordinate change. When the imaging system does not introduce a coordination distortion, i.e.,

$$p_1(x, y) = x$$
$$p_2(x, y) = y,$$

we then obtain

$$g(x, y) = \int_{-\infty}^{\infty} \int_{-\infty}^{\infty} f(\xi, \eta) h(x, y)\, \delta(x - \xi, y - \eta)\, d\xi\, d\eta \qquad (4.31a)$$

$$= h(x, y) f(x, y). \qquad (4.31b)$$

This system, then, allows for multiplicative point degradation effects.

If the impulse response becomes a function of the object coordinates (ξ, η), then some form of smearing or loss of resolution results due to the integration of the

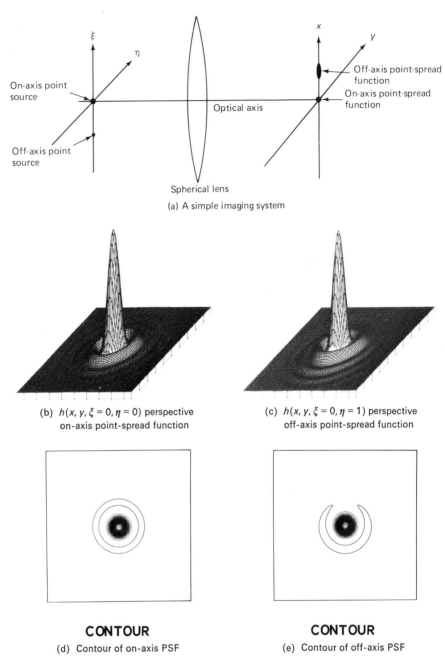

(a) A simple imaging system

(b) $h(x, y, \xi = 0, \eta = 0)$ perspective on-axis point-spread function

(c) $h(x, y, \xi = 0, \eta = 1)$ perspective off-axis point-spread function

CONTOUR

(d) Contour of on-axis PSF

CONTOUR

(e) Contour of off-axis PSF

Figure 4.6 A SVPSF optical system.

imaging system over those coordinates. Examples of these so-called spatial degradations are numerous—some of the common of which are (1) diffraction effects in optical systems; (2) first-, second-, and higher-order optical system aberrations; (3) atmospheric turbulence; (4) motion blur; and (5) defocused systems.

While the above is certainly not an exhaustive list of spatial degradations, it does provide an introduction to some of the problems faced in image restoration. The models associated with the various defects can vary from the simple SIPSF convolutions to much more complicated SVPSF representations.

Consider the model in Figure 4.6(a), to illustrate a relatively simple optical system in which deviations from diffraction limited optics introduce a SVPSF. Here due to improper lens manufacture it is noted that, by using a ray tracing algorithm [Larson (1971)], the on-axis point-spread function is symmetric and results in an image given by [see Figure 4.6(b)]

$$g(x, y) = h(x, y, 0, 0),\qquad\qquad(4.32a)$$

while an off-axis point source of light results in Figure 4.6(c) and

$$g(x, y) = h(x, y, 0, 1).\qquad\qquad(4.32b)$$

It is clear from the contour plots of the figure that the off-axis PSF is not symmetric and therefore different in shape from the on-axis PSF. Consequently a space-invariant model cannot be assumed. If this example were pursued in the discrete–discrete notation and a stacking operator on $h(x, y, \xi, \eta)$ is used to form the appropriate $[H]$ matrix of $N^2 \times N^2$ elements, then the two PSF's in Figure 4.6 would form two columns of $[H]$. The equivalent discrete–discrete representations of Equations (4.32a) and (4.32b) would become

$$\mathbf{g} = [H] \begin{bmatrix} 0 \\ \cdot \\ \cdot \\ \cdot \\ 0 \\ 1 \\ 0 \\ \cdot \\ \cdot \\ \cdot \\ 0 \end{bmatrix} \qquad\qquad(4.33a)$$

and

$$\mathbf{g} = [H] \begin{bmatrix} 0 \\ \cdot \\ \cdot \\ \cdot \\ 0 \\ 0 \\ 0 \\ \cdot \\ \cdot \\ \cdot \\ 1 \end{bmatrix} \cdot \qquad\qquad(4.33b)$$

Thus the on-axis point source generates the $\xi = \eta = 0$ column and the off-axis point source generates the $\xi = 0$, $\eta = 1$ column of $[H]$. It is clear that to describe $[H]$

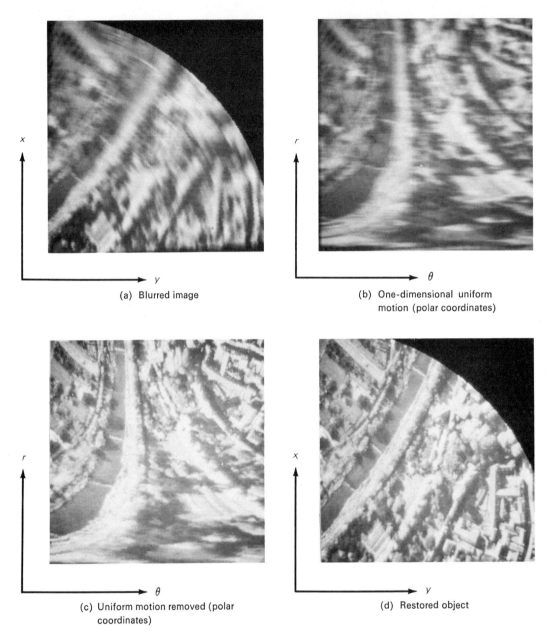

x

y

(a) Blurred image

r

θ

(b) One-dimensional uniform
motion (polar coordinates)

r

θ

(c) Uniform motion removed (polar
coordinates)

x

y

(d) Restored object

Figure 4.7 Radially symmetric SVPSF example. (After A. A.
Sawchuk, 1974.)

completely experimentally, one must allow the point source in $\mathbf{f}$ to generate all N^2
positions in order that all N^2 columns of $[H]$ be defined. While on the surface this task
is inordinately difficult, it will be seen that the relatively smooth transition of point-
spread functions from point to point in $\mathbf{f}$ and column to column in $[H]$ results in a
considerable simplification in generation and storage of $[H]$. Advantage of this property will be taken in subsequent chapters.

The SVPSF system discussed with reference to Figure 4.6 can be generalized to a variety of optical systems. One very graphic example of such systems might be that given by the aberration of coma where the on-axis PSF is in focus and the off-axis PSF's are spread out in teardrop fashion in radial symmetry. Such systems have been analytically and algorithmically inverted by Robbins and Huang (1972) and Robbins (1970). In addition, they discuss restoring images in which camera tilt between field of view and imaging plane result, and Sawchuk (1972), (1973), (1974) has generalized the SVPSF model to any geometrically distorted system under many forms of image motion (i.e., constant velocity, acceleration, etc., in rotational and rectilinear dimensions). One such example appears in the sequence of Figure 4.7. This figure illustrates a combination of geometrical coordinate transformations with one-dimensional SIPSF blur. In the image plane, however, such distortions become spatially variant. One obvious technique of restoring such distortions is to take the rotationally blurred image, Figure 4.7(a), and perform a geometrical coordinate transformation to the (r, θ) coordinate system. Now the rotational blur becomes a one-dimensional uniform motion blur in the θ coordinate [Figure 4.7(b)]. Using one-dimensional SIPSF inversion techniques, the uniform motion blur can be reduced, resulting in Figure 4.7(c). Finally performing the polar-to-rectangular coordinate transformation results in the restored object of Figure 4.7(d).

Many imaging circumstances yield a combination of both space-variant and space-invariant point-spread functions. Such a system may result from motion in the recording system, turbulence and short-term exposure effects, and motion in the field of view. In all three cases, which are illustrated in Figure 4.8, the very difficult situation of obtaining an image that has different amounts of blur in different regions of the picture is evident. If there is no *a priori* geometrical or other model describing the position and/or amount of degradation, then the restoration effort is indeed a large task. For instance, in Figure 4.8(a), the image has very little degradation in the background but due to uniform camera motion the bushes in the foreground are badly blurred. In fact, the amount of blur is really a function of the distance individual object points were from the moving camera as there must be some motion blur at each point in the image. The picture of Figure 4.8(b) also has certain regions blurred due to uniform motion. In this situation, however, an object within the field of view (the manequin head) is moving with respect to the background and as such experiences a relative motion blur, while the rest of the scene is unblurred. Since the manequin head contains a large portion of the image, then the point-spread function due to the head movement dominates the Fourier transform of the image, as illustrated in Figure 4.8(d). We shall see in Chapter 5 that a great deal of *a posteriori* information can be obtained regarding the degradation of an object by analysis in the Fourier domain. In this case, however, because the blur is space-variant (space-invariant over the manequin but variant throughout the frame), the Fourier transform method of object restoration is not applicable. Finally in Figure 4.8(c) a case is presented that is locally a SIPSF but is globally a SVPSF. This scene is of a photograph of an explosion taken from an aircraft during the exposure of which a shockwave disturbed the film plane. Fortunately, within the field of view are a series of stars that behave as local point sources

(a) Camera motion blur

(b) Partial object motion blur

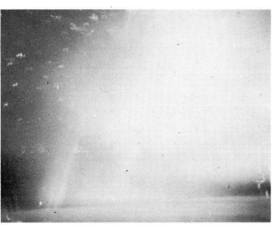

(c) Point sources and isoplanatic
     patches

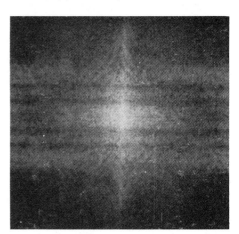

(d) Modulus of Fourier transform
     of (b)

Figure 4.8   Combined space variant and invariant PSF systems.

of light, thereby providing measures of the impulse response within the image (see Chapter 5 for a discussion of using this *a posteriori* information for image restoration). It can be seen from the image that the camera experienced significant motion during exposure. In the upper left-hand portion of the image, the star patterns form a trace of what appears to be script "w's." In the right-hand portion of the image, however, that same pattern does not repeat itself but a different star pattern results. For restoration purposes it is clear that the phenomenon is space-variant but it may be reasonable to assume an *isoplantic patch* concept in which local regions of an image are assumed to behave as if imaged from a SIPSF system. The concept of an isoplanatic patch is borrowed from uplooking photography systems in which short-term exposures tend to "stop" the atmosphere and patches of stationary atmosphere tend to blur the object differently in different regions. The isoplantic patch size can then be used as an aid in determining the extent of a SIPSF over such types of photography.

The two examples discussed above have their spatial blur defined by the object of interest, i.e., close in structure for the camera motion blur case and manequin head outline for the partial object blur case. One might be tempted to argue that such SVPSF systems with object-dependent blur are really nonlinear systems and fall into the category of Section 4.1, object-dependent point-spread functions. While this is a valid observation, if the outline of the blurred portions of the object are known from the image [as is the case for Figures 4.8(a) and (b)], then the PSF given by $h(x, y, \xi, \eta)$ will have this spatial shape information inherently imbedded within its definition. Complete knowledge of the object is then unnecessary to define $h(\cdot)$ (as was the case of Section 4.1) and thus a potentially nonlinear problem has been linearized by a *posteriori* definition of the appropriate regions of spatial blur (see Chapter 5).

The examples in Figure 4.8 are not meant to be all-inclusive of combinations of space-variant and -invariant systems. They simply serve as an illustration of typical imaging circumstances which may occur and for which the reader must be wary of the restoration difficulties involved.

Restricting attention now to spatially invariant systems, Fourier signal processing technology can be applied to the imaging equation (4.15):

$$g(x, y) = \int_{-\infty}^{\infty} \int_{-\infty}^{\infty} f(\xi, \eta) h(x - \xi, y - \eta) \, d\xi \, d\eta.$$

Since this equation is also known as a two-dimensional convolution, a mathematical transformation can be performed using the optical transfer function (OTF) of Equation (4.25) to obtain

$$G(w_x, w_y) = H(w_x, w_y) F(w_x, w_y), \tag{4.34}$$

where G, H, and F are Fourier transform pairs of their respective spatial functions. As an illustration of such SIPSF systems, three cases are physically interesting: (1) badly defocused imagery, (2) long exposure atmospheric blur, (3) uniform motion blur. Figure 4.9 presents simulations of these examples. The OTF of the three forms of SIPSF blur are given as

1. Severely defocused lens with circular aperture stop [Goodman (1968)]:

$$H(w_x, w_y) = \frac{J_1(a\rho)}{a\rho}, \qquad \rho = \sqrt{w_x^2 + w_y^2}. \tag{4.35a}$$

2. Long-term exposure of atmospheric turbulence [McGlamery (1967)]:

$$H(w_x, w_y) = \exp\left\{-\frac{1}{2} \frac{(w_x^2 + w_y^2)}{\sigma^2}\right\}. \tag{4.35b}$$

3. Uniform motion blur:

$$H(w_x, w_y) = \frac{\sin a\omega}{\omega}$$

$$\omega = w_x \cos\theta + w_y \sin\theta. \tag{4.35c}$$

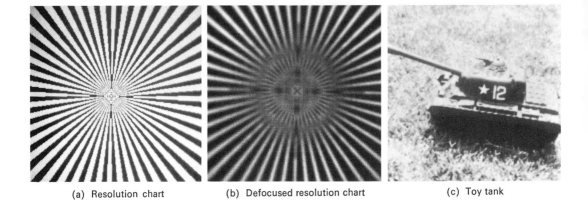

(a) Resolution chart   (b) Defocused resolution chart   (c) Toy tank

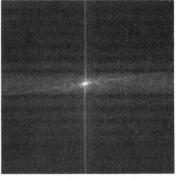

(d) Long exposure atmospheric   (e) Uniform motion blur   (f) Fourier transform modulus dis-
     blur (Gaussian PSF)   playing uniform motion blur

Figure 4.9   Space   invariant   point-spread-function   simulation
examples.

For severely defocused imaging systems, Figure 4.9(a) and (b), the first-order Bessel
function over its argument, Equation (4.35a), introduces zeros and 180° phase shifts
in particular spatial frequency regions of the object. These phase shifts result in contrast
reversals for those spatial frequency portions of the entire image. As a result certain
regions of the resolution chart, Figure 4.9(a), have contrast reversal [Figure 4.9(b)]
where those phase-reversed spatial frequencies dominate. The second example of
long-term exposure of atmospheric turbulence results in an OTF that has a Gaussian
shape and behaves as a general low-pass filter. The effects of this process, representing
a SIPSF system, are a general degradation of resolution throughout the image, as
illustrated in Figure 4.9(c) and (d). The uniform motion blur introduces a sinc function
OTF in a direction 90° to the direction of motion. The results of this OTF and blurred
image are presented in Figure 4.9(e) and (f). These examples serve to illustrate three
types of classical SIPSF phenomena and the resulting effects on various images.

4.5   Degrees of Freedom in Imaging Systems

The concept of the degrees of freedom (DOF) in an imaging system is basic to all signal processing and evolves from the desire to minimize the number of independent parameters describing an image. Basically, the intuitive meaning of degrees of freedom might be related to the concept of the number of independent samples or data points necessary to describe an image. It should be clear to the reader that simply oversampling an image by a factor of 10 does not imply that we obtain an order of magnitude increase in degrees of freedom or independent data points. Thus, in badly blurred systems, one would expect a lower number of DOF than in a well-corrected system even though the image sampling rate remains fixed. Ideally, the DOF describing an imaging system would be an excellent figure of merit for comparison purposes between such systems and would provide an invariant measure of the "resolution" of such devices. The DOF measurement would provide a quantitative evaluation of the number of independent parameters or variables obtainable from a given system without concern as to Nyquist and oversampling phenomena. Various authors [Gori and Guattari (1974), Twomey (1974)] have addressed the problem and considerable insight into imaging systems can be obtained through such concepts.

Roughly speaking, the "degrees of freedom" in an imaging system represent the minimum number of independent samples or data points required to describe the image but, from a practical viewpoint, it is desirable that the degrees of freedom measurement be valid in the presence of sensor noise. One way of defining such concepts is through a type of correlation matrix in which each point-spread function is correlated against all other point-spread functions. Using the earlier notation, such a correlation function might be defined as

1. Continuous–continuous:

$$\mathcal{R}(\alpha, \beta, x, y) = \int_{-\infty}^{\infty} \int_{-\infty}^{\infty} h(x, y, \xi, \eta) h(\alpha, \beta, \xi, \eta) \, d\xi \, d\eta. \qquad (4.36a)$$

2. Continuous–discrete:

$$[\mathcal{R}] = \int_{-\infty}^{\infty} \int_{-\infty}^{\infty} \mathbf{h}(\xi, \eta) \mathbf{h}^t(\xi, \eta) \, d\xi \, d\eta$$

or $\qquad\qquad\qquad\qquad\qquad\qquad\qquad\qquad\qquad\qquad (4.36b)$

$$\mathcal{R}_{ij} = \int_{-\infty}^{\infty} \int_{-\infty}^{\infty} h_i(\xi, \eta) h_j(\xi, \eta) \, d\xi \, d\eta, \qquad i, j = 1, \ldots, N^2.$$

3. Discrete–discrete:

$$[\mathcal{R}] = [H][H]^t$$
$$\mathcal{R}_{i,j} = \mathbf{h}_i^t \mathbf{h}_j, \qquad i, j = 1, \ldots, N^2. \qquad (4.36c)$$

The degree of freedom concept implies a discrete imaging system; as a consequence, concentration will be placed on the continuous–discrete and discrete–discrete systems in which the correlation function is a matrix $[\mathcal{R}]$ whose i, jth entries represent the effective amount of overlap of the ith PSF and the jth PSF. As an illustration from a one-dimensional example, consider the representation of Figure 4.10. In Figure 4.10(a)

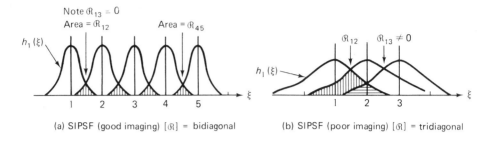

(a) SIPSF (good imaging) [ℜ] = bidiagonal   (b) SIPSF (poor imaging) [ℜ] = tridiagonal

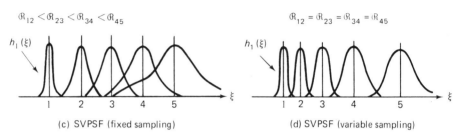

(c) SVPSF (fixed sampling)   (d) SVPSF (variable sampling)

Figure 4.10   Degrees of freedom illustration.

and (b) it is noted that for SIPSF systems the number and size of off-diagonal elements of the correlation matrix are a function of the sampling rate and spread of the PSF. Intuitively it would not be expected that many degrees of freedom would be gained for large overlaps of PSF's, which would correspond to more off-diagonal entries in [ℜ]. In the SVPSF cases in the figure, the matrix [ℜ] will not be Toeplitz as it was for the SIPSF system but will have increasing numbers of off-diagonal entries as a function of increasing indexing. Ideally, it is desirable that [ℜ] be equal to the identity matrix indicating perfect imaging. Toward this end, it is tempting to suggest a variable sampling rate, as illustrated in Figure 4.10(d), whereby the sampling interval is determined by the amount of overlap of the individual point-spread functions. Such a variable sampling process would match the degrees of freedom of a system with the PSF of the system such that a minimal number of data points would be necessary for storage of the same number of DOF.

Pursuing the DOF analysis a bit further, it is seen that the correlation matrix [ℜ] is symmetric, real and nonnegative definite [see Equations (4.36b) and (4.36c)]. This allows the investigation of the eigenvalues of [ℜ] to determine the number of linearly independent rows and therefore rank of the correlation matrix. Thus

$$[\mathfrak{R}] = [U][\Lambda][U]^t, \tag{4.37}$$

where [Λ] is a diagonal matrix of eigenvalues and [U] is an orthogonal matrix whose columns comprise the eigenvectors of [ℜ]. By observing the eigenvalue map (the plot of eigenvalues versus index in monotonic decreasing order) a feel for the number of independent samples (DOF) described by [ℜ] can be obtained. Referring to the space-

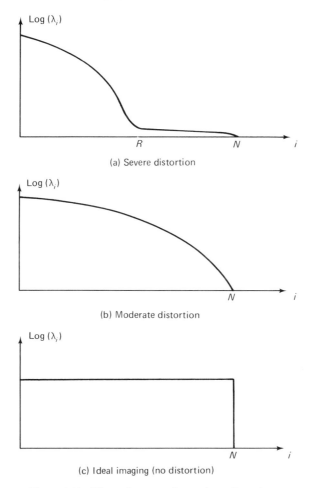

Figure 4.11   Eigenvalue maps for various distortions.

variant blurs as illustrated in Figure 4.5 where both severe and moderate distortion are demonstrated and evaluating the eigenvalues of these cases (plotted in Figure 4.11), the effect of these degradations are shown in eigenspace. The rank of the severe distortion case is about 80; whereas the moderate distortion example does not demonstrate a clear cutoff. For ideal imaging (no distortion), $[\mathfrak{R}] = [I]$ and the eigenvalue map is constant. The moderate distortion case of Figure 4.11(b) presents an interesting example of the need for a more complete definition of degrees of freedom than simply the rank of $[\mathfrak{R}]$. Specifically, it will be difficult, if not impossible, to determine the rank of $[\mathfrak{R}]$ due to measurement and computational noise. The definition of DOF could be modified to be the number of eigenvalues of $[\mathfrak{R}]$ greater than measurement and computational noise. Thus if the sensor accuracy is known to be 1 part in 10,000 and our computational accuracy is better than that, and if it is assumed that the sensor noise is uncorrelated, then a value of 10^{-4} may be set as a threshold in our eigenvalue map below which there is no confidence in further measurement and computation. In the actual distortions discussed here, the degrees of freedom for severe distortion would be DOF $= 47$; for moderate distortion, DOF $= 99$.

The eigenvalue maps discussed above will be heavily used in work in restoration. The eigenvalues of $[\mathcal{R}]$ turn out to be the singular values of the PSF matrix $[H]$; in subsequent chapters, use will be made of the singular value decomposition of $[H]$ to perform pseudo-inverse restorations of SVPSF systems. The degrees of freedom of an imaging system and the eigenspace of the PSF matrix are intimately related, and the two become extremely important concepts in linear image restoration.

In closing this section on degrees of freedom it is important to emphasize that the noise signal or error in measurement defines the smallest meaningful eigenvalue of $[\mathcal{R}]$ and implicitly defines the sampling rate of the image plane (that is, the closer the image samples, the more overlap of the point-spread functions at those samples). To increase the DOF of a system, one might resort to variable sampling (see Figure 4.10), whereby in those regions of the image plane where narrow PSF's occur, higher sampling rates become meaningful; one example might be on-axis versus off-axis imaging systems. Of course, an upper limit to the sampling rate would be the Nyquist rate associated with the object of interest $f(\xi, \eta)$, if such were known and if the PSF rate provided such high resolution imaging. The trade-off between fixed and variable sampling can be related to the mathematical problem of fixed versus variable knot interpolators, smoothers, and estimators.

4.6   Eigenanalysis of Imaging Systems

Many linear systems are effectively analyzed by using an eigenvector or eigenanalysis approach that often provides insight into the imaging process. Using the continuous–continuous model, it is known that if the imaging system has a SVPSF that is independent of the object, then the following equation holds.

$$g(x, y) = \int_{-\infty}^{\infty} \int_{-\infty}^{\infty} h(x, y, \xi, \eta) f(\xi, \eta)\, d\xi\, d\eta.$$

The eigenfunctions of such systems are defined as those waveforms that pass through the linear system unperturbed except by a scale factor or delay (shift). If the eigenfunctions of the SVPSF exist and are known, then

$$\lambda_{nm}\psi_{nm}(x, y) = \int_{-\infty}^{\infty} \int_{-\infty}^{\infty} \psi_{nm}(\xi, \eta) h(x, y, \xi, \eta)\, d\xi\, d\eta, \qquad (4.38)$$

where the $\psi(\cdot, \cdot)$ are unchanged by the linear operator $h(\cdot, \cdot, \cdot, \cdot)$. If object restoration is the objective, then an estimate of the object as a function of the eigenspace of the PSF can be developed. Expanding the object in terms of these eigenfunctions,

$$f(\xi, \eta) = \sum_{n=0}^{\infty} \sum_{m=0}^{\infty} a_{nm}\psi_{nm}(\xi, \eta), \qquad (4.39)$$

and substituting into the image forming equation yields

$$g(x, y) = \int_{-\infty}^{\infty} \int_{-\infty}^{\infty} \sum_{n} \sum_{m} a_{nm}\psi_{nm}(\xi, \eta) h(x, y, \xi, \eta)\, d\xi\, d\eta \qquad (4.40a)$$

$$= \sum_n \sum_m a_{nm}\lambda_{nm}\psi_{nm}(x, y). \tag{4.40b}$$

Multiplying and integrating both sides of Equation (4.40b) and solving for a_{nm},

$$\int_{-\infty}^{\infty} \int_{-\infty}^{\infty} g(x, y)\psi_{jk}(x, y)\, dx\, dy = \sum_{n=0}^{\infty} \sum_{m=0}^{\infty} a_{nm}\lambda_{nm} \int_{-\infty}^{\infty} \int_{-\infty}^{\infty} \psi_{nm}(x, y)\psi_{jk}(x, y)\, dx\, dy.$$

$$\tag{4.41a}$$

By the orthonormality of the eigenfunctions,

$$\int_{-\infty}^{\infty} \int_{-\infty}^{\infty} g(x, y)\psi_{jk}(x, y)\, dx\, dy = \sum_{n=0}^{\infty} \sum_{m=0}^{\infty} a_{nm}\lambda_{nm}\, \delta(j - n, k - m). \tag{4.41b}$$

Finally,

$$a_{jk} = \frac{1}{\lambda_{jk}} \int_{-\infty}^{\infty} \int_{-\infty}^{\infty} g(x, y)\psi_{jk}(x, y)\, dx\, dy \tag{4.42}$$

It is now possible to solve for the object $f(\xi, \eta)$ from Equation (4.39) using the coefficients a_{jk}.

While the analysis above is appealing in theory, there are many questions that remain unanswered. The assumption of the existence of the eigenfunctions is subject to criticism as well as assuming they are known. The two-dimensional infinite summations, of course, imply convergence considerations and computational considerations must then be investigated.

As an illustration of the possible use of the analysis above, consider the SIPSF system in which the imaging equation becomes a two-dimensional convolution [see Equation (4.15)]. In this case, the eigenfunctions become

$$\psi_{nm}(x, y) = \exp\{2\pi i(nx + my)\}, \tag{4.43}$$

which are the basis functions (and therefore kernel) for the two-dimensional Fourier transform. Consequently, filtering in the eigenspace of SIPSF systems is equivalent to processing in the Fourier transform domain.

As another illustration of such analyses, consider the ideal separable low-pass imaging system in which the PSF becomes the product of two sinc functions; i.e.,

$$h(x - \xi, y - \eta) = \frac{\sin \pi(x - \xi)}{\pi(x - \xi)} \frac{\sin \pi(y - \eta)}{(y - \eta)}. \tag{4.44}$$

In this case the eigenfunctions of such systems are the prolate spheroidal wave functions (PSWF). These functions have been extensively analyzed by Slepian and Pollak (1961) and Landau and Pollak (1961); and, as mathematical functions, they possess some very intriguing properties.

Unfortunately, the PSWF have also led to the myth of superresolution in which an attempt is made to extrapolate beyond the bandpass of a SIPSF imaging system. This is equivalent to increasing the DOF of such an imaging system, after the fact of sampling, and as such there is very little theoretical basis upon which such digital extrapolation can be anticipated. The basic problem is, again, one of signal-to-noise ratio, SNR, in which the noise of the measurement exceeds the accuracy of the knowledge of the eigenvalue of interest. As seen in Equation (4.42), the coefficients of restoration become erroneous due to the reciprocation of measurement induced inaccuracies and extremely small eigenvalues.

Consider now the SVPSF model. To obtain a better feel for the character of the eigenfunctions, it may be asked, "What waveform in two dimensions would go into a SVPSF system and come out unchanged except for a scale factor?" Maybe more specifically it might be useful to investigate the solution to the following integral equation:

$$\lambda_{nm}\Psi_{nm}(x, y) = \int_{-\infty}^{\infty}\int_{-\infty}^{\infty} \Psi_{nm}(\xi, \eta) \exp\left\{-\frac{(x - \xi)^2 + (y - \eta)^2}{\sigma^2(x, y, \xi, \eta)}\right\} d\xi\, d\eta \quad (4.45)$$

or some other suitably varying point-spread-function integral equation. Expanding the variance function $\sigma^2(\ldots)$ in a Taylor series expansion, it is seen that

$$h(x, y, \xi, \eta) = \exp\left\{[(x - \xi)^2 + (y - \eta)^2]\bigg/\left[\sum_{i=0}^{\infty}\frac{P(x, y, \xi, \eta)^i}{i!}\sigma_i^2(0, 0, 0, 0)\right]\right\}, \quad (4.46)$$

where $P(x, y, \xi, \eta)^i$ is a four-dimensional polynomial of order i with $\binom{4 + i}{i}$ terms and $\sigma_i^2(0, 0, 0, 0)$ is the ith derivative evaluated at 0. It might be noted that, for $i = 0$.

$$h_0(x, y, \xi, \eta) = \exp\left\{\frac{(x - \xi)^2 + (y - \eta)^2}{\text{constant}}\right\}, \quad (4.47)$$

which becomes a SIPSF system whose eigenfunctions are sines and cosines as indicated in Equation (4.43). Therefore, depending on the rate of variation of $\sigma^2(x, y, \xi, \eta)$, the SVPSF of Equation (4.45) may in fact result in eigenfunctions with only slightly perturbed sines and cosines.

One of the motivations for studying the eigenanalysis of imaging systems is to develop motivation for restoration in the eigenspaces of such imaging systems. In the discrete–discrete models, this means that the PSF matrix $[H]$ should be analyzed in terms of its eigenvectors, and suitable transformations should be developed to operate in the eigenspace of $[H]$. As shown in Section 4.5, the degrees of freedom of an imaging system were a function of the eigenvalues of $[\mathfrak{R}]$, which in turn were the singular values (squared) of $[H]$. It will be seen in subsequent chapters that the singular value decomposition (SVD) techniques and pseudo-inverse restorations do operate in the eigenspaces of the PSF matrices and that, for general linear systems, such eigenspaces have Fourier decomposition for SIPSF systems as their subsets. The eigenspace implementation of SVD and pseudo-inverse restoration becomes intimately related to the degrees of freedom of the imaging system and the eigenanalysis of that system.

4.7 Stochastic Point-Spread Functions

Traditionally the point-spread function of an imaging system, whether it be linear or nonlinear or space-variant or -invariant, is assumed to be known deterministically. Realistically speaking, however, the analyst is often faced with imprecise knowledge of $h(x, y, \xi, \eta)$ and it is desirable to know the effect of the degree of imprecision on any restoration results. One method of establishing such a measure is through a perturbation analysis, on $h(x, y, \xi, \eta)$. The first-order perturbation might be defined using a Taylor series expansion

$$h(x + \Delta x, y + \Delta y, \xi + \Delta\xi, \eta + \Delta\eta)$$

$$\cong h(x_0, y_0, \xi_0, \eta_0) + \frac{\partial h}{\partial x}\Delta x + \frac{\partial h}{\partial y}\Delta y + \frac{\partial h}{\partial \xi}\Delta\xi + \frac{\partial h}{\partial \eta}\Delta\eta, \quad (4.48)$$

where the partial derivatives are all evaluated at $(x_0, y_0, \xi_0, \eta_0)$. If there are no singularities in the first-order perturbation, then the analysis might expand to high-order effects. Normally, however, the first- and second-order effects will give an indication as to the effect due to imprecise knowledge of a given variable (x, y, ξ, η).

An alternative approach to imprecise knowledge of $h(x, y, \xi, \eta)$ is through a statistical description of h, i.e., $p(h)$. If the PSF was confidently known, then the probability density function of $h(\cdot)$ would be quite close to a Dirac delta function.

On other occasions our knowledge of $h(\cdot)$ may be very imprecise, and the density function would vary around some nominal $h_0(\cdot)$ over the space of allowable point-spread functions (see Chapter 8 for constraints on this space). Knowledge of $p(h)$ may in fact be limited but second-order moments of $h(\cdot)$ may still be available. Slepian (1967) has investigated the use of such second-order moment information on the PSF for defining minimum mean-square filters. Without further knowledge of these moments it is difficult to describe the effect of these "average" filters other than to note that an "average" restoration will obviously be suboptimal to a "deterministic" restoration, but it will be better than no restoration at all. It is difficult to provide further analysis on such statistically described PSF's without further knowledge of $p(h)$. Once such information is available, minimum mean-square error, maximum *a posteriori*, and maximum likelihood filters can be developed.

Chapter 5

A Posteriori Determined Degradation Parameters

5.0 Introduction

This chapter might be described as utilizing the "art" of image processing for restoration. Specifically, the available image at hand is used to develop parameters to describe the imaging system. The "art" enters by virtue of the fact that the degree of restoration success is dependent on the cleverness and insight of the individual developing algorithms to extract the pertinent degradation parameters from a given image. Chapter 4 might be the basis for utilizing *a priori* knowledge concerning the effect imposed by an imaging system. *A posteriori* knowledge often plays a role greater than many choose to admit in the practical day-to-day processing of real-world imagery, however. Obvious examples might include point-spread-function determination from edges or points in the image that are known to exist in the object. The PSF determination is often done with test scenes such as resolution charts and point targets (stars and other point sources). Other examples of *a posteriori* image use might include estimates of the noise variance and possible power spectra obtained from relatively smooth regions in the image. A third example might be one in which scanner-induced noise (jitter) becomes immediately evident in the Fourier transform of the image although such noise is subtly obscured in the spatial representation of the image.

One of the first processes that might be attempted for correction is the point process nonlinearity correction to compensate for the nonlinear response of film, amplifiers, and other devices through which the object passed before becoming a sampled image within the computer. Ideally an intensity wedge (i.e., a ramp of brightness changes) would be desirable if imaged along with the original object. Naturally this is usually not feasible for the object plane but is a valid approach for z-axis linearization of the

90

digitization process. Figure 5.1 indicates the steps desirable for such a compensation procedure. While the analytic nature of such a process is not very exciting [the only restriction is that the curve in Figure 5.1(c) be monotonic increasing], the practical importance of this phase of image restoration cannot be overestimated. A similar procedure should be employed upon image recovery from the computer (image display) such that linearization is maintained throughout the restoration process. Stockham (1972) has addressed this subject to considerable extent and the details are left to that reference [also McGlamery (1967)].

5.1   Point-Spread-Function Measurements

Probably the next degree of sophistication in *a posteriori* image restoration is the attempt to determine the point-spread function from the available image. The more sophisticated techniques in this area lie in determination of SIPSF parameters, the SVPSF systems being (in general) orders of magnitude more complex to model and analyze. Before proceeding to some of the SIPSF techniques, however, one diversion to the SVPSF case is noteworthy. Specifically with an interactive type of image processing facility, it is possible to allow human intervention to define obvious local regions of an image that are subject to a SIPSF degradation; whereas the entire image may not be equivalently distorted. Figure 5.2 might illustrate this procedure. Specifically Figure 5.2(a) depicts a full image, while the Fourier transform of this scene is presented in Figure 5.2(b). Notice from the Fourier transform that the obvious linear motion blur of the lower portion of the image [that of Figure 5.2(c)] does not show up clearly in the Fourier domain. By removing the majority of that portion of the image that is not motion blurred and Fourier transforming [see Figure 5.2(d)], however, the effect of the zeros of the sinc function, indigenous to motion blur modulating the Fourier transform of the image, is seen. Subsequent discussions will illustrate next steps following this stage of the processing. The point for emphasis is the ability of the user to define subregions of an image that are subject to SIPSF distortions, thereby lending themselves to existing techniques (some to be described below).

Probably the simplest and most common SIPSF blurs for *a posteriori* determination are defocus aberrations and linear motion blur. Badly defocused SIPSF imagery behaves as if its Fourier transform had been multiplied by an optical transfer function given by a first-order Bessel function divided by its argument. Thus

$$H(\rho, \theta) = \frac{J_1(a\rho)}{a\rho}, \tag{5.1}$$

where

$$\rho = \sqrt{w_x^2 + w_y^2} \tag{5.2a}$$

$$\theta = \tan^{-1}\frac{w_y}{w_x}. \tag{5.2b}$$

Consequently,

$$G(\rho, \theta) = H(\rho, \theta)F(\rho, \theta), \tag{5.3}$$

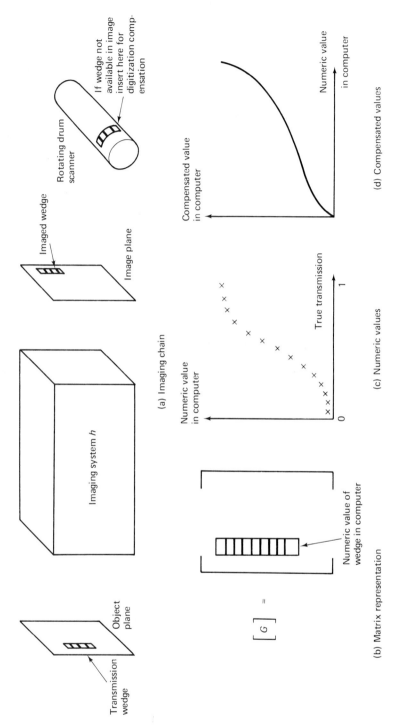

Figure 5.1 Point process (z axis) compensation.

Transmission wedge

Object plane

Imaging system h

Image plane

Imaged wedge

Rotating drum scanner

If wedge not available in image insert here for digitization compensation

(a) Imaging chain

$$[\,G\,] =$$

Numeric value of wedge in computer

(b) Matrix representation

Numeric value in computer

True transmission

(c) Numeric values

Compensated value in computer

Numeric value in computer

(d) Compensated values

92

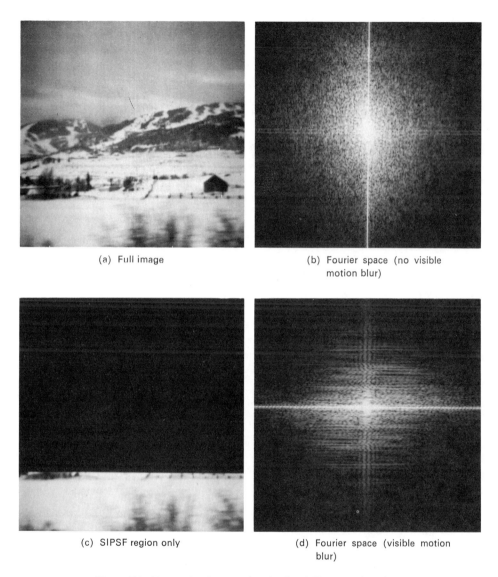

(a) Full image

(b) Fourier space (no visible motion blur)

(c) SIPSF region only

(d) Fourier space (visible motion blur)

Figure 5.2   Interactive intervention for local SIPSF region determination.

where the traditional SIPSF relationship is represented by the Fourier domain in polar coordinate notation. Figure 5.3 presents examples of such blur in which the 180° phase reversal [negative lobe in Figure 5.3(a)] causes a contrast reversal (light to dark and dark to light) in the image [Figure 5.3(b)]. The original object (see Figure 4.9(a)] is formed with increasing dominant spatial frequencies toward the center and the contrast reversal phenomenon becomes obvious in the spatial domain. Such would not be the case for normal imagery in which a contrast reversal at certain spatial frequencies would occur but the general effect on the object would be blurred imagery. In Figure 5.3(c) and (d), less severe defocus occurs and no phase reversals result. A general blurring but no contrast reversal is apparent in the resulting image. One suggestion that has been made to measure such distortion is to integrate out the effect of the object as a function of θ, thereby leaving an approximation to the OTF [Adams and Barrett (1970)]. Taking complex logarithms to separate the multiplicative processes into additive processes yields

$$\log |\hat{H}(\rho)| \cong \frac{1}{2\pi} \int_{-\pi}^{\pi} \log |G(\rho, \theta)| \, d\theta \tag{5.4a}$$

$$\cong \frac{1}{2\pi} \int_{-\pi}^{\pi} \log |F(\rho, \theta)| \, d\theta + \log \left| \frac{J_1(a\rho)}{a\rho} \right| + j\pi(a\rho), \tag{5.4b}$$

where it is assumed that the phase of the image $F(\rho, \theta)$ averages to zero and the OTF is not a function of θ. It is clear from the approximation (5.4b) that the estimate of the logarithm of the OTF is biased by an image-dependent term. The objective is, however, to find a better feeling for the zeros of the OTF. The determination of the value of the parameter a may be more readily obvious from Equation (5.4b). Naturally the rectification (absolute value operator) to allow the logarithm operation must be dealt with cautiously as logarithms of zero are not well-behaved.

A similar technique can be devised for determination of the zeros of the OTF associated with linear motion blur (see Figures 4.9 and 5.2). Here the OTF is given by

$$H(w_x, w_y) = \frac{\sin a\omega}{a\omega}, \tag{5.5}$$

where

$$\omega = w_x \cos \psi + w_y \sin \psi \tag{5.6}$$

and ψ is the direction of motion blur of the object with respect to the image plane. Again the objective is to determine the value of the parameter a, which in this case defines the periodic placement of zeros in the frequency domain. Using logarithms to separate out the multiplicative phenomenon and performing a one-dimensional Fourier transform yields

$$\hat{h}_x(x, y) \cong \int_{-\infty}^{\infty} \log |F(w_x, w_y)| \exp (jw_y y) \, dw_y + j \int_{-\infty}^{\infty} \gamma(w_x, w_y) \exp (jw_y y) \, dw_y$$

$$+ \int_{-\infty}^{\infty} \log \left| \frac{\sin a\omega}{a\omega} \right| \exp (jw_y y) \, dw_y + j \int_{-\infty}^{\infty} \pi(a\omega) \exp (jw_y y) \, dw_y. \tag{5.7}$$

It is obvious that the first two terms are image-dependent and will result in some arbitrary function. The second two terms are periodic in w_y, however, as is evident from the equation for ω (Equation 5.6), and as such will result in a line of large amplitude parallel to the x axis in the $\hat{h}_x(x, y)$ function (see Figure 5.4). Taking absolute values and integrating out the x dimension to average out the image-dependent term yields

$$\hat{h}(y) \cong \int_{-\infty}^{\infty} |\hat{h}_x(x, y)| \, dx.$$

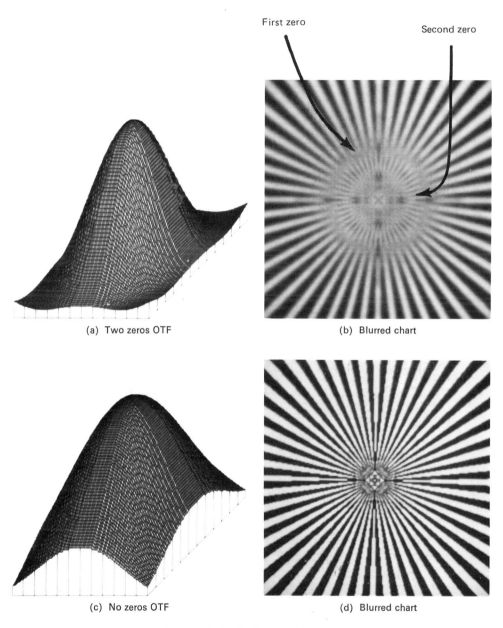

Figure 5.3   Badly defocused OTF.

The resulting function should have a pronounced peak at the periodic rate of $a \sin \psi$ in the xy direction. Thus

$$\max_{y} \hat{h}(y) = a \sin \psi \tag{5.8a}$$

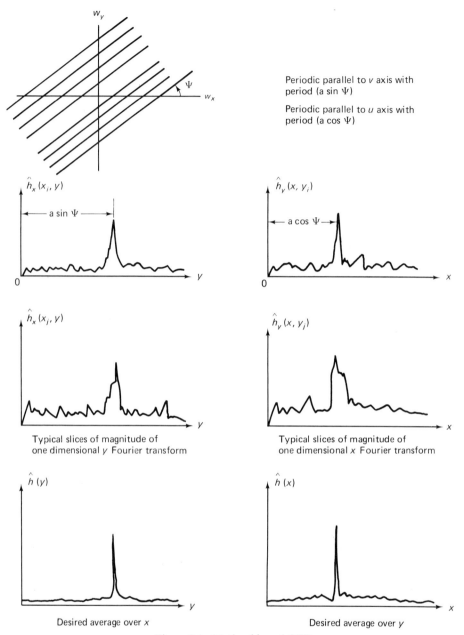

Periodic parallel to v axis with
period (a sin Ψ)

Periodic parallel to u axis with
period (a cos Ψ)

Typical slices of magnitude of
one dimensional y Fourier transform

Typical slices of magnitude of
one dimensional x Fourier transform

Desired average over x

Desired average over y

Figure 5.4   Motion blurred OTF.

and by symmetry

$$\max_{x} \hat{h}(x) = a \cos \psi, \tag{5.8b}$$

where *by symmetry* is meant the entire Fourier transform plane and averaging processes
are done in the complement coordinates. Consequently both the period and direction
of motion blur are theoretically available from this Cepstrum-like technique [Bogert,
et al. (1963)].

The motivation behind the techniques described above is simply that of averaging out an unwanted signal (image-dependent pheonomena) and retaining a desired signal (OTF and image-independent). The technique has been generalized to all types of phaseless imagery by Cole (1973) and Cannon (1974) and is based, again, upon averaging image-dependent terms from common OTF responses. The technique of segmentation [Huang (1971); Stockham, Ingebretzen, and Cannon (1975)] suggests that an image be partitioned into a set of smaller images, indexed by i, each of which is disturbed by the same SIPSF. Thus

$$g_i(x, y) = h(x, y) \circledast f_i(x, y), \tag{5.9}$$

where $\circledast$ implies two-dimensional convolution. Taking Fourier transforms and averaging logarithms of the resulting magnitudes yields a log power spectrum estimate

$$\hat{P}_{\ln(g)}(w_x, w_y) = \sum_{i=1}^{M} \log \{|G_i(w_x, w_y)|^2\} \tag{5.10a}$$

$$= \sum_{i=1}^{M} \log |F_i(w_x, w_y)|^2 + M \log |H(w_x, w_y)|^2. \tag{5.10b}$$

Again we are faced with an image-dependent term that must be removed. Cole (1973) has shown that, by subtracting a "typical" object prototype $a(x, y)$ for the first term in Equation (5.10b), one can obtain a reasonable estimate of the OTF as

$$\hat{P}_{\ln(g)}(w_x, w_y) = M \log |H(w_x, w_y)|^2 + \sum_{i}^{M} \log |F_i(w_x, w_y)|^2$$

$$- \sum_{i=1}^{M} \log |A_i(w_x, w_y)|^2 \tag{5.11a}$$

$$\cong M \log |H(w_x, w_y)|^2. \tag{5.11b}$$

The technique above for determining phaseless OTF's for SIPSF systems has come to be known as an *averaged-log-spectrum* method. A parallel approach, investigated by Cannon (1974), is illustrated in Figure 5.5. A power spectral analysis is used here for motivation for the desired filter. Specifically, the power spectrum of the image is given by

$$P_g(w_x, w_y) = P_f(w_x, w_y)|H(w_x, w_y)|^2 + P_n(w_x, w_y). \tag{5.12}$$

The restoration filter $w(x, y)$ causes the restored object to have a power spectrum of

$$P_f(w_x, w_y) = P_g(w_x, w_y)|W(w_x, w_y)|^2. \tag{5.13}$$

Constraining the power spectrum of the object to equal that of the estimated object yields

$$|W(w_x, w_y)| = \left[\frac{P_f(w_x, w_y)}{P_f(w_x, w_y)|H(w_x, w_y)|^2 + P_n(w_x, w_y)} \right]^{1/2}. \tag{5.14}$$

This particular restoration filter will be examined as a subset of a family of such filters in Chapters 7 and 8. Note here, however, that the power spectrum of the object might be unknown. Again experimental results indicate that a "typical" object prototype $a(x, y)$ can be used for determining the needed power spectrum [i.e., $P_f(w_x, w_y) = P_a(w_x, w_y)$]. The advantage of the two techniques above is that no knowledge as to the type of distortion (other than phaseless and SIPSF) need be available for the methods to work. If the OTF does contain phase, then possible combination of the

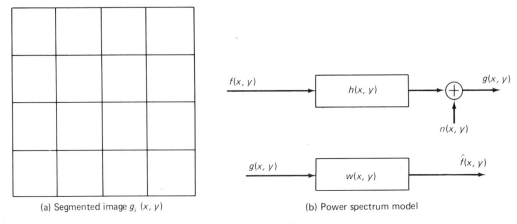

(a) Segmented image $g_i(x, y)$ (b) Power spectrum model

Figure 5.5 Phaseless SIPSF filter determination.

techniques above to determine the magnitude of the OTF with other phase determination criteria (such as those described earlier in the chapter or by human observation of the Fourier domain) may provide valuable restoration filter parameterization
[Cannon (1974)]. The technique is referred to as *averaged-magnitude-spectrum* methods
as contrasted to the averaged-logarithmic-spectrum methods described previously.

The utility of the SIPSF phaseless filter determination described above is a function
of the importance, or lack thereof, of the phase of the OTF. The OTF is the Fourier
transform of the PSF and, as such, will have a phase component whenever the PSF
is not symmetric. One technique that has considerable success under these circumstances is to measure the PSF directly at the time of exposure. McGlamery (1967)
has illustrated this technique by imaging a point source of light simultaneously with
normal object exposure. A point source is in the field of view and if such a point source
is remote (not overlapping) from the rest of the object of interest, then the localized
point source becomes the PSF that must then be Fourier transformed to obtain the
OTF. For short-term exposure situations, such as experienced in atmospheric turbulence, this technique will yield a viable PSF.

Naturally the point source and resulting PSF are subject to the assumption of a
SIPSF imaging system as well as the existence of a true point source. Even in certain
SVPSF systems, however, for regions within isoplanatic patches, these same tech-
niques can be applicable.

As an example of the use of other than point sources for OTF determination,
consider the technique of derivation of the transfer function of a two-dimensional
linear system from a degraded edge [Tatian (1965)]. Under these conditions, an appropriate edge (known to be an edge in the object, *a priori*) is determined in the image and
a one-dimensional PSF is calculated. Then by assumption of circular symmetry the
rotation of the one-dimensional PSF becomes the two-dimensional version. As an
illustration of the technique, consider the resolution chart illustrated in Figure 5.6(a)
[Tescher and Andrews (1973)]. The horizontal edge of the rectangle in the upper half
of the resolution chart was used in the application of the edge-gradient analysis. Here

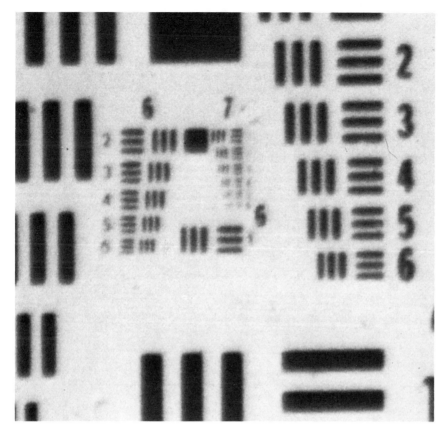

1024 × 1024 Digital image

Figure 5.6   Edge determined PSF.

160 vertical edges from the indicated rectangle were available for the determination of an effective transfer function. In order to miminize the significant amount of noise present in the image, the individual edges were averaged. The resultant edge is shown in Figure 5.7. The edge is investigated in a 32-sample observation window. The result of smoothing with Hanning filter weights is shown in Figure 5.7. Next, the line-spread function was obtained by numerically differentiating the edge, and the final estimate of the transfer function was taken as the modulus of the frequency terms of the line-spread Fourier transform (Figure 5.7). The abscissa units for this figure are in harmonics where the largest value, 16 for the 32-point segment, corresponds to the highest spatial frequency in the original image. The lack of symmetry in the line-spread function is due to the nonlinearity in the scanning process on the z axis and as such indicates improper transmission density compensation. Naturally, this should be corrected prior to any PSF parameter determination.

In closing this section on point-spread-function measurements, it is instructive to view the effect of the point-spread function on reducing the degrees of freedom avail-

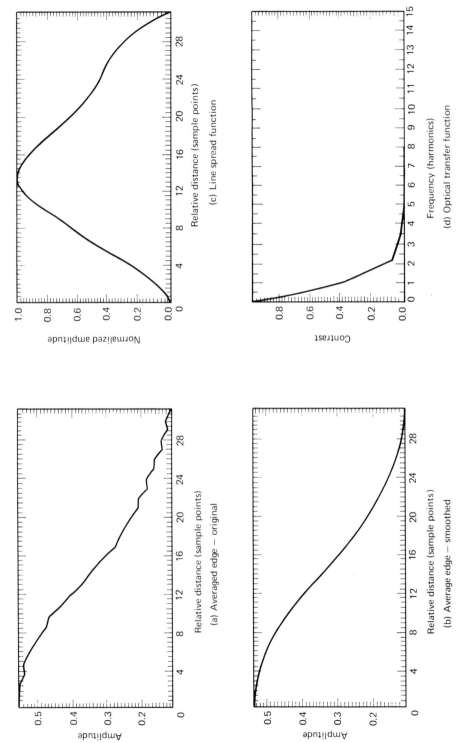

Figure 5.7 Line spread function and OTF.

able in the image from which the *a posteriori* measurements are to be taken. Using a discrete–discrete model, the rank of an image can be investigated *a posteriori* and some facts regarding the imaging system can be inferred. As an example, consider the discrete–discrete model (SIPSF or SVPSF) given by

$$[G] = [A][F][B]^t. \qquad (5.15)$$

From linear algebra it is known that the rank of the image is bounded above by the minimum of the ranks of the various degradations and that of the object. Thus

$$R[G] \leq \min \{R[A], R[F], R[B]\}. \qquad (5.16a)$$

It might be argued that the original object must have large rank or number of degrees of freedom (at least for objects of sufficient detail to be of interest) and, as such, under the nonsingular object model,

$$R[G] \leq \min \{R[A], R[B]\}. \qquad (5.16b)$$

Measuring the rank of the image results in a qualitative assessment of the various degrees of freedom in the system. Thus

$$R[A] \geq R[G]$$
$$R[B] \geq R[G] \qquad (5.17)$$
$$R[F] \geq R[G].$$

A large rank image consequently implies effective imaging. Notice that by increasing the sampling rate (i.e., larger matrices) the degrees of freedom will not necessarily increase with more samples and consequently oversampling will not improve the restoration.

5.2   Noise Measurements

Naturally it would be desirable to be able to evaluate an imaging system such that the noise parameters associated with the data gathering process were well-defined. As indicated in Chapters 2 and 4, however, there are a variety of models and mechanisms by which errors can enter the image acquisition process and the model assumed for such noise sources may dramatically affect the restoration process. Consequently, it would be desirable to confirm the noise model and even parameterize that model by *a posteriori* techniques associated with the image at hand. Possibly the most basic question might concern the multiplicative versus additive (or their combinations) aspect of the noise in the system. Certainly the stationarity versus non-stationarity of the noise process is a relevant concern.

One desirable aspect of an image for noise measurement purposes is that it have regions of relatively unchanging object content since, in these regions, noise parameters can be calculated. To illustrate the point, consider again the resolution chart depicted in Figure 5.6. From *a priori* knowledge it is known that the chart is binary in intensity and characteristics of the noise in the light and/or dark regions can be measured. It is also fortunate that such regions exist at the extremes of transmission since if the noise parameters measured in the light regions do not equal those in the dark regions, it is possible to determine that a multiplicative process exists (as opposed to an additive process). If, indeed, it is determined that the noise is multiplicative, then a logarithm operation, with the appropriate constant for gamma correction, would separate the signal from the noise. Subsequent linear filtering in this homo-morphic process would then allow traditional noise suppression [Oppenheim, *et al.* (1968)]. Conversely, filters can be developed for Wiener filtering of multiplicative noise processes as opposed to additive logarithm noise processors [Franks (1969)].

To illustrate these points, the resolution chart of Figure 5.6 has been used as an example image for noise evaluation. A relatively flat subsection of the image has been extracted [see Figure 5.8(a)]. A singular value decomposition of the noise section indicates a relatively wide-band level by virtue of the fairly flat portion of the eigen-value plot. This is further confirmed by virtue of the display of the postulated noise power spectrum [Figure 5.8(c) and (d)]. These functions were obtained from the Fourier analysis of the subsection region and also indicate a relatively broad-band noise process. The entire experiment, indicated in Figure 5.8, was repeated in the dark portion of the resolution chart, and these results are shown in Figure 5.9. It is clear that the SVD noise level is considerably lower and the respective power spectra displays provide the same conclusion. (The bright vertical energy in the power spec-trum is due to the artificial edge introduced in the subsection region by a bright upper border.) In this circumstance, it is concluded that the noise process changes as a func-tion of the underlying object brightness and as such it is believed that the noise is multiplicative[1] (at least has a signal dependent component). Since there are only two data points on the transmission curve, i.e., light and dark regions, then it would be desirable to find other regions in an image with other underlying brightnesses to obtain additional confirmation of the multiplicative hypothesis. This is not possible in a binary object, but in general forms of imagery such a constraint may not exist.

An additional conclusion concerning the experiment above reflects on the con-cept of oversampling. The noise power spectra developed above in conjunction with the PSF on the tribar resolution chart indicate that most of the spatial frequency energy beyond one-quarter the Nyquist rate is due to noise. The fact that the transfer function has an effective cutoff at one-fourth of the frequency that is permitted by the specific sampling used indicates that the data are grossly oversampled. In fact, if it is assumed that the derived transfer function is rotationally symmetric, the loca-tion of the cutoff indicates a twenty-fold oversampling of the image.

In order to obtain a higher confidence level in the derived transfer function and noise models, the following simple experiment was performed. After a Fourier trans-form of the resolution chart was obtained, all terms in the frequency plane outside the circular region of radius of one-fourth frequency that would be allowed by the

[1]The bright and dark sections of the opaque prints correspond to dark and bright sections in the original negative; hence, noise variance is greater at higher film density (darker regions), as discussed in Chapter 2.

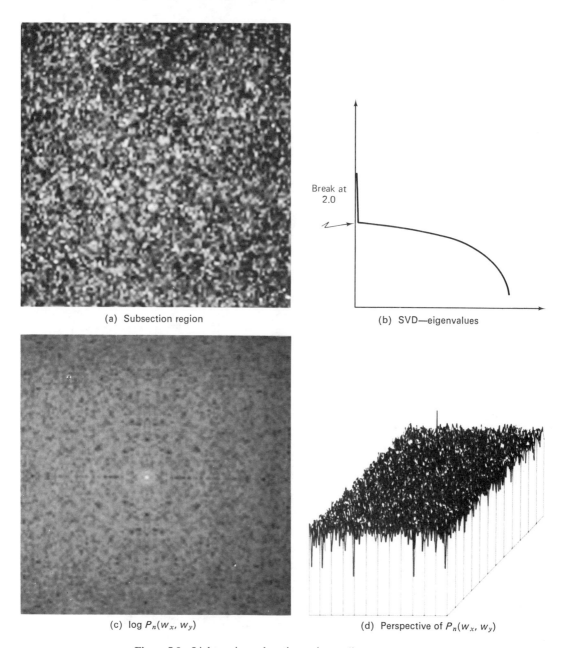

(a) Subsection region

(b) SVD—eigenvalues

Break at
2.0

(c) $\log P_n(w_x, w_y)$

(d) Perspective of $P_n(w_x, w_y)$

Figure 5.8 Light region subsection noise studies.

sampling theorem were replaced with zero. The low-pass filtered image is obtained by the inverse Fourier transform. The observed image [Figure 5.10(a)] shows no loss in resolution in terms of apparent signal-to-noise ratio.

The derivation of the transfer function can be repeated using the set of edges from the low-pass filtered image. The results of the analysis are shown in Figure 5.10(b)

103

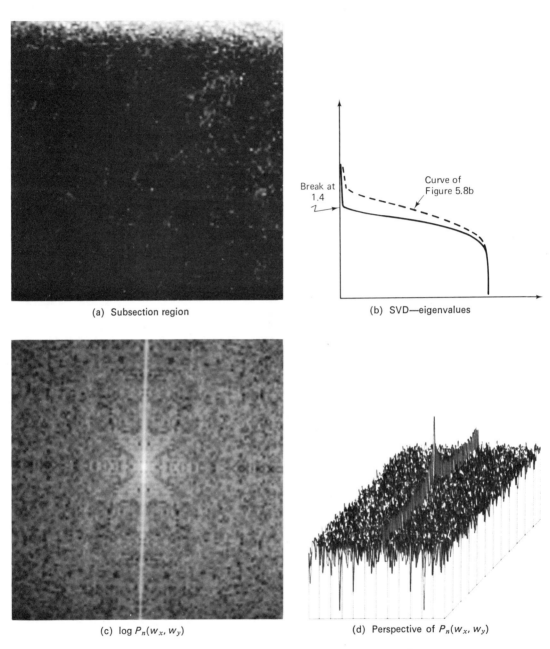

(a) Subsection region

(b) SVD—eigenvalues

(c) $\log P_n(w_x, w_y)$

(d) Perspective of $P_n(w_x, w_y)$

Figure 5.9 Dark region subsection noise studies.

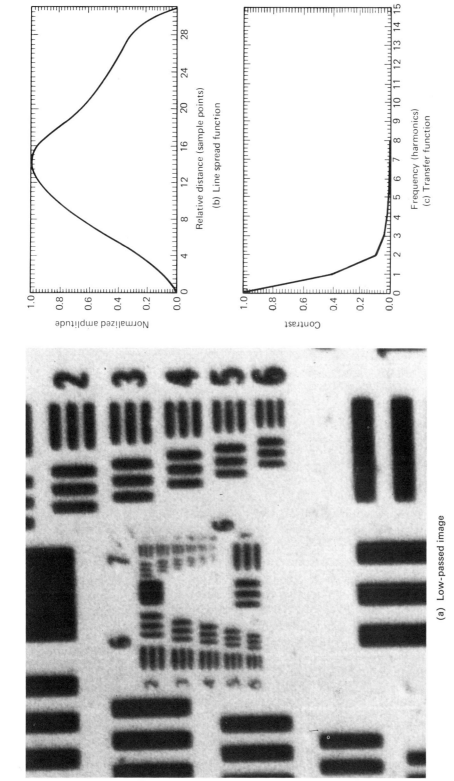

(b) Line spread function

(c) Transfer function

(a) Low-passed image

Figure 5.10 Low-pass resolution chart.

and (c). The agreement between transfer functions is very good, indicating a high confidence level in the obtained results.

5.3 Scanner Evaluation

This section of the chapter is devoted to a dividend that often accompanies the analysis of a digitized image for degradation parameters. Specifically it is relatively simple to evaluate the effect of the digitization or scanning process through some simple observations on the digitized image. Four specific aspects for observation include

1. Signal-to-noise determination.
2. Gray scale distribution.
3. Scanner-induced artifacts (spatial frequency).
4. Scanning aperture effects.

The first aspect above can be evaluated by a simple examination of the bit planes of an image. A rule of thumb is if any spatial correlation exists in a bit plane, then that bit carries signal information. If, on the other hand, a given bit plane is determined to be random and uncorrelated, then it might be surmised that the particular plane carried little signal information and might be governed only by noise. Figure 5.11 presents an illustration of this point with an eight-bit image in which the least significant bit still shows some spatial structure, thereby implying a signal-to-noise ratio of greater than $256 : 1$.

Figure 5.12 addresses the second aspect of scanner evaluation in which the zero-order histograms, i.e., estimates of the probability density function, $p(g)$, for two different images are presented. The first obvious observation is that the baboon image is "better distributed" than the face image. The biased and saturated nature of Figure 5.12(d) indicates that the z-axis scanning response was not properly adjusted and consequently the full potential of the range of transmission values is not being used. Another aspect of histogram observation that should be mentioned is the possibility of "sticky bits" in the analog-to-digital converter (in the scanning process). This defect is characterized by gaps in the histograms as illustrated in Figure 5.12(e). What appears to be a smoothly increasing or decreasing curve is roughened by evenly spaced gaps that indicate the hesitancy of certain bits to convert (i.e., every two gray-level gaps imply least significant bit problems; every four gray-level gaps imply second least significant bit problems, etc.).

The third topic associated with improper scanning is that of scanner-induced spatial frequency artifacts. Unfortunately, users often ignore the question of scanner integrity and may be completely unaware of artificially induced effects on their digital images, which may be completely unrelated to the pictorial information under analysis.

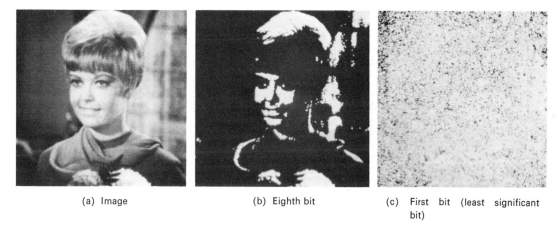

(a) Image   (b) Eighth bit   (c) First   bit   (least   significant
                                                                   bit)

Figure 5.11   Significant bit determination of digital imagery.

The particular image, which is of concern here, appears in Figure 5.13 and is known *a priori* to be binary in nature due to the use of black and white paint (no gray shades) in the definition of the Air Force resolution chart. Effects of the atmosphere, imaging camera, film, and scanner obviously produce an image in the computer that is far from binary. By observing the histogram of the digitized image it is possible to pick out levels of gray that are due to noise and levels that are due to signal. By clipping and stretching in the appropriate regions of the histogram, it is possible to define a non-linear mapping that yields an enhanced image that is more binary in histogram nature than the nonenhanced versions [see Figure 5.13(b) and (e)]. Note, however, that we refer to such images as enhanced rather than restored, as there is no unique clipping and stretching routine to binarize properly the image to become the object again.

One possible condition for introducing energy perfectly aligned with the frequency domain axes (see Figure 5.13) might be due to jitter in the scanner itself. If the start of each scan line is random in some sense to its neighbor, an artificial spatial shift of that line results. The shifted line then introduces artificial high-frequency edges within the image that are perfectly normal (perpendicular) to the scan axis. Naturally, the worse the jitter, the more artificial high-frequency energy will be generated, and the scanner signature will be stronger along the horizontal or vertical spatial frequency axis.

In Figure 5.13 the Fourier domain of both images demonstrates two interesting phenomena concerning the device used for scanning. First, there is a significant amount of image energy along the horizontal axis in the Fourier domain. This energy is due to the scanner-line jitter phenomenon described in the paragraph above. Note how it occurs in both scenes and tends to have a periodic structure indicating a possible periodic electronic oscillation defining the starting position of each scan line. A second way for the Fourier axis to have so much energy is that one of the borders of

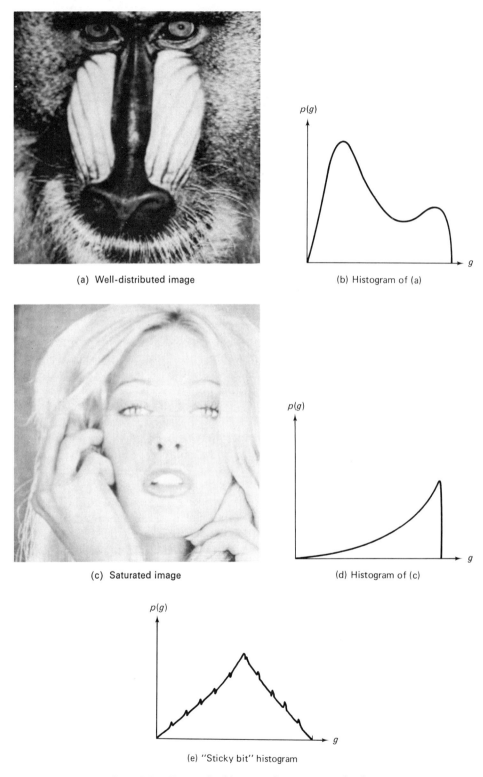

(a) Well-distributed image

(b) Histogram of (a)

(c) Saturated image

(d) Histogram of (c)

(e) "Sticky bit" histogram

Figure 5.12 Zero-order histogram for scanner evaluation.

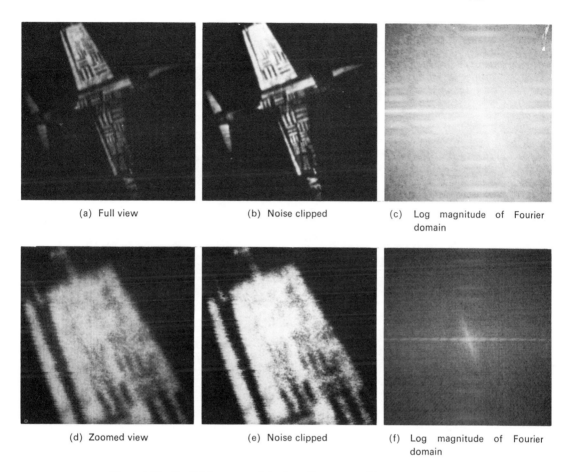

(a) Full view   (b) Noise clipped   (c) Log magnitude of Fourier
                                                                        domain

(d) Zoomed view   (e) Noise clipped   (f) Log magnitude of Fourier
                                                                        domain

Figure 5.13   Spatial frequency detection of scanner artifacts.

the image is brighter than its opposite border. Because the left and right edges of both scenes are black, the characteristic does not show up in the vertical Fourier axis. The same phenomenon occurs for top and bottom window borders but is masked in these cases by the scan-line-jitter synchronization problem.

The fourth scanner artifact mentioned in the introduction to this section was that of aperture effects. Another unnatural display of Fourier energy still to be explained is the periodic faint horizontal stripes that occur along both horizontal and vertical axes where energy is again perfectly parallel or normal to the spatial frequency axes. From this effect in Figure 5.13(c) and (f) it might be claimed that the pattern was similar to a $(\sin aw_x/aw_x)(\sin bw_y/bw_y)$ double sinc function. If this were a multiplicative envelope in the Fourier domain, it might imply some sort of linear two-dimensional scan motion blur. Scanning aperture modulations often occur in this manner in the Fourier domain [Hunt and Breedlove (1975)]. It is interesting to note that without Fourier transforming the original image, it would have been virtually impossible to know that such an aperture degradation was being introduced, although the scanning jitter was fairly obvious in this case in the spatial domain.

Part III

RESTORATION

Chapter 6

Preliminary Concepts
In Image Restoration

6.0 Introduction

By the end of this book a large number of diverse methods will have been proposed
for image restoration; keeping track of all the methods and their relations to one
another is not an easy task. It is the function of this chapter to present some of the
fundamental or common principles that underlie the many methods of image restoration that will be encountered in the remaining chapters.

The motivation of this chapter is clearly pragmatic. The great variety of methods
proposed for image restoration can make sense only if some of the common benchmarks or points of reference are established. Even with these benchmarks, it will
be difficult to provide a unified view of image restoration. This is due to the nature of
the problem. Image restoration is ill-conditioned and, as such, it lacks a unique solution. The number of possible solution methods is limited only by human ingenuity.
In this sense, the problem of image restoration results in an unmanageable and diverse
field. It simultaneously results in a field that is still rich in new concepts and ideas.
It seems to be a truism that an unruly problem provides an environment for ferment
in intellectual endeavor.

6.1 The Ill-Conditioned Nature of Restoration

One of the most essential problems is the fact that image restoration is an ill-conditioned problem at best and a singular problem at worst. These terms will be left
undefined for the moment, their specific meaning to be presented below.

As discussed in Section 2.6, a complete model for image restoration must include image sensor, nonlinear effects, and noise. Since the problem of image restoration initially should be considered independent of sensor effects, a linear sensor with no inherent noise will be assumed. The result is an equation such as the following:

$$g(x, y) = \int_{-\infty}^{\infty} \int_{-\infty}^{\infty} h(x, \xi, y, \eta) f(\xi, \eta) \, d\xi \, d\eta. \tag{6.1}$$

The problem of *image restoration* is the determination of the original object distribution f given the recorded image g and knowledge about the point-spread-function h.

A common method of analysis of equations such as (6.1) is by operator theory. Given a space of functions on which f is defined and a space of functions on which g is defined, then the problem of the transformation or operator T that maps f into g can be posed as

$$T\{f\} \longrightarrow g, \tag{6.2}$$

where obviously for images

$$T\{f\} = \int_{-\infty}^{\infty} \int_{-\infty}^{\infty} h(x, \xi, y, \eta) f(\xi, \eta) \, d\xi \, d\eta. \tag{6.3}$$

The problem of image restoration is then to find the inverse transformation T^{-1} such that

$$T^{-1}\{g\} \longrightarrow f. \tag{6.4}$$

In a mathematical sense, the problem of image restoration corresponds to the existence and uniqueness of an inverse transformation. Both existence and uniqueness are important. If the inverse transformation does not exist, then there is no mathematical basis for asserting that f can be exactly recovered from g. (Although there may be no mathematical basis for exactly recovering f, there may be a practical basis for asserting that something very close to f can be recovered.) Problems for which there is no inverse transformation, i.e., T^{-1} does not exist, are said to be *singular*. On the other hand, T^{-1} may exist but not be unique; i.e., there may be more than one T^{-1}, the nature of which is used being dependent on f. Finally, even if T^{-1} exists and is unique, it may be *ill-conditioned*, by which we mean that a trivial perturbation in g can produce nontrivial perturbations in f. That is, there exists ϵ, which can be made arbitrarily small such that

$$T^{-1}\{g + \epsilon\} = f + \delta, \tag{6.5}$$

where $\delta \gg \epsilon$; δ is *not* arbitrarily small and is *not* negligible. Thus, an ill-conditioned problem is one in which inherent data perturbations can result in undesirable effects in the solution by inverse transformation. As will be seen, image restoration problems are of this class at best and are frequently singular.

The ill-conditioned aspect of image restoration can be demonstrated by means of the Riemann–Lebesgue lemma. If $h(\xi, \eta)$ is an integrable function, then it can be shown that

$$\lim_{\beta \to \infty} \lim_{\alpha \to \infty} \int_a^b \int_a^b h(\xi, \eta) \sin(\alpha\xi) \sin(\beta\eta) \, d\xi \, d\eta = 0. \tag{6.6}$$

Now, assume a function h with parameters x, y. Then from (6.6) it follows that

$$\lim_{\beta \to \infty} \lim_{\alpha \to \infty} \int_a^b \int_a^b h(x, y, \xi, \eta) \sin (\alpha \xi) \sin (\beta \eta) \, d\xi \, d\eta = 0. \tag{6.7}$$

The implications to the image restoration problem are direct.

$$\lim_{\beta \to \infty} \lim_{\alpha \to \infty} \int_a^b \int_a^b h(x, y, \xi, \eta)[f(\xi, \eta) + \sin (\alpha \xi) \sin (\beta \eta)] \, d\xi \, d\eta$$

$$= \int_a^b \int_a^b h(x, y, \xi, \eta) f(\xi, \eta) \, d\xi \, d\eta = g(x, y). \tag{6.8}$$

In other words, a sinusoid of infinite frequency can be added to the object distribution f and the resulting sum is identical to the image distribution g.

The demonstration of Equation (6.8) is very general since it requires only integrability of the point-spread function. A direct implication of the result is that if a small value $\epsilon_1 > 0$ is chosen, then there exists a value A such that

$$\int_a^b \int_a^b h(x, y, \xi, \eta) \sin (\alpha \xi) \sin (\beta \eta) \, d\xi \, d\eta < \epsilon_1 \tag{6.9}$$

whenever $\alpha, \beta \geqq A$. Thus,

$$\int_a^b \int_a^b h(x, y, \xi, \eta)[f(\xi, \eta) + \sin (\alpha \xi) \sin (\beta \eta)] \, d\xi \, d\eta$$

$$= \int_a^b \int_a^b h(x, y, \xi, \eta) f(\xi, \eta) \, d\xi \, d\eta + \epsilon = g(x, y) + \epsilon \tag{6.10}$$

for all values of $\alpha, \beta \geqq A$, where $|\epsilon| < \epsilon_1$. Thus, if an infinitesimally small value ϵ is chosen and added to the image distribution g, this cannot be separated, in the sense of image restoration, from an original object distribution that has an additional component of a sinusoid with frequency $\alpha \geqq A$. Since ϵ can be made infinitesimally small, then a trivial perturbation in the image cannot be distinguished from a finite, nontrivial perturbation in the original object distribution. Thus, the statement that image restoration is an *ill-conditioned* problem is justified.

The use of the Riemann–Lebesgue lemma to demonstrate this ill-conditioned behavior, which is a property of integral equations of the first kind in general, was by Phillips (1962). The Riemann–Lebesgue lemma is discussed in Apostol (1958).

The source of the term ϵ in Equation (6.10) is easily identified in an image restoration problem. The sensor noise is always unavoidable in a realistic image formation and recording system and the existence of noise means *a priori* that there must be a fixed amount of uncertainty in the restoration to obtain object distribution f.

An image restoration problem can also be *singular*, depending on the nature of the point-spread function or *kernel* of the underlying integral equation. Two functions are said to *orthogonal* over the interval $[a, b]$ if

$$\int_a^b \int_a^b h(\xi, \eta) f(\xi, \eta) \, d\xi \, d\eta = 0. \tag{6.11}$$

If the function h possesses parameters x and y, then $h(x, y, \xi, \eta)$ and $f(\xi, \eta)$ are orthogonal over the interval $[a, b]$ if

$$\int_a^b \int_a^b h(x, y, \xi, \eta) f(\xi, \eta) \, d\xi \, d\eta = 0 \qquad \forall \; x, y. \tag{6.12}$$

In this case $h(x, y, \xi, \eta)$ is termed singular with respect to $f(\xi, \eta)$ and, obviously, the restoration of f is impossible. If an object distribution is composed of the sum of a function f which is orthogonal to h and a function c which is not, then

$$\int_a^b \int_a^b h(x, y, \xi, \eta)[f(\xi, \eta) + c(\xi, \eta)] \, d\xi \, d\eta = \int_a^b \int_a^b h(x, y, \xi, \eta) c(\xi, \eta) \, d\xi \, d\eta \tag{6.13}$$

and the existence of the orthogonal component cannot be determined by observing the image distribution. *Singularity* is also common in image restoration.

We wish to forget for a moment the discussion above to touch upon the third aspect of the image restoration problem. Assume that the image sensing and recording system is linear, so that the only effect of the image recording process is the introduction of noise. Thus, the image distribution g has had added a random process n, symbolizing the sensor noise. Thus,

$$g(x, y) = \int_a^b \int_a^b h(x, y, \xi, \eta) f(\xi, \eta) \, d\xi \, d\eta + n(x, y) \tag{6.14}$$

describes the relation between the recorded image and the initial object distribution. In the ideal case of $n(x, y) \equiv 0$ in the interval, the association between g and f can be unique (if singularity is not present). If the noise is not zero, however, there can be no unique association. Every possible function in the ensemble of the random process $n(x, y)$ is potentially the function added to $g(x, y)$. There is an infinite family of object distributions, the elements of the family being derived from each element of the ensemble of the noise process $n(x, y)$.

Analytical methods for dealing with ill-conditioned and singular behavior have been studied in integral equations of the first kind ever since the pioneering work of Volterra (1959). The presence of noise means that one must also select the "proper" solution from within an infinite family of candidate solutions. Quotes around the word *proper* were used to alert the reader; there is literally no proper solution but only solutions that can be derived from various combinations of available *a priori* information and desired criteria of performance in the solution.

6.2 Discrete Formulation of Restoration

As discussed in detail in Chapter 4, the discrete–discrete model for image and object correspondence leads to descriptions of the linear relations as matrix-vector equations:

$$\mathbf{g} = [H]\mathbf{f}, \tag{6.15}$$

where $\mathbf{g}$ and $\mathbf{f}$ are lexicographically ordered vectors created from the sampled object and image field and $[H]$ is the matrix resulting from the point-spread-function samples. In terms of the complete model including sensor response and noise,[1] the following matrix-vector equation description may apply:

$$g = s\{[H]f\} + n \tag{6.16}$$

and g is the response in Figure 2.9 sampled and converted into a lexicographically ordered vector and the detector response function is s (the notation $s\{b\}$ means that each element of the vector b is componentwise transformed by the same function). Thus

$$s\left\{\begin{bmatrix} b_1 \\ b_2 \\ \cdot \\ \cdot \\ \cdot \\ b_N \end{bmatrix}\right\} \triangleq \begin{bmatrix} s(b_1) \\ s(b_2) \\ \cdot \\ \cdot \\ \cdot \\ s(b_N) \end{bmatrix}. \tag{6.17}$$

To examine the explicit mathematical properties of restoration it will be assumed that s is the identity function and Equation (6.16) becomes

$$g = [H]f + n. \tag{6.18}$$

It is evident that the problems of digital restoration are determined by the properties of the matrix equation in (6.18).

First, the same point can be made with respect to the lack of a unique solution as was made in Section 6.1. Given the existence of a noise process, the multivariate sample vector n, there is a family of solutions generated by every possible sample vector from the multivariate random process that underlies the sampled noise process in the vector n. Aside from questions of ill-conditioned and/or singular behavior in the matrix $[H]$, the problem of digital image restoration is still characterized by choosing the "proper" solution from the family of possible solutions.

What about ill-conditioned behavior in the matrix $[H]$? Assume a simple linear point-spread function:

$$g(x, y) = \int_a^b \int_a^b h(x, y, \xi, \eta) f(\xi, \eta) \, d\xi \, d\eta \tag{6.19}$$

The digital representation can be derived by subdividing the interval $[a, b]$ into a discrete number of N points and then approximate Equation (6.19), using a rectangular integration rule, as

$$g(x, y) = \sum_{x=0}^{N-1} \sum_{y=0}^{N-1} h(x, y, \xi, \eta) f(\xi, \eta), \tag{6.20}$$

which leads to a linear set of equations, expressible in the vector-matrix form of Equation (6.15) as

$$g = [H]f. \tag{6.15}$$

---

[1]In Equation (6.16), signal-independent sensor noise is shown. As discussed in Section 2.6, sensor noise is signal-dependent. The independent model in this section is used to simplify the discussion, and the realistic nature of the assumption is discussed in Section 6.4.

Here x, y, ξ, η take on only integer values. Consider the elements of the matrix $[H]$. If it is assumed that the point-spread-function $h(x, y, \xi, \eta)$ possesses a Taylor series expansion, then it is possible to show that the rows of the matrix $[H]$ satisfy the approximation:

$$h(x + 1, y, \xi, \eta) \cong h(x, y, \xi, \eta) + [h(x, y, \xi, \eta) - h(x - 1, y, \xi, \eta)]. \qquad (6.21)$$

In the matrix $[H]$, index x is a row index and (6.21) shows that the $(k + 1)$th row of $[H]$ is approximately a linear combination of the kth and $(k - 1)$ rows [Hunt (1972)].

The relation (6.21) is of importance for the following reason: Since the rows of the matrix $[H]$ are approximately linear combinations of one another, the matrix $[H]$ is very nearly singular. From matrix theory it is known that equations with near-singular matrices are extremely difficult to solve; i.e., they are *ill-conditioned*. The property of a matrix's condition is formally defined in a matrix theory by the condition number. Suppose that in the equation

$$\mathbf{g} = [H]\mathbf{f} \qquad (6.15)$$

the matrix $[H]$ is square of size $N^2 \times N^2$. Then it is known from elementary matrix theory that the *rank* of $[H]$ is equal to the number of nonzero eigenvalues of $[H]$. Let $\{\lambda\}$ be the set of eigenvalues of $[H]^T[H]$; then the *condition number* may be defined as

$$c([H]) = \left(\frac{\lambda_{\max}}{\lambda_{\min}}\right)^{1/2} \qquad (6.22)$$

[Lancaster (1969)]. From (6.22) it is obvious that as $\lambda_{\min} \rightarrow 0$, the condition number approaches infinity. Thus, even though the matrix $[H]$ may not be singular, near-singularity is associated with very small eigenvalues and the solution of the resulting linear equations becomes difficult. In the presence of noise (whether sensor noise or computational noise in the solution process) the matrix $[H]$ can become singular within the bounds of uncertainty imposed by the noise. Solution of the digital restoration problem is thus tied to the solution of ill-conditioned (near-singular) systems of linear equations and computational methods become important [Ralston (1965)].

The matrix equation corresponding to the digital restoration problem may be, of course, singular. In such a case $[H]^{-1}$ does not exist, which is equivalent to $[H]$ being of less than full rank, and of $\lambda_{\min}$ in (6.22) being 0, i.e., infinite condition number.

Both ill-conditioned and singular image restoration problems are common; thus, the discrete domain and the use of the digital computer does not free us of any of the fundamental problems noted in Section 6.1.

6.3 Deterministic versus Stochastic Approaches to Restoration

Either Equation (6.16) or (6.18) can be used to state the digital image restoration problem; (6.18) differs from (6.16) only in the assumption of a linear function for s. For either (6.16) or (6.18) the question posed marks a philosophical attitude: Should the restoration problem be solved in a deterministic or stochastic framework? To illustrate the philosophical attitude, consider (6.18):

$$\mathbf{g} = [H]\mathbf{f} + \mathbf{n}. \qquad (6.18)$$

The deterministic approach implies the result of viewing (6.18) as a problem in the solution of linear equations, while the stochastic approach implies the result of viewing (6.18) as a problem in the estimation of a vector subject to random disturbances.

Concentrating on the former approach, assume initially that the matrix $[H]$ is square and nonsingular. An estimate of $\mathbf{f}$ can be generated by

$$\hat{\mathbf{f}} = [H]^{-1}\mathbf{g}, \tag{6.23}$$

and from (6.18)

$$\hat{\mathbf{f}} = [H]^{-1}([H]\mathbf{f} + \mathbf{n})$$
$$= \mathbf{f} + [H]^{-1}\mathbf{n}. \tag{6.24}$$

Thus, the estimate is composed of two parts: the actual object distribution and a term involving the inverse acting on the noise.

In an algebraic analysis, the Equation (6.18) is considered as a linear system with uncertainty or errors in the data; i.e., the data is "good" to a limited number of digits of significance because of the measurement errors. If $[H]$ has a large condition number, i.e., near-singular, then the inverse $[H]^{-1}$ will have very large entries {since the determinant of $[H]$ is small}, and consequently the term $[H]^{-1}\mathbf{n}$ can dominate the term containing the solution $\mathbf{f}$. Problems such as this are analyzed in great detail in treatises on numerical analysis [Ralston (1965)]. Suffice it to say that in the presence of an inherent error such as $\mathbf{n}$ there is a large inherent uncertainty in the solution.

To illustrate, consider an example where bounds are imposed on the size of the errors with respect to the data. Assume that in (6.18)

$$\|\mathbf{g}\| = \|[H]\mathbf{f} + \mathbf{n}\| \leq \|[H]\mathbf{f}\| + \|\mathbf{n}\|, \tag{6.25}$$

where $\|\mathbf{g}\|$ is the Euclidean norm of the vector $\mathbf{g}$. As in Chapter 4, assume that $[H]$ preserves energy in $\mathbf{f}$; hence

$$\|[H]\mathbf{f}\| = \|\mathbf{f}\|, \tag{6.26}$$

so that the relative signal-to-noise ratio (SNR) (defined in terms of norms) is

$$\frac{\|\mathbf{f}\|}{\|\mathbf{n}\|} = \alpha. \tag{6.27}$$

Now in the solution,

$$\|\hat{\mathbf{f}}\| = \|\mathbf{f} + [H]^{-1}\mathbf{n}\| \leq \|\mathbf{f}\| + \|[H]^{-1}\|\|\mathbf{n}\|, \tag{6.28}$$

where an Euclidean norm for both vectors and matrices is used [Lancaster (1969)]. If the norms of the two terms in (6.28) are compared,

$$\frac{\|\mathbf{f}\|}{\|[H]^{-1}\|\|\mathbf{n}\|} = \beta, \tag{6.29}$$

then even though $[H]$ preserves energy in $\mathbf{f}$, $[H]^{-1}$ does not demonstrate such properties in general. Indeed, it is typical of an ill-conditioned problem that

$$\|[H]^{-1}\| \gg 1. \tag{6.30}$$

Thus, even though the original data's signal-to-noise ratio was α, the solution possesses a signal-to-noise ratio of β and ratio of these two gives the deterioration in signal-to-noise between data and solution:

$$\left(\begin{array}{c}\text{Deterioration factor in SNR}\\ \text{from data to solution}\end{array}\right) = \frac{\alpha}{\beta} = ||[H]^{-1}||. \tag{6.31}$$

For example, suppose that originally $||\mathbf{f}|| = 100$, $||\mathbf{n}|| = 1$, and $||[H]^{-1}|| = 10$. Then $\alpha = 100$, $\beta = 10$, and deterioration factor $= 10$. Thus, even very good signal-to-noise ratios can be deteriorated by ill-conditioning. ($||[H]^{-1}|| = 10$ would be considered very mild in a restoration problem; $||[H]^{-1}|| = 1000$ or more is typical, meaning the noise would dominate the solution for the hypothetical case posed in this example.)

The linear systems or deterministic approach also provides interesting insight into the restoration problem in the case where $[H]$ in (6.18) is singular. Formally, the solution does not exist since the matrix $[H]^{-1}$ does not exist. In matrix theory it is demonstrable that the singular behavior is a function of linear dependence in the rows (or columns) of $[H]$; i.e., the rows of $[H]$ do not span the entire vector space. Linear systems with such properties can still be solved, however, by the use of the so-called *generalized inverse* and its related matrices [Graybill (1969), Lancaster (1969), Rao and Mitra (1971)]. Such techniques, stated briefly, find a solution by projection into the subspace that is spanned by the linear-independent rows of $[H]$. A particularly appealing demonstration of this property will be shown when linear algebraic methods in restoration are examined in Chapter 8. All the problems of singular behavior are not eliminated by the use of generalized inverses. The existence of noise in the data is still of concern.

The stochastic viewpoint of solving (6.16) or (6.18) takes into account the nature of the random disturbance inasmuch as is possible. For example, in (6.16), if it is assumed that the solution $\mathbf{f}$ is a nonrandom quantity but the observed quantity of the product $[H]\mathbf{f}$ is corrupted by the noise term $\mathbf{n}$, then the multivariate probability density function of $\mathbf{n}$ can be used to determine the conditional density of $\mathbf{f}$ given the recorded data $\mathbf{g}$:

$$p_n(\mathbf{f}|\mathbf{g}),$$

where p_n is the density function of $\mathbf{n}$ and the density of $\mathbf{f}$ given $\mathbf{g}$ is simply the density of $\mathbf{n}$ centered about $\mathbf{g}$ since $\mathbf{g}$ is *nonrandom*.

Similar analyses for assumptions of both $\mathbf{f}$ and $\mathbf{n}$ being random quantities can be derived. Detailed exposition of these topics will be relegated to later sections and chapters, in a complete framework of statistical approaches to image restoration.

6.4   Theoretical versus Practical Aspects of Image Restoration

Returning to the basic discrete formulation of restoration, Equation (6.16),

$$\mathbf{g} = s\{[H]\mathbf{f}\} + \mathbf{n}, \tag{6.16}$$

the restoration problem will be examined from the viewpoint of the distinctions between theory and practice. From the theoretical viewpoint, questions concerning the types of processing to be used in carrying out the restoration should be asked. From the practical viewpoint, questions regarding useful approximations that can be utilized should be answered.

As an illustration, suppose it is proposed to carry out the restoration by a linear system. The sampled recorded image, $\mathbf{g}$, is acted upon by a matrix $[L]$ to produce a restoration $\hat{\mathbf{f}}$:

$$\hat{\mathbf{f}} = [L]\mathbf{g} = [L](s\{[H]\mathbf{f}\} + \mathbf{n}). \tag{6.32}$$

Even in the absence of noise, we know from system theory that there exists no linear system $[L]$ such that $\hat{\mathbf{f}} = \mathbf{f}$. If the noise were zero, $\mathbf{n} = \mathbf{0}$, then $\hat{\mathbf{f}} = \mathbf{f}$ would be true only if $[L] = [H]^{-1}$ and if

$$s\{[H]\mathbf{f}\} = [H]s\{\mathbf{f}\}. \tag{6.33}$$

Since linear and nonlinear processes do not, in general, commute, Equation (6.33) cannot be satisfied and theoretically it is unlikely that a linear system exists that satisfies the requirements sought in restoration.

As a second illustration, suppose that it is decided to carry out the processing for restoration by using a nonlinear system, which we signify by the function T operating on the vector $\mathbf{g}$. Then,

$$\hat{\mathbf{f}} = T\{\mathbf{g}\} = T\{s\{[H]\mathbf{f}\} + \mathbf{n}\}. \tag{6.34}$$

In the absence of noise, $\mathbf{n} = \mathbf{0}$, then the choice of T to be $[H]^{-1}s^{-1}$ gives perfect restoration since

$$\hat{\mathbf{f}} = [H]^{-1}s^{-1}\{s\{[H]\mathbf{f}\}\}, \tag{6.35}$$

assuming s is a nonlinear operator with an inverse. The equation above implies that the nonlinearity is "backed out" of the system prior to the linear inversion. Since noise cannot be overlooked, then

$$\hat{\mathbf{f}} = [H]^{-1}s^{-1}\{s\{[H]\mathbf{f}\} + \mathbf{n}\}. \tag{6.36}$$

If it could be assumed that

$$s^{-1}\{\mathbf{p} + \mathbf{q}\} = s^{-1}\{\mathbf{p}\} + s^{-1}\{\mathbf{q}\}, \tag{6.37}$$

then

$$\hat{\mathbf{f}} = \mathbf{f} + [H]^{-1}s^{-1}\{\mathbf{n}\}. \tag{6.38}$$

Equation (6.37) is *never* satisfied in the theoretical sense, however, and thus such results cannot be derived. Since s is a nonlinear sensor response function, s^{-1} is nonlinear and Equation (6.37) is a property of linearity that cannot hold.

The practical importance of the discussions above can be most readily observed in the case of images sensed and recorded on photographic film. As discussed in Chapter 2, the image sensed by the film is an *intensity image*; i.e., an image in light intensity carries the picture information. The properties of photographic film result in a recorded image, however, which it is natural to describe as a *density image*, i.e., an image in optical density that is proportional to the actual mass of silver deposited on the film. Thus in image restoration with photographic film, should the process be considered with an intensity image or a density range? Processing a density image with a linear system is equivalent to Equation (6.32), the density image being the term $(s\{[H]\mathbf{f}\} + \mathbf{n})$. On the other hand, processing an intensity image with a linear system is equivalent to Equation (6.36); the function s^{-1} is constructed by using the characteristic curve (the D–log E curve discussed in Chapter 2) to transform film densities back to the light intensity domain where the linear processing may be applied.

As discussed in a footnote dealing with Equation (6.16), the model that (6.16) represents is one of signal-independent noise. Some length in Chapter 2 was dedicated to describing the signal-dependent properties of film–grain and photoelectron noise. The purpose in doing so was to ensure that the reader was aware of the true nature of the problem; image sensor noise is complicated and the informed reader should be knowledgeable of such; however, there are equally important reasons that allow a simplification of the signal-dependent noise problem. First, there is no real wealth of mathematical knowledge on dealing with signal-dependent noise as compared to that for signal-independent noise. Second, what little knowledge of signal-dependent noise processing exists [Walkup (1974)] indicates that processing with signal-dependent models results in little gain in the accuracy of the solution. Consequently, the signal-independent noise model of Equation (6.16) shall be used.

Return now to Equations (6.32) and (6.36), and analyze the behavior under small variations. Considering the function s, let $\bar{g} + \Delta g$ signify perturbations about a constant $\bar{g}$. Then,

$$s\{\bar{g} + \Delta g\} \cong s\{\bar{g}\} + \frac{\partial s}{\partial g}\bigg|_{\bar{g}} \Delta g \tag{6.39}$$

follows directly from a Taylor series expansion and indicates the behavior is linear in Δg since $s\{\bar{g}\}$ and the derivative are constants.[2] In applications of this to the imaging problem, recall the discussion in Chapter 3 concerning models. In that chapter it was noted, in conjunction with parametric statistical models, that random fluctuations about a mean value can be a description of a class of image models. Further, for Gaussian models, the fluctuations should be small with respect to the mean to minimize the negative values generated by such a model. Using Equation (6.39) directly it can be stated that

$$s\{[H](\mathbf{f} + \bar{\mathbf{f}})\} \cong k_1[H]\mathbf{f} + \mathbf{k}_2, \tag{6.40}$$

k_1 and $\mathbf{k}_2$ are constants and $\bar{\mathbf{f}}$ and $\mathbf{f}$ are the mean and fluctuations about the mean. Neglecting the constants, which affect only a constant bias and scaling, the use of Equation (6.40) in Equation (6.32) gives

$$\hat{\mathbf{f}} \cong [L][H]\mathbf{f} + [L]\mathbf{n} \tag{6.41}$$

and now if $[L] = [H]^{-1}$, then

$$\hat{\mathbf{f}} \cong \mathbf{f} + [H]^{-1}\mathbf{n} \tag{6.24}$$

and analysis such as in Section 6.2 can be carried out. Similar arguments can be applied to (6.36).

A different analysis, but based on the same principle, can be carried out for (6.36) in the case of high signal-to-noise ratio. Expanding by Taylor's series,

$$s^{-1}\{s\{[H]\mathbf{f}\} + \mathbf{n}\} \cong s^{-1}\{s\{[H]\mathbf{f}\}\} + \frac{\partial s^{-1}}{\partial g}\bigg|_{g=s\{[H]\mathbf{f}\}} \mathbf{n}, \tag{6.42}$$

i.e., an approximate linearization in the form of (6.37), so that Equation (6.38) becomes

$$\hat{\mathbf{f}} \cong \mathbf{f} + [H]^{-1}k_3\mathbf{n}, \tag{6.43}$$

---

[2]Of course for linear sensors, e.g., film with $\gamma = -1$, or a photoelectronic system with $\gamma = 1$, s is a linear function and linear approximations are not required. Equation (6.44) can then be used directly and is exact.

where the constant k_3 is to account for the derivatives in the Taylor expansion. Again the form of (6.43) is familiar.

The point of the discussion above is the following: In addition to the signal-independent-noise assumption, it is often justifiable to make a linear approximation to the nonlinear sensor response. The approximation is referred to as the *low-contrast assumption*. The following heuristic procedure is suggested as a test for exploring the extent to which the linear assumptions may be valid. If both density and intensity versions of the image are processed, assuming the approximate linear model,

$$\mathbf{g} \cong [H]\mathbf{f} + \mathbf{n}, \qquad (6.44)$$

then regions in the two processed versions that appear significantly different are regions where low-contrast assumption and/or high signal-to noise ratio assumptions break down.

Equations (6.16) and (6.44) are fundamental. The former poses the restoration problem in its complete, nonlinear form; the latter is a useful and very often valid approximation. It would obviously be advantageous to quantify the transition between the use of the two. Such remains undone. There is no hard rule to state that on the basis of some computation that the linear approximation breaks down or that the signal-to-noise ratio is insufficient. There is, indeed, a sufficient amount of experimental evidence to suggest that linear processing of a linear approximation to (6.32) is desirable in all cases, whether the approximation is valid or not [Cannon (1974)]. Since (6.32) is associated with the processing of density images as with photographic film, then the suggestion of processing of density images as though the nonlinear response function was not present follows. Density image processing always results in restorations without negative numbers since the data is exponentiated in converting to light intensity for display. The pragmatic justification of the use of an equation in the form of (6.44) is appealing; it is pleasing to find so convenient an approximation borne out by experimental evidence and is probably the most important of the trade-offs between theoretical and practical aspects discussed in this section.

6.5   An Overview of Image Restoration Methods

Given the two basic formulations of the digital image restoration problem,

$$\mathbf{g} = s\{[H]\mathbf{f}\} + \mathbf{n}, \qquad (6.16)$$

$$\mathbf{g} = [H]\mathbf{f} + \mathbf{n}, \qquad (6.44)$$

the basic problem still remains, that of ill-conditioned behavior. As shown in previous sections this can result in a deterioration of the signal-to-noise ratio between the original data and the solution. This is also compatible with the view of Section 6.1, namely, the dominance of the noise results from a poor choice of a solution in the infinite family. There is no *unique* solution in view of noise and ill-conditioning, and some meaningful rationale must be employed to pick a better solution. It is the purpose of this section to give a broad perspective on rationales for controlling ill-conditioned behavior.

Given the view of the infinite family of solutions that can be generated from a noisy, ill-conditioned solution, the selection of a specific solution from the family must be guided by some criterion or a set of criteria. Analytic and numerical formulation of criteria is a topic discussed in the study of *optimization theory* and will be relied upon extensively in this book. Virtually all image restoration schemes can be posed as the solution of some particular optimization problem. The restoration schemes will differ, therefore, in the choice of criteria functions and/or the specific side conditions included as problem constraints.

As an example, consider the model posed by Equation (6.44): In the total absence of any knowledge about the noise term $\mathbf{n}$, the philosophy might be adopted that a criterion for solution would be based on an estimate of the restored object distribution, $\hat{\mathbf{f}}$, that would satisfy Equation (6.44) consistent with the noise term $\mathbf{n}$ being minimal in some sense. Picking the measure of $\mathbf{n}$ as the norm of the vector, then the criterion stated in the previous sentence is equivalent to finding a solution $\hat{\mathbf{f}}$ such that

$$(\mathbf{g} - [H]\hat{\mathbf{f}})'(\mathbf{g} - [H]\hat{\mathbf{f}}) = \mathbf{n}'\mathbf{n} \qquad (6.45)$$

is a minimum. This is the so-called *least-squares* solution philosophy. As an example of the stochastic approach to restoration, suppose the object distribution $\mathbf{f}$ is assumed to be a random, stochastic entity, modeled by a scheme such as discussed in Chapter 3. Then a criterion of a solution is to construct an estimate such that over the ensemble of estimates and object distributions the expected value of the difference between estimate and the original object distribution is minimized. This is equivalent to finding a solution $\hat{\mathbf{f}}$ such that

$$\epsilon = \mathcal{E}\{(\mathbf{f} - \hat{\mathbf{f}})'(\mathbf{f} - \hat{\mathbf{f}})\} \qquad (6.46)$$

is a minimum. The stochastic nature of this approach is evident since it can be expected that the minimization process over the ensemble must take into account ensemble statistics (mean, covariance, etc.).

Finally, it is possible to conceive of methods that combine some elements of both deterministic and stochastic methods. Suppose it is known that the object distribution $\mathbf{f}$ comes from a random process that has a fixed amount of energy in the distribution, i.e., over the ensemble

$$\mathcal{E}\{\mathbf{f}'\mathbf{f}\} = e. \qquad (6.47)$$

Adopting the least-squares criterion subject to a fixed energy constraint gives the problem

$$\begin{aligned} \text{Minimize} \quad & (\mathbf{g} - [H]\hat{\mathbf{f}})'(\mathbf{g} - [H]\hat{\mathbf{f}}) \\ \text{Subject to} \quad & \mathcal{E}\{\hat{\mathbf{f}}'\hat{\mathbf{f}}\} = e, \end{aligned} \qquad (6.48)$$

which is an optimization problem with a side constraint. It is also a hybrid restoration process that is both deterministic and stochastic, using a deterministic criterion function with a side constraint that depends on the ensemble statistic e.

Finally, it should be noted that whatever properties of image modeling are known or assumed can be included into the formulation of the restoration problem (indeed, it is *the* place to include such model information). For example, even such weak assumptions as positivity of the restored object distribution values and upper bound for total energy model properties are appropriately included here. Including such in (6.48), for example, gives

$$\text{Minimize} \quad (\mathbf{g} - [H]\hat{\mathbf{f}})^t(\mathbf{g} - [H]\hat{\mathbf{f}})$$

$$\text{Subject to:} \quad \mathcal{E}\{\hat{\mathbf{f}}^t\hat{\mathbf{f}}\} \leq e \qquad\qquad\qquad (6.49)$$

$$\hat{\mathbf{f}} \geq 0, \qquad \text{i.e., } \hat{f}_1 \geq 0, \hat{f}_2 \geq 0, \text{ etc.} \dots .$$

There are, of course, image restoration techniques that are not explicitly formulated as optimization problems. That is, the development of the technique might have been made on a heuristic or analytic basis separate from the optimization viewpoint, and, with hindsight, it is not discernible how to translate the resulting restoration method into a problem in optimization. The fact that the corresponding optimization problem has not been formulated, however, does not invalidate the viewpoint that underlies the optimization approach: the use of a criterion to select a solution from the infinite family of solutions presented by the data.

Chapter 7

Noniterative Methods Implemented by Fourier Computation

7.0 Introduction

In this chapter begins a discussion of specific image restoration methods. The concentration will be upon methods which are noniterative and which can be implemented by the use of Fourier computations. The distinction is necessary; as shall be seen in a later chapter, there are methods that are iterative and/or require the use of computation methods other than those of the Fourier domain.

The chapter describes least-squares and minimum mean-square restoration in the context of space-invariant imaging systems. Thus Toeplitz, circulant, and discrete Fourier transforms (DFT) are brought to bear on the restoration process. The interested reader is directed to the appendices for detailed references on the necessary approximations to utilize DFT techniques for computational efficiency. Caution is necessary in this process as wraparound and end effects can plague the restoration process if care is not taken to be aware of such artifacts that sampled DFT techniques introduce.

7.1 Least-Squares Restorations

A model will be assumed for image formation and recording in which the low-contrast linear approximation and the signal-independent-noise assumptions are valid. In addition (as discussed in Appendix A), assume that the restoration effects in a segment cut from a larger image can be localized. Thus border regions of an image where such effects occur can be safely neglected. Thus the imaging equation is

$$\mathbf{g} = [H_{BT}]\mathbf{f}, \tag{7.1}$$

where the subscript refers to *block Toeplitz* and is included here for emphasis. See Appendix A for a detailed discussion on $[H_{BT}]$. Equation (7.1) specifies the image formation process in a digital form. When recording effects are included, the following version results

$$\mathbf{g} = s\{[H_{BT}]\mathbf{f}\} + \mathbf{n}. \tag{7.2}$$

Here $\mathbf{n}$ is a noise vector and $s\{\cdot\}$ is the memoryless nonlinear operator describing sensor effects. Making the low-contrast linear assumption,

$$\mathbf{g} = [H_{BT}]\mathbf{f} + \mathbf{n}. \tag{7.3}$$

The image restoration problem is to estimate $\mathbf{f}$ given the samples of the recorded image, $\mathbf{g}$.

Invoking the least-squares solution criterion is equivalent to a solution that is consistent with minimizing the norm of the noise term $\mathbf{n}$. The rationale is, in the absence of any specific knowledge about $\mathbf{n}$, select a solution that is consistent with assuming that $\mathbf{n}$ is as small as possible given the data $\mathbf{g}$. Thus,

$$\mathbf{n} = \mathbf{g} - [H_{BT}]\mathbf{f},$$

and seek the solution

$$\underset{\mathbf{f}}{\text{minimize}} \ \mathbf{n}'\mathbf{n} = (\mathbf{g} - [H_{BT}]\hat{\mathbf{f}})'(\mathbf{g} - [H_{BT}]\hat{\mathbf{f}}). \tag{7.4}$$

Equation (7.4) describes a quadratic form in $\hat{\mathbf{f}}$. Differentiation with respect to $\hat{\mathbf{f}}$ and solving for $\hat{\mathbf{f}}$ yields

$$\hat{\mathbf{f}} = ([H_{BT}]'[H_{BT}])^{-1}[H_{BT}]'\mathbf{g}. \tag{7.5}$$

But by matrix inverse properties,

$$\hat{\mathbf{f}} = [H_{BT}]^{-1}\mathbf{g} \tag{7.6}$$

is the least-squares estimate since the matrix $[H_{BT}]$ is square.

The solution in (7.6) is the so-called *inverse filter* since the restoration is obtained with the inverse of $[H_{BT}]$. As in Chapter 6,

$$\hat{\mathbf{f}} = [H_{BT}]^{-1}([H_{BT}]\mathbf{f} + \mathbf{n}) = \mathbf{f} + [H_{BT}]^{-1}\mathbf{n} \tag{7.7}$$

and the effects of noise are of concern. It is assumed, of course, that the inverse $[H_{BT}]^{-1}$ exists. If it does not, then inverse filter restoration does not exist.

Since $[H_{BT}]$ is block Toeplitz, Equation (7.6) requires the solution of an $N^2 \times N^2$ set of linear equations. Suppose that the image was digitized so that $N = 500$, then (7.6) requires inverting a 250,000 $\times$ 250,000 matrix, clearly an impossibility. On the other hand, suppose $[H_{BT}]$ is replaced with a circulant approximation:

$$\hat{\mathbf{f}} = [H_{BC}]^{-1}\mathbf{g}. \tag{7.8}$$

A direct algorithm for computing the restoration by using DFT's follows from the appendices.

1. Compute the two-dimensional DFT of the recorded image

$$G(w_x, w_y) = \sum_{x=0}^{N-1} \sum_{y=0}^{N-1} g(x, y) \exp\left\{\frac{-2\pi i}{N}(w_x x + w_y y)\right\}, \tag{7.9}$$

where a square array $N \times N$ is assumed and N is a highly composite number for use in a fast Fourier transform algorithm.

2. Compute the two-dimensional DFT of the PSF matrix:

$$H(w_x, w_y) = \sum_{x=0}^{N-1} \sum_{y=0}^{N-1} h(x, y) \exp \left\{ \frac{-2\pi i}{N} (w_x x + w_y y) \right\}, \qquad (7.10)$$

where zeros may be added to $h(x, y)$ to make it of size $N \times N$. In step (7.10) any spurious phase effects can be corrected in the previous analysis *by the way* h(x, y) *is placed in the matrix of size* N $\times$ N. Thus if $h(x, y)$ is symmetric about the origin of quadrants, then a circulant can be constructed based on origin symmetry and this will be effected in the DFT domain.

3. Compute the inverse two-dimensional DFT:

$$\hat{f}(x, y) = \frac{1}{N^2} \sum_{w_x=0}^{N-1} \sum_{w_y=0}^{N-1} \frac{G(w_x, w_y)}{H(w_x, w_y)} \exp \left\{ \frac{2\pi i}{N} (x w_x + y w_y) \right\}, \qquad (7.11)$$

which is the inverse filter restoration, constructed by DFT calculations.

The ill-conditioned nature of image restoration is not aided by the use of the least-squares criterion, shown in (7.11). The DFT quantities $H(w_x, w_y)$ are the eigenvalues of $[H_{BC}]$ and are an approximation to the eigenvalues of $[H_{BT}]$. As the eigenvalues $H(w_x, w_y)$ become small, the inverse becomes large and the result is an amplification of the noise in the eigenspace of the PSF, indicated in the image space by Equation (7.7); hence the inverse filter restoration is likely to be troublesome. In an extremely high signal-to-noise ratio situation, e.g., SNR = 1000:1 or more, and with small amounts of image blur, the inverse filter will perform well, provided there are no singularities; i.e., $H(w_x, w_y) \neq 0$ for any values of w_x and w_y. It is difficult, however, to quantify such cases in terms of values of SNR or extent of blur to use as a decision tool.

Figure 7.1 shows an original digital image, sampled as a 500 × 500 matrix. Figure 7.2 is the result of blurring Figure 7.1 by a mild low-pass filter; noise has also been added to Figure 7.2 after blurring, with SNR = 2000:1 (33 dB) measured in terms of image variance divided by noise variance. Figure 7.3 is the inverse filter restoration. Much of the detail has been regained but there is also a great amplification of the noise. Figure 7.4 is restoration by inverse filter with the same blur, but with SNR = 200:1 (23 dB). It is typical of the loss of image to expect when the SNR falls too low.[1]

An important aspect of the three-step algorithm above for computing the inverse filter restoration by Fourier methods is the choice of N. Note the following points.

1. The choice of N is usually motivated by the type of fast Fourier transform routine that is available. In the usual case N will be an integral power of 2. Fast Fourier transform (FFT) routines for arbitrary factors are possible, of course, but usually suffer greatly in computational efficiency over a well-optimized radix-2 or radix-4 routine.

---

[1] The border effects in Figure 7.2 and 7.4 are due to segment effects, as discussed in the appendices. They are localized, as argued there.

Figure 7.1 Original image.

2. The solution of (7.6) is equivalent to convolving the circulant approximation of the inverse PSF matrix with the recorded image. Since the convolution is *circular* [Rader and Gold (1969)], there is an additional edge effect from convolution *wraparound* at the image borders. The addition of zeros in steps 1 and 2 on pages 127 and 128 results in the suppression of wraparound, as demonstrated in standard works on digital filtering [Rader and Gold (1969)].

3. Even in cases where N is chosen such that wraparound is not suppressed, the resulting artifacts are usually noted at the edges of the image only and are readily recognized.

If $[H_{BC}]$ is singular, it is known, from matrix theory, that this is equivalent to the matrix $[H_{BC}]$ having at least one zero eigenvalue. Most likely, any number of eigenvalues may be zero. In such cases the comparison of the eigenvalue map of $[H_{BC}]$ with the DFT of the data **g** can be beneficial. For example, an eigenvalue (Fourier) spectrum

(a)

(b)

Figure 7.2 (a) Original blurred with high SNR. (b) Original blurred with low SNR.

Figure 7.3 Restoration of Figure 7.2(a) by inverse filter.

Figure 7.4 Restoration of Figure 7.2(b) by inverse filter.

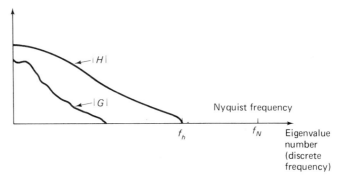

Nyquist frequency

f_h f_N Eigenvalue
                              number
                              (discrete
                              frequency)

Figure 7.5   Eigenvalue and data transform comparisons.

for a hypothetical PSF is shown in Figure 7.5, plotted with the transform in the eigenvalue (Fourier) space of the data **g**. Clearly, since the upper limit of the spectrum of G is less than that of H, then it can reasonably be concluded that the original data was limited in the spectrum space. The effect is probably a property of the underlying original object distribution **f** and not a property induced by the PSF.

On the other hand, Figure 7.6 presents a case where the data spectrum is nonzero. It is a reasonable conjecture that inherent noise prevents observation of the spectrum as it approaches zero.

In the case of Figure 7.5 there is a clear course of action. Even though there are many zero eigenvalues in the range between f_h and the Nyquist frequency, the data spectrum is band-limited and the singularity of the restoration is no problem. The restoration can be carried out by computing the inverse two-dimensional DFT of $G(w_x, w_y)/H(w_x, w_y)$ for those values of G that are nonzero.

Figure 7.6 is more troublesome. Section 7.2 will show that singularities can be handled by a more powerful optimization criterion than the simple least-squares criterion.

7.2 Minimum Mean-Square-Error Restoration

Assume again the linear, signal-independent-noise model of image formation and recording:

$$\mathbf{g} = [H_{BT}]\mathbf{f} + \mathbf{n}. \tag{7.3}$$

Rather than seeking a solution consistent with minimum contamination by noise, we wish to attack the restoration problem directly and propose a criterion that explicitly evaluates how close the restoration is to the original object intensity distribution. A number of criteria can be posed for this optimization; however, the criterion to be used here is the minimum mean-square error (MMSE).

Assume an estimate of the original object intensity distribution, **f**. Call this estimate **f̂**. The error of the estimate is defined as

$$\boldsymbol{\epsilon} = \mathbf{f} - \mathbf{\hat{f}}. \tag{7.12}$$

The MMSE criterion requires the total error of estimation to be a minimum over the entire ensemble of all possible images. The error as defined in (7.12) can fluctuate both

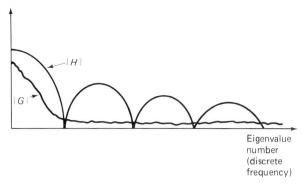

Eigenvalue
number
(discrete
frequency)

Figure 7.6 Eigenvalue and data transform comparisons.

positive and negative. Consider the positive quantity $\boldsymbol{\epsilon}'\boldsymbol{\epsilon}$, and pose the optimization problem

$$\underset{\hat{\mathbf{f}}}{\text{minimize}} \; \mathcal{E}\{\boldsymbol{\epsilon}'\boldsymbol{\epsilon}\} = \mathcal{E}\{Tr\,(\boldsymbol{\epsilon}\boldsymbol{\epsilon}')\}. \qquad (7.13)$$

Since the transformation $[H_{BT}]$ is linear, pragmatism indicates a linear estimate. That is, an estimate of $\hat{\mathbf{f}}$ derived by a linear operation on the recorded image

$$\hat{\mathbf{f}} = [L]\mathbf{g}, \qquad (7.14)$$

where $[L]$ is to be derived such that (7.13) is minimized.

Substituting into (7.14) from (7.3), (7.12), and (7.14) yields

$$\underset{\hat{\mathbf{f}}}{\text{minimize}} \; \mathcal{E}\{Tr\,\{\boldsymbol{\epsilon}\boldsymbol{\epsilon}'\}\} = \mathcal{E}\{Tr\,\{(\mathbf{f} - [L]\mathbf{g})(\mathbf{f} - [L]\mathbf{g})'\}\}$$

$$= \mathcal{E}\{Tr\,\{(\mathbf{f} - [L]([H_{BT}]\mathbf{f} + \mathbf{n}))(\mathbf{f} - [L]([H_{BT}]\mathbf{f} + \mathbf{n}))'\}\}$$

$$= \mathcal{E}\{Tr\,\{(\mathbf{f}\mathbf{f}' - [L]([H_{BT}]\mathbf{f}\mathbf{f}' + \mathbf{n}\mathbf{f}') - (\mathbf{f}\mathbf{f}'[H_{BT}]' + \mathbf{f}\mathbf{n}')[L]'$$

$$+ [L]([H_{BT}]\mathbf{f}\mathbf{f}'[H_{BT}]' + \mathbf{n}\mathbf{f}'[H_{BT}]' + [H_{BT}]\mathbf{f}\mathbf{n}' + \mathbf{n}\mathbf{n}')[L]'\}\}.$$

Notice that $Tr\,\{A\} = Tr\,\{A'\}$ and since the trace is linear, it interchanges with the expectation operator $\mathcal{E}$. Then,

$$\underset{\hat{\mathbf{f}}}{\text{minimize}} \; \mathcal{E}\{Tr\,(\boldsymbol{\epsilon}\boldsymbol{\epsilon}')\} = Tr\,\{[\mathcal{R}_f] - 2[L][H_{BT}][\mathcal{R}_f]$$

$$+ [L][H_{BT}][\mathcal{R}_f][H_{BT}]'[L]' + [L][\mathcal{R}_n][L]'\}, \qquad (7.15)$$

where the signal-independent noise was assumed, e.g.,

$$\mathcal{E}\{\mathbf{f}\mathbf{n}'\} = \mathcal{E}\{\mathbf{n}'\mathbf{f}\} = [0], \qquad (7.16)$$

and the autocorrelation matrices have been defined as

$$\mathcal{E}\{\mathbf{f}\mathbf{f}'\} = [\mathcal{R}_f]; \qquad \mathcal{E}\{\mathbf{n}\mathbf{n}'\} = [\mathcal{R}_n]. \qquad (7.17)$$

Differentiating (7.15) with respect to $[L]$ and setting the result equal to zero, the mean-square-error solution is

$$[L] = [\mathcal{R}_f][H_{BT}]^T([H_{BT}][\mathcal{R}_f][H_{BT}]^T + [\mathcal{R}_n])^{-1}. \qquad (7.18)$$

The minimum mean-square-error estimate was first derived in image processing problems by Helstrom (1967). An alternative form of (7.18) may be derived under the assumption that $[H_{BT}]$, $[\mathcal{R}_f]$, and $[\mathcal{R}_n]$ each have an inverse:

$$[L] = ([H_{BT}]^T[\mathcal{R}_n]^{-1}[H_{BT}] + [\mathcal{R}_f]^{-1})^{-1}[H_{BT}]^T[\mathcal{R}_n]^{-1}. \qquad (7.19)$$

In terms of the modeling discussion of Chapter 3, $[\mathcal{R}_f]$ and $[\mathcal{R}_n]$ are required for restoration. The implicit modeling assumption associated with (7.18) is a nonparametric statistical model used to describe both image and noise; i.e., the matrices $[\mathcal{R}_f]$ and $[\mathcal{R}_n]$ encompass the model information necessary to carry out the restoration process.

In the form of either (7.18) or (7.19), the MMSE restoration is a very large matrix computation, as was the case with the simple least-squares estimate of section 7.1. Thus, means to convert Equations (7.18) or (7.19) into discrete frequency relations must be found.

Inspecting the matrices $[\mathcal{R}_f]$ and $[\mathcal{R}_n]$, the following characteristics are noted. $[\mathcal{R}_f]$ and $[\mathcal{R}_n]$ are both symmetric, by the definitions (7.17). Since **f** is a lexicographically ordered image vector, then

$$[\mathcal{R}_f] = \begin{bmatrix} [\mathcal{R}_{00}] & [\mathcal{R}_{01}] & \cdots & [\mathcal{R}_{0,N-1}] \\ [\mathcal{R}_{10}] & [\mathcal{R}_{11}] & & \cdot \\ \cdot & & \cdot & \cdot \\ \cdot & & & \cdot \\ \cdot & & & \cdot \\ [\mathcal{R}_{N-1,0}] & \cdots & & [\mathcal{R}_{N-1,N-1}] \end{bmatrix}, \tag{7.20}$$

where each matrix $[\mathcal{R}_{ij}]$ is of size $N \times N$,

$$[\mathcal{R}_{ij}] = \mathcal{E}\{\mathbf{f}_i \mathbf{f}_j^t\}, \tag{7.21}$$

and $\mathbf{f}_i$, $\mathbf{f}_j$ are the ith and jth column partitions of the ordered vector **f**. Since $[\mathcal{R}_{ij}] = [\mathcal{R}_{ji}]$, then (7.20) is a symmetric matrix. The blocks $[\mathcal{R}_{ii}]$ on the diagonal describe the variation of each column partition (row of the original matrix F) with itself. Blocks off the diagonal describe the "correlation" of rows in the matrix separated by $|i - j|$. Likewise, the *covariance matrices* $[\phi_f]$ and $[\phi_n]$ can be defined in a fashion directly analogous to (7.20) and (7.21) by removing the means:

$$[\phi_f] = \mathcal{E}\{(f - \bar{f})(f - \bar{f})^t\}, [\phi_n] = \mathcal{E}\{(n - \bar{n})(n - \bar{n})^t\}.$$

Often, pixels in an image possess no predictable correlation beyond a correlation distance, d. That is,

$$\mathcal{E}\{f(x_1, y_1)f(x_2, y_2) - \bar{f}(x_1, y_1)\bar{f}(x_2, y_2)\} \cong 0 \quad \text{for } [(x_1 - x_2)^2 + (y_1 - y_2)^2]^{1/2} \geqq d.$$

Typically d will be about 20–30 pixels [Wintz (1972)]. Thus writing the corresponding covariance matrices approximately yields

$$[\phi_f] \cong \begin{bmatrix} [\phi_{00}] & \cdots & [\phi_{0,d-1}] & & & 0 \\ \cdot & \cdot & & \cdot & \\ \cdot & & \cdot & & \cdot \\ \cdot & & & \cdot & \\ [\phi_{d-1,0}] & & \cdot & [\phi_{n-1+d,N-1}] \\ & & \cdot & & \cdot \\ 0 & \cdot & & & \cdot \\ & [\phi_{N-1,N-1+d}] & \cdots & [\phi_{N-1,N-1}] \end{bmatrix} \tag{7.22}$$

and each matrix $[\phi_{ij}]$ has the structure

$$[\phi_{ij}] = \begin{bmatrix} \phi_{00}^{ij} & \cdot & \cdot & \cdot & \phi_{0,d-1}^{ij} & & & 0 \\ \cdot & \cdot & & & & \cdot & & \\ \cdot & & \cdot & & & & \cdot & \\ \cdot & & & \cdot & & & & \\ \phi_{d-1,0}^{ij} & & & & \cdot & \phi_{N-1+d,N-1}^{ji} & & \cdot \\ & & & & \cdot & & & \\ 0 & \cdot & & & & \cdot & & \cdot \\ & & \cdot & & & & \cdot & \\ & & & \phi_{N-1,N-1+d}^{ij} & \cdot & \cdot & \cdot & \phi_{N-1,N-1}^{ij} \end{bmatrix} \quad (7.23)$$

The matrices in (7.22) and (7.23) are obviously symmetric, just as were the related matrices in (7.20). The property exploited for Fourier computation in section 7.1 was not symmetry, however, but the Toeplitz structure. Toeplitz properties can be invoked for (7.22) and (7.23) only if

$$\mathcal{E}\{f(x_1, y_1)f(x_2, y_2) - \bar{f}(x_1, y_1)\bar{f}(x_2, y_2)\} = [\phi_{x_1-x_2, y_1-y_2}]; \quad (7.24)$$

i.e., interpixel correlation depends only on the distance between two pixels and not the actual location of the pixels. This is sometimes referred to as weak stationarity (about the mean) of the second-order statistic (the covariance statistic). If (7.24) is satisfied, then (7.22) and (7.23) are block Toeplitz and Toeplitz matrices, respectively. Then it is possible to approximate these covariance matrices by circulants.

Approximating $[\phi_f]$ by a circulant is not the same as approximating $[\mathcal{R}_f]$. We must examine the effect of the mean term $[\bar{f}\bar{f}^t]$ in using the circulant approximation. Specifically,

$$[\mathcal{R}_f] = [\phi_f] + [\bar{f}\bar{f}^t]. \quad (7.25)$$

Three cases are important:

Case 1: $\bar{f} = 0$. A zero-mean process is most desirable since then $[\mathcal{R}_f] = [\phi_f]$ and approximation is direct. Since f is the vector of samples from the image, however, then the positivity of images makes $\bar{f} = 0$ impossible. This can be reconciled in terms of the next case.

Case 2: $\bar{f} = \mu$, a constant vector. If it is assumed as part of the initial model assumptions that the underlying random process for f is stationary (*cf.* the discussion in Chapter 3), then $\bar{f} = \mu$ and $[\phi_f]$ is Toeplitz. Since the model produces random fluctuations about a constant mean, then the constant mean cannot be affected (except for a change in scale) by the action of the PSF matrix. Thus a restoration process would be performed as though the data was zero mean to which a constant (positive) bias had been added. This means, assuming $[\mathcal{R}_f] = [\phi_f]$ and making the circulant approximations, the restored image would be a zero-mean process plus an additive constant.

Case 3: $\bar{f} \neq \mu$, a constant vector. In terms of the discussion of Chapter 3, the model is nonstationary. If the covariance statistic is stationary ($[\phi_f]$ Toeplitz), then the stationary random process fluctuates about a nonuniform mean. Since the mean is nonuniform, then it has been affected by the PSF matrix and the restoration process must modify the nonuniform mean. In such a case the sum $[\mathcal{R}_f] = [\phi_f] + [\tilde{\mathbf{f}}\tilde{\mathbf{f}}^t]$ must be used. But $[\tilde{\mathbf{f}}\tilde{\mathbf{f}}^t]$ will not be Toeplitz and $[\mathcal{R}_f]$ is thus not Toeplitz. We cannot use the circulant approximation and there is no simplification of (7.18) or (7.19) for rapid computation.

Case 3 cannot be handled because the underlying model of the image and object distribution is too weak. In Chapter 9 a more powerful model (multivariate Gaussian) will be used to develop a restoration process that will handle the case of nonuniform mean. Thus, the assumption for the remainder of this section is that case 2 prevails.

Note, finally, that the above is a concern only for $[\mathcal{R}_f]$. Since it is known from Chapter 2 that, in image recording, noise is usually assumed to be zero mean, then $[\mathcal{R}_n] = [\phi_n]$ with no difficulty.

Substituting into (7.18) for $[\mathcal{R}_f]$ and $[\mathcal{R}_n]$

$$[L] = [\phi_f][H_{BT}]^T ([H_{BT}][\phi_f][H_{BT}]^T + [\phi_n])^{-1} \qquad (7.26)$$

Since $[\phi_f]$ and $[\phi_n]$ are assured to be Toeplitz with the forms of (7.22) and (7.23), then the circulant approximations are easily constructed by adding elements to the upper right and lower left corners of the matrices in (7.22) and (7.23) to create the circular shift structure on the rows of the matrices. (See Appendices A and B.) Designate the circulants so constructed as $[C_f]$ and $[C_n]$. Then

$$[L] \cong [C_f][H_{BC}]^T ([H_{BC}][C_f][H_{BC}]^T + [C_n])^{-1} \qquad (7.27)$$

is the circulant approximation to the MMSE restoration process.

The circulant approximation is used for the rapid Fourier computation. Since all circulants have the same set of eigenvectors, then it is obvious that sums, products, and inverses of circulants are also circulants. Thus if $[C_1]$ and $[C_2]$ are circulants with eigenvalue matrices $[\Lambda_1]$ and $[\Lambda_2]$, then

$$[C_1] + [C_2] = [\mathcal{F}]([\Lambda_1] + [\Lambda_2])[\mathcal{F}]^{-1}$$
$$[C_1][C_2] = [\mathcal{F}][\Lambda_1][\Lambda_2][\mathcal{F}]^{-1}.$$

Therefore,

$$[L] \cong [\mathcal{F}_{N^2}][\Lambda_f][\Lambda_h^*]([\Lambda_h][\Lambda_f][\Lambda_h^*] + [\Lambda_n])^{-1}[\mathcal{F}_{N^2}]^{-1}, \qquad (7.28)$$

where $[\mathcal{F}_{N^2}]$ is the two-dimensional DFT matrix as defined in Appendix B and * denotes complex conjugate. The fact was used that if $[C]$ is a circulant with eigenvalue matrix $[\Lambda]$, then

$$[\Lambda] = [\mathcal{F}][C][\mathcal{F}]^{-1},$$

which implies

$$[\Lambda^*] = [\mathcal{F}][C]^t[\mathcal{F}]^{-1}.$$

Substituting into (7.14) gives

$$[\mathcal{F}_{N^2}]^{-1}\hat{\mathbf{f}} = [\Lambda_f][\Lambda_h^*]([\Lambda_h][\Lambda_f][\Lambda_h^*] + [\Lambda_n])^{-1}[\mathcal{F}_{N^2}]^{-1}\mathbf{g}. \qquad (7.29)$$

Since Equation (7.29) is a relation in diagonal matrices and $[\mathcal{F}_{N^2}]^{-1}\hat{\mathbf{f}}$ and $[\mathcal{F}_{N^2}]^{-1}\mathbf{g}$ are recognizable as two-dimensional DFT's, then the matrix equation in (7.29) can be written in terms of Fourier quotients, just as in Section 7.1. Proceeding directly results in the following algorithm:

1. Compute the two-dimensional DFT's $G(w_x, w_y)$ and $H(w_x, w_y)$ as in Equations (7.9) and (7.10). The same considerations with respect to the choice of N still apply as discussed in Section 7.1. Identical comments pertaining to the shifting of $h(x, y)$, for spatial delay and phase considerations, are applicable here as presented with (7.10).
2. The covariance matrices, approximated in Equations (7.22) and (7.23), define the functions that must be transformed. It is obvious that (7.22) and (7.23) are symmetric circulants and must be transformed without any shifting, which is legitimate only for h. In the matrix of size $N \times N$, Equations (7.22) and (7.23) obviously define symmetry about the $(N/2, N/2)$ center point. The transforms are then

$$P_f(w_x, w_y) = \sum_{x=0}^{N-1} \sum_{y=0}^{N-1} \phi_f(x, y) \exp\left[-\frac{2\pi i}{N}(w_x x + w_y y)\right], \qquad (7.30a)$$

$$P_n(w_x, w_y) = \sum_{x=0}^{N-1} \sum_{y=0}^{N-1} \phi_n(x, y) \exp\left[-\frac{2\pi i}{N}(w_x x + w_y y)\right], \qquad (7.30b)$$

where ϕ_f and ϕ_n are the covariance matrices of the original object intensity distribution and the noise, respectively. By definition, the transforms P_f and P_n are the corresponding *power spectra* of signal and noise [Davenport and Root (1958)].

3. The estimate in the Fourier domain is

$$\hat{F}(w_x, w_y) = \frac{P_f(w_x, w_y)H^*(w_x, w_y)G(w_x, w_y)}{H^*(w_x, w_y)H(w_x, w_y)P_f(w_x, w_y) + P_n(w_x, w_y)}$$

$$= \frac{H^*(w_x, w_y)G(w_x, w_y)}{|H(w_x, w_y)|^2 + [P_n(w_x, w_y)/P_f(w_x, w_y)]}. \qquad (7.31)$$

4. The estimate of the restored image is thus the inverse DFT:

$$\hat{f}(x, y) = \frac{1}{N^2} \sum_{w_x=0}^{N-1} \sum_{w_y=0}^{N-1} \hat{F}(w_x, w_y) \exp\left\{\frac{2\pi i}{N}(xw_x + yw_y)\right\}. \qquad (7.32)$$

Several important points about the MMSE estimate of the restored image include

1. There is no ill-conditioned behavior associated with the MMSE estimate. Even though $H(w_x, w_y)$ may become small or even zero, the denominator of (7.31) cannot fall below the lower limit defined by the ratio P_n/P_f. Thus, the matrix $[H_{BT}]$ and its circulant approximation $[H_{BC}]$ can actually be singular and a restored image can still be generated, even in the presence of noise. Indeed,

the existence of noise makes the restoration possible in the presence of the P_n term in the denominator.

2. If the noise approaches zero, then $P_n \rightarrow 0$ and

$$\hat{F}(w_x, w_y) \longrightarrow \frac{G(w_x, w_y)}{H(w_x, w_y)}, \qquad (7.33)$$

which is recognized as the inverse filter. Thus, in cases of high signal-to-noise ratio, the MMSE filter approaches the inverse filter justifying the comments made in Section 7.1 concerning the use of the inverse filter.

3. As the signal power spectrum approaches zero, $P_f \rightarrow 0$, then

$$\hat{F}(w_x, w_y) \longrightarrow 0. \qquad (7.34)$$

This is also reasonable behavior because we cannot expect to recover information from spatial frequencies where the noise was completely dominant. Relation (7.34) can hold at isolated points [e.g., the zeros of $(\sin x/x)$] or over a broad range of frequencies.

4. If the PSF matrix is a Dirac function, e.g., a unity value at one location, with all other locations zero, then

$$H(w_x, w_y) = 1$$

and then

$$\hat{F}(w_x, w_y) = \frac{G(w_x, w_y)}{1 + [P_n(w_x, w_y)/P_f(w_x, w_y)]}, \qquad (7.35)$$

which is the MMSE estimate of a signal contaminated by noise. The original results for this problem were derived by Wiener (1942).

The MMSE estimate has desirable properties since it controls ill-conditioning in a fashion that is explicitly determined by the signal-to-noise ratio as a function of spatial frequency in the term P_n/P_f. There has been much success in applying the MMSE restoration to pictures from a variety of real-world problems. There is only one drawback to the MMSE (or Wiener) estimate. In low signal-to-noise ratio cases, the results generated do not appear as good visually as those produced by other criteria. The shortcoming may be due to several factors, including

1. The MMSE estimate is based on linear assumptions and there are nonlinearities in image recording and in the human visual system that evaluates images.
2. The MMSE is not the criterion that the human visual system naturally employs. MMSE restorations in low SNR cases appear too smooth; the human eye is often willing to accept more visual noise in exchange for the additional image structure lost in the process.
3. The MMSE estimate assumes stationary random process models, which is probably insufficient to describe the meaningful structure adequately in images of interest, and uses only the covariance information of the stationary model in the estimate.

Figures 7.7 and 7.8 are the images of Section 7.1 restored by using the MMSE estimates. Again Fourier computations, using the FFT algorithm in the steps described

Figure 7.7 Restoration of Figure 7.2(a) by the Wiener filter.

Figure 7.8 Restoration of Figure 7.2(b) by the Wiener filter.

above, were employed to implement the restoration process. The superiority of the MMSE restoration over the inverse filter is quite evident. The minimum expected error is found, by substituting (7.27) into (7.13), and after some manipulation,

$$\text{Expected min error} \cong Tr\,\{[\phi_f] - [L][H_{BC}][\phi_f]\}, \tag{7.36}$$

which approaches zero as the SNR approaches infinity and approaches $Tr\,\{[\phi_f]\}$ as the SNR approaches zero.

In the discussion of this section the two most important assumptions underlying the development were stationarity of the random process models and the assumption of a linear operation to compute the estimate. If the underlying models of the random processes are not stationary, then the Fourier computations are not necessarily valid. The space–domain form of Equation (7.18) is valid in the nonstationary case but the resulting matrix calculations are difficult to carry out unless the PSF is separable. Note that the linear processor for the estimate $[L]$ was a result of the linearity of the model in (7.3). One can always conceive of a nonlinear processor to generate the estimate but the resulting equations to minimize the mean-square error become difficult to solve. Results have been derived using a signal-dependent *multiplicative* noise model and a linear processor to generate the estimate [Walkup and Choens (1974)] and also a signal-independent multiplicative noise model [Franks (1969)]. The estimate has the same general form as (7.31) and shows no marked improvement in simulations of mean-square-error performance.

7.3 Homomorphic Filter Restoration

The following restoration technique to be discussed can be associated with the generic term of *homomorphic filtering* [Oppenheim, Schafer, and Stockham (1968)]. The technique is one in which a signal is mapped from its original representation space into another space where desired processing operations are more easily undertaken. As applied to image processing [Cole (1972)], it was shown to be possible to estimate the behavior of an unknown point-spread function by homomorphic operations on a recorded image. Cannon (1974) extended the work and demonstrated that a filter like the homomorphic filter could be derived by a much simpler argument and procedure. The development of Cannon will be followed in this section. For relations between the method discussed herein and the earlier work of Cole, the reader should consult the paper by Stockham, Ingebretsen, and Cannon (1975).

As always, a restoration criterion is required to motivate the development of the method. The criterion assumed is that of *power spectrum equalization*. The model is of the form

$$\mathbf{g} = [H_{BT}]\mathbf{f} + \mathbf{n}; \tag{7.3}$$

consider its circulant approximation

$$\mathbf{g} \cong [H_{BC}]\mathbf{f} + \mathbf{n}. \tag{7.37}$$

The criterion of power spectrum equalization is to find a linear operator $[L]$ such that acting upon the recorded image with $[L]$ generates an image with a power spectrum equal to the power spectrum of the original object intensity distribution. In terms of the discrete frequency domain,

$$L(w_x, w_y)G(w_x, w_y) = \hat{F}(w_x, w_y) \tag{7.38}$$

and the criterion is

$$P_{\hat{f}}(w_x, w_y) = P_f(w_x, w_y) \tag{7.39}$$

as described in Chapter 5. This leads to

$$|L(w_x, w_y)|^2 P_g(w_x, w_y) = P_f(w_x, w_y);$$

hence

$$|L(w_x, w_y)| = \left[\frac{P_f(w_x, w_y)}{P_g(w_x, w_y)}\right]^{1/2}. \tag{7.40}$$

The result specifies the magnitude of the filter only, and phase either is assumed to be zero [Cole (1972)] or is specified only for a fixed number of PSF's (focus defect, motion blur) and estimated separately [Cannon (1974)]. The P's are real functions and (7.40) is consistent.

Under the assumption of (7.37), the power spectrum of g is defined as

$$\mathcal{E}\{G(w_x, w_y)G(w_x, w_y)^*\} = P_g(w_x, w_y)$$
$$= \mathcal{E}\{(H(w_x, w_y)F(w_x, w_y) + N(w_w, w_y))(H(w_x, w_y)F(w_x, w_y)$$
$$+ N(w_x, w_y))^*\}, \tag{7.41}$$

which follows directly from the linearity of the Fourier transform and the ensemble averaging operations. A stationary random process is assumed as the image model, treating the situation exactly as in case 2 of Section 7.2. Expanding,

$$P_g(w_x, w_y) = |H(w_x, w_y)|^2 P_f(w_x, w_y) + P_n(w_x, w_y). \tag{7.42}$$

Equation (7.40) becomes

$$|L(w_x, w_y)| = \left[\frac{P_f(w_x, w_y)}{|H(w_x, w_y)|^2 P_f(w_x, w_y) + P_n(w_x, w_y)}\right]^{1/2}. \tag{7.43}$$

The resemblance of this filter to the MMSE filter is very evident. This filter takes on a geometrical mean connotation in Chapter 8.

The most interesting development in the filter is the generation of the denominator and numerator of (7.43) without detailed knowledge of H and P_n, as Cannon demonstrated. A recorded image **g** is broken up into a number of (possibly overlapping) blocks, the so-called magnitude squared of the Fourier transform of each block is then computed. Chapter 5 developed the mechanics of the process in Section 5.1.

The limiting behavior of the homomorphic restoration filter is of interest. Spatial frequencies in the region where the noise is near zero gives rise to the following assumptions:

$$P_n(w_x, w_y) \cong 0;$$

then

$$|L(w_x, w_y)| \longrightarrow \frac{1}{|H(w_x, w_y)|}, \tag{7.44}$$

which is the magnitude only (no phase angle effects are possible) of the inverse filter encountered in Section 7.1. The behavior is the same as the MMSE (Wiener) restoration filter in Section 7.2. Likewise if the power spectrum P_f is zero in any spatial frequency, then $|L(w_x, w_y)| = 0$ at the same spatial frequencies. A distinct difference, however, between the MMSE and homomorphic estimates is in the case of zero response in H. From Equation (7.31) we see that if $H(w_x, w_y) = 0$, then the MMSE estimate is zero. In the case of the homomorphic filter, however,

$$|L(w_x, w_y)| \longrightarrow \left[\frac{P_f(w_x, w_y)}{P_n(w_x, w_y)}\right]^{1/2}; \qquad (7.45)$$

i.e., the filter response is proportional to the ratio of the power spectra of signal and noise.

Figures 7.9 and 7.10 show the result of restoring the images originally presented in Section 7.1 by use of the homomorphic filter. Even though the criterion of power spectrum equalization seems a rather weak criterion, when compared to the strong criterion of minimum mean-square error the results of the restoration are of good quality. In fact, there is some justification in judging the restoration results from homomorphic processing to be preferable to those of the MMSE restoration, as close inspection of the two images in Figures 7.9 and 7.10 relative to Figures 7.7 and 7.8 will indicate.

The previous paragraph points up a difficulty that is inherent in comparing different image restoration techniques. Presumably, the results of Section 7.2 should lead to better restoration since the mean-square error has been minimized. There is experimental evidence [Cole (1972), Cannon (1974), Hunt and Andrews (1973)], however, that the Wiener filter does not always lead to optimum restorations. The differences lie, no doubt, in the extent to which the Weiner filter assumptions are satisfied by a given image and in the way the human visual system demands more information than the Wiener estimate permits.

The computation of the homomorphic filter restoration can be described in a simple algorithm as in Sections 7.1 and 7.2. There are two cases of interest: the case where $\mathcal{R}_f$ and $\mathcal{R}_n$ {and, equivalently, the covariance matrices $[\phi_f]$ and $[\phi_n]$} and the PSF $[H_{BT}]$ are assumed to be known and the case where they are assumed to be unknown and estimated from the recorded image and a prototype image. In the former case, the construction of the filter is virtually identical to the algorithm in Section 7.2 (the MMSE restoration). In the latter case, the necessity of deriving an estimate forces a change and the algorithm below is available:

1. Divide recorded image up into Q (possibly overlapping) blocks of size $M \times M$, and compute the Fourier transform of the ith block:

$$G_i(w_x, w_y) = \sum_{x=0}^{M-1} \sum_{y=0}^{M-1} g_i(x, y) \exp\left[\frac{-2\pi i}{M}(w_x x + w_y y)\right].$$

2. Compute the average power spectrum estimate:

$$P_g(w_x, w_y) = \frac{1}{Q} \sum_{i=1}^{Q} G_i(w_x, w_y) G_i(w_x, w_y)^*.$$

This is the estimate of the denominator of (7.43).

3. The prototype spectrum is assumed known, as $P_f(w_x, w_y)$.

4. The restoration is computed from the inverse DFT of the quantity

Figure 7.9 Restoration of Figure 7.2(a) by Cannon's filter.

Figure 7.10 Restoration of Figure 7.2(b) by Cannon's filter.

$$\hat{F}(w_x, w_y) = \left[\frac{P_f(w_x, w_y)}{P_g(w_x, w_y)}\right]^{1/2} G(w_x, w_y). \tag{7.46}$$

Since the image **g** is of size $N \times N$, the computations must be performed with an $N \times N$ transform. $P_g(w_x, w_y)$ is of size $M \times M$, from step 1 above, however, and $P_f(w_x, w_y)$ may be known on a different-sized transform grid also. It is necessary, therefore, to interpolate P_f and P_g to a grid size of $N \times N$. Simple interpolation schemes, (e.g., linear, quadratic, cubic spline, etc.) are sufficient for the computation in (7.46), as well as interpolation by the DFT.

Note that the homomorphic filter method results in a magnitude-only filter; whereas the MMSE restoration is capable of retaining phase information, as (7.31) demonstrates with complex quantities. For example, the PSF of motion blur and out-of-focus blur results in Fourier transforms that have negative values, as we see in Figure 7.11. This corresponds to a phase angle of zero for the positive lobes and $\pm\pi$ for the negative lobes. Cannon has shown that it is possible to detect phase angles of this form and construct a magnitude and phase version of (7.43) to use in restoration. More general phase angle estimates are impossible because of the nonunique nature of the phase angle of the complex numbers [Cannon (1974)].

7.4   Concluding Comments

The MMSE estimate of Section 7.2 requires explicit knowledge of the power spectra P_f and P_n; similar requirements are seen in the homomorphic filter, although the prototype and estimation concepts free one of the requirements.

The comments made in Section 7.3 concerning the prototype are equally applicable to the MMSE restoration in 7.2. If one has an undegraded, low-noise image of the same ensemble class as the given degraded image, then it may be used to estimate P_f. But what if an appropriate undegraded ensemble member is not available? And how can P_n be determined? The following procedure has been shown by experimental test to be of utility.

Figure 7.12 shows the power spectrum estimate that might be constructed by applying the averaging process discussed in Section 7.3 to a given recorded (hence, noisy and presumably degraded) image. It is known that

$$P_g(w_x, w_y) \cong |H(w_x, w_y)|^2 P_f(w_x, w_y) + P_n(w_x, w_y).$$

If it is assumed that the film–grain noise is a white process (which is true if digital samples are taken at distances greater than the average film–grain correlation distance), then $P_g(w_x, w_y)$ should be composed of a sum of a constant (the white-noise term) plus the term involving P_f. This is usually easy to identify, as the power spectrum becomes approximately flat beyond some frequency. The mean level about which the fluctuations occur can be identified as the spectral power associated with P_n. The other term is the associated "hump" at the lower frequencies. Experience shows that spectra of unblurred images possess the same behavior, i.e., a low-frequency hump that decays quickly as a function of frequency. This is an obvious result of interpixel correlation.

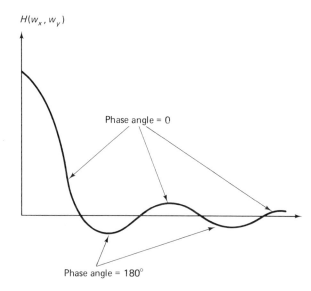

$H(w_x, w_y)$

Phase angle = 0

Phase angle = 180°

Figure 7.11   Phase angles associated with negative values of $H(w_x, w_y)$.

The effect of the factor $|H(w_x, w_y)|^2$ in the product $|H(w_x, w_y)|^2 P_f(w_x, w_y)$ is usually to accelerate the decay toward zero. The power spectrum P_f is above the curve $|H(w_x, w_y)|^2 P_f(w_x, w_y)$, as the dotted line in Figure 7.12 shows. If $H(w_x, w_y)$ is known, this knowledge can be used to estimate P_f from a plot such as Figure 7.12. (In both P_f and P_n, it is usually desirable to smooth local variations in a spectral plot such as Figure 7.12 unless particular features, e.g., periodic spikes, are known to be significant. Simple least-squares polynomials, e.g., quadratic and cubic, are usually sufficient to smooth the spectra for determination of P_f and P_n.) Finally, if the blur of the image is small, then $H(w_x, w_y) \cong 1$ can be assumed and the visible low-frequency hump used as P_f.

A crude approximation is to use the observed low-frequency hump as P_f and then multiply each point by some scalar >1 to increase P_f and correct for the effects of $|H(w_x, w_y)|$. If this is done, it is advisable to try restorations with several correlation factors and to observe which one seems most favorable in terms of the visual quality of the restored image.

All the results in this chapter were developed under the assumption that the Fourier processing is accomplished by taking fast transforms of a size comparable to the image to be restored, i.e., transforms of size $N \times N$ and greater. For a large digital image, $N = N = 500$ or more, the resulting number of digital image samples becomes so large as to require considerable effort in software development to make efficient use of the computer and its resources. In particular, transforms with FFT's of size 512×512 and greater require attention to computation problems; such considerations are covered in detail in papers in the literature [Hunt (1972), Hunt and Trussell (1973)]. Since this book is not devoted primarily to such topics, we refer the

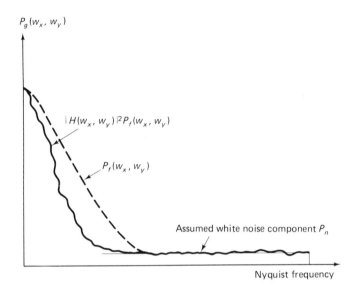

Figure 7.12   Typical power spectrum estimate.

reader to the cited papers, as well as the papers by Eklundh (1972) and Twogood and Ekstrom (1975). It should be noted, however, that transforms of size $N \times N$ can be avoided if more effort is used in designing the digital filters.

As discussed in the appendices, the structure of the PSF matrix that is the convolution inverse to another PSF matrix can be shown to result in a localized structure. That is, the inverse circulant $[H_{BC}]^{-1}$ can be approximated with a banded circulant structure (a matrix with zeros everywhere except in the vicinity of the diagonal). This is equivalent to a convolution with a finite-size PSF matrix, where the size is chosen to satisfy a suitable truncation criterion. But, given any truncated PSF matrix, size $M \times M$, it is possible to filter an image of size $N \times N$ using transforms of size $X \times X$, where $N > X > M$. The technique to do so is two-dimensional [Gold and Rader (1968)] and a published algorithm is available in the literature [Hunt (1971)], known as *block-mode* image filtering, which is an extension to two dimensions of the original one-dimensional sectioning algorithm of Stockham.

Thus, it is possible to filter an image with a 32×32 PSF matrix using 64×64 transforms. The errors that result from doing so in image restoration are governed by the truncation properties of the PSF matrix, which is inverse in convolution to the given PSF. For example, if an inverse PSF is truncated to within 1% integrated error on a matrix of size 64×64, it will generate a better restoration than a similar truncation to size 40×40, for example, with 5% integrated error. More extensive design procedures are also required since spatial windows and spectral smoothing are necessary to make the truncation well-behaved. The paper by Merserau and Dudgeon (1975) should be consulted for more comments on truncated PSF design.

Chapter 8

Linear Algebraic Restoration

8.0 Introduction

This chapter is devoted to the use of linear algebra applied to the image restoration problem. One of the advantages of the algebraic approach is a relatively new viewpoint to the task of image restoration in which cross-pollination from the field of numerical analysis and linear algebra provides new and deeper insights into restoration attempts. Specifically the concepts of degrees of freedom, singularity, pseudo-inversion, etc., map over from the linear algebra space into physically meaningful parameters in digital image restoration. This chapter addresses a few of the algebraic concepts applicable to image restoration in a linear framework.

While the linear algebraic approaches developed in this chapter may initially appear somewhat artificial, it is hoped that the reader is shown that the power of such approaches encompasses most of the more traditional signal processing analyses and techniques. The traditional filters of Fourier signal processing fame will take on new meaning in the more powerful linear algebraic structure. The chapter develops around the least-squares derivation of a large class of restoration filters including the inverse, Wiener, constrained least squares and a variety of other filters, followed by examples for illustrative purposes.

8.1 Discrete–Discrete Model: Least-Squares Techniques

In setting the framework for this section, reference will be made to the discrete–discrete model of Table 4.1 with additive noise. Thus,

147

$$\mathbf{g} = [H]\mathbf{f} + \mathbf{n}, \tag{8.1}$$

where $\mathbf{g}$, $\mathbf{f}$, and $\mathbf{n}$ are stacked vectors $N^2 \times 1$ and $[H]$ is an $N^2 \times N^2$ point-spread-function matrix. The filters that will be derived all have the property that they can be developed from least-squares Lagrangian methods resulting in spatial domain representations. Then investigation into the diagonalization of the resulting filters results in Fourier and other eigenspace scalar processing for specific assumptions and conditions. By using the least-squares approach it will be possible to develop and make comparisons among the inverse, constrained, parametric Wiener, weighted least-squares, geometric mean (see Chapters 5 and 7), and maximum entropy filters all in a common concise notation. Of course, one of the major motivations for such a comparative filter development lies in the belief that in two-dimensional signal processing there is far greater motivation for non-Wiener filter solutions than in the one-dimensional (radar, speech, communication, etc.) case. Toward this end, the following derivations are presented.

Inverse Filter

In the inverse filter derivation the objective function utilized for minimization becomes

$$W(\mathbf{f}) = \|\mathbf{g} - [H]\mathbf{f}\|^2. \tag{8.2}$$

In other words, seek the $\hat{\mathbf{f}}$ that minimizes the norm of the difference between the reblurred estimated object $[H]\hat{\mathbf{f}}$ and the given data (image) $\mathbf{g}$. Taking partial derivatives with respect to $\mathbf{f}$ and setting equal to zero, as in Chapter 7, yields

$$\frac{\partial W(\mathbf{f})}{\partial \mathbf{f}} = 0 = -2[H]^{*t}(\mathbf{g} - [H]\mathbf{f}) \tag{8.3}$$

and solving for that $\mathbf{f}$ that satisfies the minimum of the objective function yields

$$\hat{\mathbf{f}} = ([H]^{*t}[H])^{-1}[H]^{*t}\mathbf{g}. \tag{8.4}$$

Thus the inverse filter becomes

$$\boxed{([H]^{*t}[H])^{-1}[H]^{*t} = \text{inverse filter.}}$$

Note that if $[H]$ is singular, then so is $[H]^{*t}[H]$ and the inverse becomes indeterminant as is the expected situation in the more traditional Fourier inverse filter for those optical transfer functions that contain zeros (singularities).[1]

Constrained Least-Squares Filter

In order that the restoration filter have more effect than simple inversions, a constrained least-squares filter might be developed in which the constraint allows the

---

[1] Note that $[H]^{*t}$ is used to include the completely general case of complex elements in the point-spread function; such is not required for ordinary processing but may prove useful in the coherent imaging situation.

designer additional control over the restoration process. Such filters first appeared in the image processing literature for SIPSF systems but are easily generalized to the cases at hand [Hunt (1973)]. Specifically, minimize some linear operator on the object **f** (i.e., [Q]**f**) subject to some other conditions. For instance, the norm of the noise signal $||\mathbf{n}||^2$ may be known or measurable *a posteriori* from the image (see Chapter 5). Thus the constrained least-squares problem could be formulated as minimize $||[Q]\mathbf{f}||^2$ subject to $||\mathbf{g} - [H]\mathbf{f}||^2 = ||\mathbf{n}||^2$. Then using the method of Lagrange multipliers,

$$W(\mathbf{f}) = ||[Q]\mathbf{f}||^2 - \lambda(||\mathbf{g} - [H]\mathbf{f}||^2 - ||\mathbf{n}||^2). \tag{8.5}$$

Again taking derivatives of the objective function with respect to **f**,

$$\frac{\partial W(\mathbf{f})}{\partial \mathbf{f}} = \mathbf{0} = 2[Q]^{*t}[Q]\mathbf{f} + 2\lambda(H^{*t}(\mathbf{g} - [H]\mathbf{f})). \tag{8.6}$$

Solving for that **f** that provides the minimum of the objective function yields

$$\hat{\mathbf{f}} = ([H]^{*t}[H] + \gamma[Q]^{*t}[Q])^{-1}[H]^{*t}\mathbf{g}, \tag{8.7}$$

where $\gamma = 1/\lambda$ for simplification. It is concluded that

$$\boxed{([H]^{*t}[H] + \gamma[Q]^{*t}[Q])^{-1}[H]^{*t} = \text{constrained least-square filter.}}$$

The reciprocal Lagrangian multiplier γ must be adjusted such that the constraint $((\mathbf{g} - [H]\mathbf{f}))^2 = ||\mathbf{n}||^2$ is satisfied. This is often done in an iterative fashion [Hunt (1973)]. The derivation of the filter above was deceptively simple and may overshadow the significance of the result. The generality of the linear operator [Q] on the object allows the development of a variety of constraints that have the same structure as Equation (8.7). For instance,

1. $[Q] = [I]$. In this case a minimum norm solution on **f** subject to the noise norm equality constraint is sought. Thus

$$\hat{\mathbf{f}} = ([H]^{*t}[H] + \gamma[I])^{-1}[H]^{*t}\mathbf{g}, \tag{8.8}$$

   which leads to the pseudo-inverse filter. This solution will be investigated in considerable detail later as a means of avoiding the problem of singular point-spread-function matrices.

2. $[Q] = $ [finite difference matrix]. It may be chosen to minimize the second (or higher-order) difference energy of the estimated object. In this case, for the second difference,

$$[Q] = [Q_1] \otimes [Q_1]$$

   and

$$[Q_1] = \begin{bmatrix} -2 & 1 & & & & & \\ 1 & -2 & 1 & & & & \\ 0 & 1 & -2 & & & 0 & \\ & & & \ddots & \ddots & & \\ & 0 & & \ddots & \ddots & & \\ & & & & 1 & -2 & 1 \\ & & & & & 1 & -2 \end{bmatrix},$$

which is a tridiagonal matrix. For fourth differences,

$$[Q_1] = \begin{bmatrix} 6 & -4 & 1 & & & & & \\ -4 & 6 & -4 & 1 & & & 0 & \\ 1 & -4 & 6 & -4 & 1 & & & \\ & \cdot & \cdot & \cdot & \cdot & \cdot & & \\ & & \cdot & \cdot & \cdot & \cdot & \cdot & \\ & & & 1 & -4 & 6 & -4 & 1 \\ & 0 & & & 1 & -4 & 6 & -4 \\ & & & & & 0 & 1 & -4 & 6 \end{bmatrix},$$

which is a five-diagonal matrix. Such operator constraints guarantee that the object estimate $\hat{\mathbf{f}}$ does not oscillate wildly in the constrained solution by minimizing higher-order differences.

3. $[Q] =$ [eye model]. One may desire that the restoration be appealing to a human from a perceptual viewpoint. In this case $[Q]$ is a block circulant whose properties in the Fourier domain match the spatial frequency response of the psychophysics of the human visual system [Hunt (1975)].

4. $[Q] = [\phi_f]^{-1/2}[\phi_n]^{1/2}$. This case results in a parametric Wiener filter that reduces to the traditional Wiener filter for $\gamma = 1$. Here $[\phi_f]$ and $[\phi_n]$ are the signal and noise covariance matrices, respectively. This filter is further discussed below.

Parametric Wiener Filter

Because of the emphasis placed on the Wiener filter in one-dimensional signal processing [Davenport and Root (1958)], it is instructive to develop a linear algebraic version of such a filter here. If the effective noise-to-signal ratio of the estimated object $\hat{\mathbf{f}}$ is minimized while simultaneously minimizing the residual norm between the image and the reblurred estimated object, the objective function becomes

$$W(\mathbf{f}) = \| [\phi_f]^{-1/2}[\phi_n]^{1/2}\mathbf{f} \|^2 + \| \mathbf{g} - [H]\mathbf{f} \|^2. \tag{8.9}$$

Here the $[\phi_f]^{-1/2}$ and $[\phi_n]^{1/2}$ matrices exist due to the symmetry and positive definiteness of the respective covariance matrices. Proceeding with the traditional differentiation with respect to $\mathbf{f}$ yields

$$\frac{\partial W(\mathbf{f})}{\partial \mathbf{f}} = 0 = 2([\phi_f]^{-1/2}[\phi_n]^{1/2})^t[\phi_f]^{-1/2}[\phi_n]^{1/2}\mathbf{f} - 2H^{*t}(\mathbf{g} - [H]\mathbf{f}). \tag{8.10}$$

Utilizing the symmetries of the covariance matrices, their inverses, and circulant approximation,

$$\hat{\mathbf{f}} = ([H]^{*t}[H] + [\phi_f]^{-1}[\phi_n])^{-1}[H]^{*t}\mathbf{g}. \tag{8.11}$$

Thus the Wiener filter becomes

$$\boxed{([H]^{*t}[H] + [\phi_f]^{-1}[\phi_n])^{-1}[H]^{*t} = \text{Wiener filter.}}$$

Had the objective function for the constrained least-squares approach been chosen, the parametric Wiener filter would have resulted:

$$([H]^{*t}[H] + \gamma[\phi_f]^{-1}[\phi_n])^{-1}[H]^{*t} = \text{parametric Wiener filter},$$

where $\gamma = 1$ defines the traditional filter. It is interesting to note the effect of γ on the filter as it tends to emphasize ($\gamma > 1$) or de-emphasize ($\gamma < 1$) the noise and signal statistics, respectively. It is also interesting to note that for SIPSF's systems {i.e., $[H]$ is block Toeplitz} and for stationary separable and independent signal-and-noise covariances {i.e., $[\phi_f]$ and $[\phi_n]$ are block Toeplitz}, then the Wiener filter can be further simplified. For large dimensions, the block Toeplitz matrices tend to be block circulant and, as such, the Wiener filter is diagonalized by the block Fourier matrix (see Appendices A and B). Therefore, the Fourier domain allows scalar Wiener filtering only under the Toeplitz circulant assumptions above for both point-spread-function (deterministic) as well as signal-and-noise covariance (statistical) matrices. Under these assumptions the traditional Fourier version of the Wiener filter becomes applicable: i.e., the entries on the N^2 diagonal matrix resulting from $[\mathcal{F}_{N^2}]$ operating on the matrix version yield

$$\frac{H(w_x, w_y)^*}{|H(w_x, w_y)|^2 + [P_n(w_x, w_y)/P_f(w_x, w_y)]} = \text{Fourier Wiener filter.}$$

Therefore indices w_x and w_y count out all N^2 diagonal elements for the scalar multiplicative matrix equivalent operation.

Geometrical Mean Filters

The filters discussed in Chapters 5 and 7 that result in *a posteriori* determination of the point-spread function from subpicture averaging in the Fourier domain have a generalization to the SVPSF and nonstationary statistic filters being developed in this chapter. One interpretation of these filters is by a geometric mean argument in which the filter designer might wish to parameterize the ratio of inverse filter to Wiener filter effect on the restoration. The motivation for such a parameterization is the desire to de-emphasize the low-frequency dominance of the Wiener filter while avoiding the early singularity of the inverse filter. One such parameterization might yield an estimate of the object as

$$\hat{\mathbf{f}} = (\text{inverse filter})^{\alpha}(\text{parametric Wiener filter})^{1-\alpha}\mathbf{g}, \qquad (8.12)$$

where $0 \leq \alpha \leq 1$ and the filters are defined in their scalar or diagonal spaces.

While the filter above may not be obvious in its current form, we can develop its Fourier diagonalized equivalent {i.e., $[H]$ is a SIPSF and $[\phi_f]$ and $[\phi_n]$ are from stationary processes}:

$$\hat{F}(w_x, w_y)$$

$$= \left(\frac{H(w_x, w_y)^*}{|H(w_x, w_y)|^2}\right)^{\alpha}\left(\frac{H(w_x, w_y)^*}{|H(w_x, w_y)|^2 + \gamma[P_n(w_x, w_y)/P_f(w_x, w_y)]}\right)^{1-\alpha}G(w_x, w_y). \qquad (8.13)$$

Now for $\gamma = 1$ as α varies from 0 to 1, the filter changes continuously from a totally Wiener filter to a totally inverse filter [Stockham (1973)]. If $\alpha = 1/2$ (the geometrical mean of the filter) then, for a symmetric blur [i.e., $H(w_x, w_y)$ is phaseless],

$$\hat{F}(w_x, w_y) = \left(\frac{P_f(w_x, w_y)}{P_f(w_x, w_y)\,|\,H(w_x, w_y)|^2 + P_n(w_x, w_y)}\right)^{1/2} G(w_x, w_y). \qquad (8.14)$$

This is the filter developed in Chapters 5 and 7 and perfected by Cole (1973) and Cannon (1974). The most general representation of this class of filters [i.e., Equation (8.12)] requires considerable insight to understand the utility of the matrix formulation and parameters α and γ. It should be clear to the reader, however, that as $[H]$ becomes singular, the inverse portion of the filter will become large and the user will wish to de-emphasize this effect by setting α close to zero. At the other extreme, for low-noise nonsingular PSF images, one might choose $\alpha = \frac{1}{2}$ and $\gamma = 0$ in which case the inverse filter dominates. Another way to achieve the inverse filter is by letting $\alpha = 1$. It is interesting to observe the filter as a function of α, γ space. Figures 8.1 through 8.4 present experimental results of such observations. Figure 8.1 presents two different one-dimensional hypothetical optical transfer functions from a SIPSF imaging system. Figure 8.1(c) displays the α–γ space and the stability regions of the geometrical mean filter. Figures 8.2(a) and (d) develop the filter in the α–ω space for γ fixed, while the rest of the figure presents γ–ω spaces for various versions of fixed α (i.e., $\alpha = \frac{1}{2}$, $\alpha = 0$). The instability of the filter (inverse filter dominance) is evident at the zeros of $H(\omega)$. Figure 8.3 shows one-dimensional slices of the α–ω plane illustrating the filter response at various values of α. Figure 8.4 presents slices of the γ–ω plane for various values of γ. The two-dimensional geometric mean filter for $\alpha = \frac{1}{2}$, $\gamma = 1$ is developed in Figure 8.6 to be discussed shortly.

Maximum Entropy Filters

One filter that has yet to be discussed is that developed from a maximum entropy argument. The resulting filter guarantees positive (although not necessarily bounded) restoration and is based on modeling the object as a probability density function through Maxwell–Boltzmann statistical arguments [Frieden (1972), Hershel (1971)]. If the object $\mathbf{f}$ is normalized to unit energy, then each f_i scalar value can be interpreted as a probability (possibly the probability that so many photons or silver grains were present at the ith sample of the object assuming the object was light quanta or film, respectively). Then the entropy of the object would be given by

$$\text{Entropy} = -\sum_{i=1}^{N^2} f_i \ln f_i \qquad (8.15a)$$

or

$$\text{Entropy} = -\mathbf{f}^t \ln \mathbf{f}, \qquad (8.15b)$$

where $\ln \mathbf{f}$ refers to componentwise natural logarithms. If constrained least-squares approaches are applied as before, then the negative of the entropy could be minimized

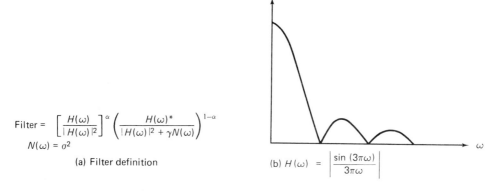

$$\text{Filter} = \left[\frac{H(\omega)}{|H(\omega)|^2}\right]^{\alpha} \left(\frac{H(\omega)^*}{|H(\omega)|^2 + \gamma N(\omega)}\right)^{1-\alpha}$$

$$N(\omega) = \sigma^2$$

(a) Filter definition

(b) $H(\omega) = \left|\dfrac{\sin(3\pi\omega)}{3\pi\omega}\right|$

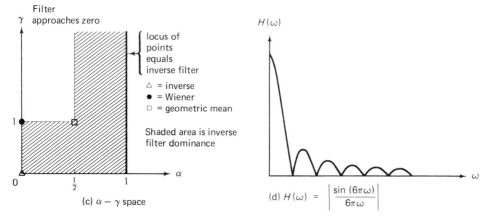

(c) $\alpha - \gamma$ space

(d) $H(\omega) = \left|\dfrac{\sin(6\pi\omega)}{6\pi\omega}\right|$

Figure 8.1   Geometric restoration filters.

subject to the constraint that $\|\mathbf{g} - [H]\mathbf{f}\|^2 = \|\mathbf{n}\|^2$. Thus the objective function becomes

$$W(\mathbf{f}) = \mathbf{f}^t \ln \mathbf{f} - \lambda\{\|\mathbf{g} - [H]\mathbf{f}\|^2 - \|\mathbf{n}\|^2\}. \tag{8.16}$$

Performing the necessary differentiation and setting the derivative to zero yields

$$\frac{\partial W(\mathbf{f})}{\partial \mathbf{f}} = \mathbf{0} = \mathbf{1} + \ln \mathbf{f} + \lambda(2[H]^{*t}(\mathbf{g} - [H]\mathbf{f})). \tag{8.17}$$

Solving for the estimate of the object that satisfies the optimization,

$$\ln \hat{\mathbf{f}} = -\mathbf{1} - 2\lambda[H]^{*t}(\mathbf{g} - [H]\hat{\mathbf{f}}) \tag{8.18a}$$

or

$$\boxed{\hat{\mathbf{f}} = \exp\{-\mathbf{1} - 2\lambda[H]^{*t}(\mathbf{g} - [H]\hat{\mathbf{f}})\}} \tag{8.18b}$$

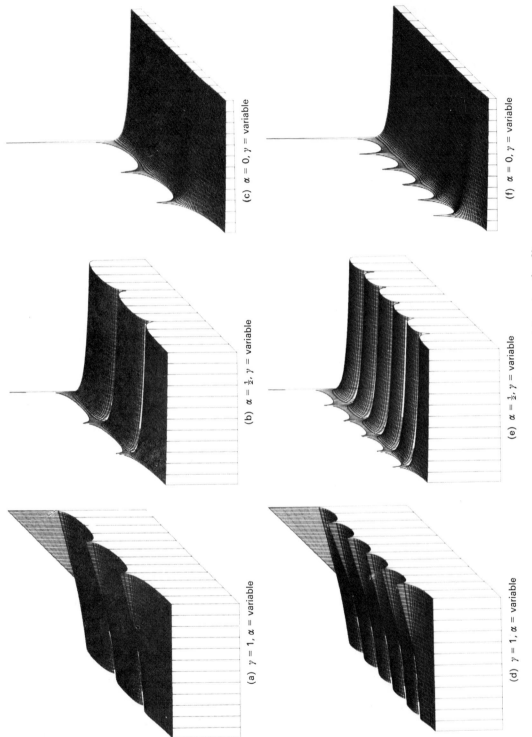

(c) $\alpha = 0$, γ = variable

(f) $\alpha = 0$, γ = variable

(b) $\alpha = \frac{1}{2}$, γ = variable

(e) $\alpha = \frac{1}{2}$, γ = variable

(a) $\gamma = 1$, α = variable

(d) $\gamma = 1$, α = variable

Figure 8.2 α-γ space perspectives for geometric restoration filters.

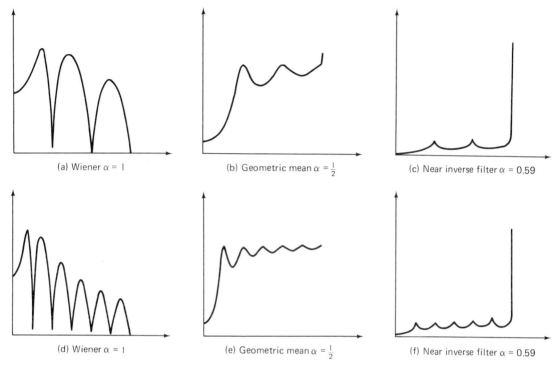

(a) Wiener $\alpha = 1$

(b) Geometric mean $\alpha = \frac{1}{2}$

(c) Near inverse filter $\alpha = 0.59$

(d) Wiener $\alpha = 1$

(e) Geometric mean $\alpha = \frac{1}{2}$

(f) Near inverse filter $\alpha = 0.59$

Figure 8.3   Geometric filters parametric in α ($\gamma = 1$).

and the solution is transcendental in $\hat{\mathbf{f}}$; however, the exponential guarantees the positiveness of the restoration. It is interesting to examine the linear approximation form of this filter by observing the first two terms in the Taylor series expansion of $\exp(\cdot)$. In this case,

$$\hat{\mathbf{f}} \cong -1 - 2\lambda[H]^{*t}(\mathbf{g} - [H]\hat{\mathbf{f}}). \tag{8.19}$$

Now solving explicitly for $\hat{\mathbf{f}}$ yields

$$\hat{\mathbf{f}} = ([H]^{*t}[H] + \gamma[I])^{-1}[H]^{*t}\mathbf{g}. \tag{8.20}$$

The observant reader will note that this solution was achieved earlier, Equation (8.8), and will be the basis for the pseudo-inverse filter. Of course, the approximation obtained by the two-term Taylor series no longer guarantees positive restoration but the authors feel it is significant that the two-term approximation to the maximum entropy filter is intimately related to the pseudo-inverse filter. Detailed discussion of maximum entropy estimates in the context of nonlinear restoration will be presented in Chapter 9.

Pseudo-Inverse Filter

In the constrained least-squares formulation the objective function, Equation (8.5), was designed to minimize the norm of a linear operation on $\mathbf{f}$ subject to a Lagrangian equality constraint. Thus,

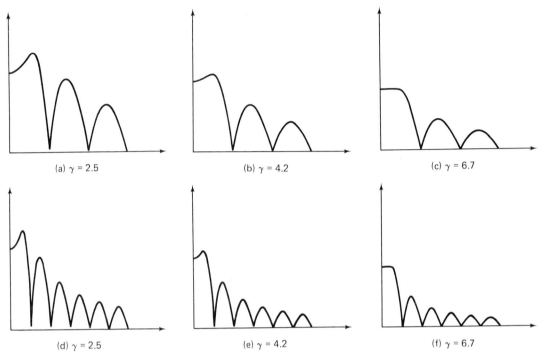

(a) $\gamma = 2.5$

(b) $\gamma = 4.2$

(c) $\gamma = 6.7$

(d) $\gamma = 2.5$

(e) $\gamma = 4.2$

(f) $\gamma = 6.7$

Figure 8.4   Parametric Wiener filter ($\alpha = 0$).

$$W(\mathbf{f}) = ||\,[Q]\mathbf{f}\,||^2 - \lambda(||\,\mathbf{g} - [H]\mathbf{f}\,||^2 - ||\,\mathbf{n}\,||^2)$$

and the solution resulted in the constrained least-squares filter of

$$([H]^{*t}[H] + \gamma[Q]^{*t}[Q])^{-1}[H]^{*t}.$$

If it is desired to minimize the norm of $\mathbf{f}$; i.e., $[Q] = [I]$; then an estimate $\hat{\mathbf{f}}$ is given by

$$\hat{\mathbf{f}} = ([H]^{*t}[H] + \gamma[I])^{-1}[H]^{*t}\mathbf{g}. \tag{8.21}$$

In the limit as $\gamma \longrightarrow 0$, equivalently as $\lambda \longrightarrow \infty$, the resulting filter is defined as the pseudo-inverse filter [Albert (1972)] denoted as

$$[H]^+ = \lim_{\gamma \to 0} ([H]^{*t}[H] + \gamma[I])^{-1}[H]^{*t}, \tag{8.22}$$

where the [ ]$^+$ notation refers to the inverse of the matrix or *pseudo-inverse* of the matrix if the inverse does not exist [Albert (1972)]. Referring to the objective function, the Lagrangian constraint begins to dominate the minimization problem as $\gamma \longrightarrow 0$. Consequently, the pseudo-inverse is equivalent to minimizing the difference between the image $\mathbf{g}$ and the estimated object $\hat{\mathbf{f}}$ reblurred through the point-spread-function $[H]\hat{\mathbf{f}}$ subject to a minimum norm on $\hat{\mathbf{f}}$. In the absence of noise this is equivalent to stating that the best estimate of $\mathbf{f}$ given $\mathbf{g} = [H]\mathbf{f}$ and assuming $[H]$ is singular is that provided by the pseudo-inverse. Because $[H]$ is singular, there will be a possible infinite number of **f**'s which will provide the given **g** and the pseudo-inverse provides that object which is smallest and, when passed through [H], also equals the image **g**.

The definition of Equation (8.22) is not as convenient as one might like and another version of the pseudo-inverse may serve as well. That definition is provided through the use of the singular value decomposition (SVD) of the point-spread-function matrix. Given the SVD of [H] as

$$[H] = [U][\Lambda^{1/2}][V]^t, \tag{8.23}$$

where

$$[H][H]^t = [U][\Lambda][U]^t, \tag{8.24a}$$

$$[H]^t[H] = [V]^t[\Lambda][V], \tag{8.24b}$$

and

$$[U]^t[U] = [V][V]^t = [I], \tag{8.24c}$$

then [U] and [V] are the respective eigenvector matrices of the [H][H]^t and [H]^t[H] products and [Λ] is the diagonal matrix of singular values (eigenvalues) common to all three expansions above. From previous chapters it was observed that Equation (8.23) could be rewritten as

$$[H] = \sum_{i=1}^{R} \lambda_i^{1/2} \mathbf{u}_i \mathbf{v}_i^t, \tag{8.25}$$

where R is the rank of [H]. The alternative pseudo-inverse definition now becomes

$$\boxed{[H]^+ = \sum_{i=1}^{R} \lambda_i^{-1/2} \mathbf{v}_i \mathbf{u}_i^t,} \tag{8.26}$$

where it is clear that no zero eigenvalues have been reciprocated because of the summation truncating at R, the rank of [H]. The pseudo-inverse filter will be investigated in considerably more detail in subsequent sections of this chapter. The alternative definition of the filter is shown here for completeness.

In closing this section on various filter structures, reference to Table 8.1 becomes useful. The table lists the filters discussed above and indicates their interrelationships as functions of the various parameters involved. In addition, the objective functions are listed, where applicable, in order that the reader may readily refer to the minimization procedure that defines the resulting filter. To this point the usefulness and applicability to image restoration of each of the individual filters has yet to be demonstrated. The motivation for the generation of so many filters lies in the belief that, in two-dimensional signal processing, the best filter is not necessarily a single filter. In addition, the derivations above were presented in their linear algebraic form to include the most complex forms of linear degradation. Thus SVPSF matrices as well as second-order nonstationary signal and noise covariances can all be included in the analyses above. It is important, however, to emphasize that not all degradations are as complex as space-variant point-spread functions and nonstationary signal and noise models. For those situations that are characterized by SIPSF's and stationary signal and noise covariances, considerable simplification in filter implementation results. Because such processes result in Toeplitz matrices {for [H], [ϕ_f], and [ϕ_n]} and because, for large

TABLE 8.1

Filter Name	Objective Function	Optimal Filter	Parametric Settings	Comments
Inverse filter	$W(\mathbf{f}) = \|\mathbf{g} - [H]\mathbf{f}\|^2$	$\hat{\mathbf{f}} = ([H]^*[H])^{-1}[H]^*\mathbf{g}$		Related to $[H]^+$
Constrained least-squares filter	$W(\mathbf{f}) = \|[Q]\mathbf{f}\|^2 - \lambda(\|\mathbf{g} - [H]\mathbf{f}\|^2 - \|\mathbf{n}\|^2)$	$\hat{\mathbf{f}} = ([H]^*[H] + \gamma[Q]^*[Q])^{-1}[H]^*\mathbf{g}$	$[Q] = [I]$ $[Q]$ = finite difference matrix $[Q]$ = eye model $[Q] = [\phi_f]^{-1/2}[\phi_n]^{1/2}$	Related to $[H]^+$ Smoother Psychophysical viewing Parametric Wiener filter
Parametric Wiener filter	$W(\mathbf{f}) = \|[\phi_f]^{-1/2}[\phi_n]^{1/2}\mathbf{f}\|^2 + \lambda\|\mathbf{g} - [H]\mathbf{f}\|^2$	$\hat{\mathbf{f}} = ([H]^*[H] + \gamma[\phi_f]^{-1}[\phi_n])^{-1}[H]^*\mathbf{g}$	$\gamma = 1$ $[\phi_f]^{-1}[\phi_n] = [I]$	Wiener filter Related to $[H]^+$
Geometrical mean filters	Not applicable, user defined	$\hat{\mathbf{f}} = (([H]^*[H])^{-1}[H]^*)^\alpha$ $(([H]^*[H] + \gamma[\phi_f]^{-1}[\phi_n])^{-1}[H]^*)^{1-\alpha}\mathbf{g}$ $[H], [\phi_f], [\phi_n]$ are in diagonal form	$\gamma = 1, \alpha = 0$ $\gamma = 1, \alpha = \frac{1}{2}$ $\alpha = 1$ $\alpha = 0$	Wiener filter Geometric mean Inverse filter Parametric Wiener
Maximum entropy filters	$W(\mathbf{f}) = \mathbf{f}^t \ln \mathbf{f} - \lambda(\|\mathbf{g} - [H]\mathbf{f}\|^2 - \|\mathbf{n}\|^2)$	$\hat{\mathbf{f}} = \exp\{-\mathbf{1} - 2\lambda[H]^*(\mathbf{g} - [H]\hat{\mathbf{f}})\}$	First two Taylor series terms	Related to $[H]^+$
Pseudo-inverse filters	$\lim_{\gamma \to 0} W(\mathbf{f})$ where $W(\mathbf{f}) = \|\mathbf{f}\|^2 - \lambda\|\mathbf{g} - [H]\mathbf{f}\|^2$	$\hat{\mathbf{f}} = [H]^+\mathbf{g} = \lim_{\gamma \to 0} ([H]^*[H] + \gamma[I])[H]^*\mathbf{g}$ or $\hat{\mathbf{f}} = \sum_{i=1}^R \lambda_i^{-1/2}\mathbf{v}_i\mathbf{u}_i^t\mathbf{g}$, where $[H] = [U][\Lambda]^{1/2}[V]^t$	Constrained least-squares approach Singular value decomposition approach	

dimensions, circulants are good approximations to Toeplitz forms, the Fourier series signal processing techniques become immediately applicable. Under these circumstances, all the filters derived above become diagonalized by the Fourier matrix $[\mathfrak{F}_{N^2}]$ and the filtering process becomes one of scalar (not vector) multiplication in the Fourier domain. Computationally such simplifications are quite important and the examples presented below illustrate many of the filters above under the Toeplitz/ circulant assumptions and subsequent Fourier implementations.

The different filter structures discussed above are derived on the basis of various objective criteria. There is no knowledge, however, to what extent a given criterion for development of a filter results in a restored object that is pleasing to the human observer. Consequently the ranking of one filter against another can be done only on an empirical basis; such will always be the case until a comprehensive model of the human visual system is known that can be employed in developing criteria for restoration filter design. With these ideas in mind, consider some experimental results. Figure 8.5(a) shows the original object that was digitized by a scanning microdensitometer. The object was passed through a defocusing SIPSF whose OTF was a first-order Bessel function divided by its argument. The OTF was circularly symmetric with a single zero crossing at three-fourths of the Nyquist rate forcing the PSF matrix to be singular. Noise was then added to the defocused image such that the variance signal-to-noise ratio was 10 dB with the noise concentrated in the high-frequency portion of the image (high-pass noise). It is readily observed from Figure 8.5(b) that the amount of defocus is only of moderate extent and does not produce severe distortion of the object. On the other hand, the signal-to-noise ratio of 10 dB is quite low. For very fine grain films and optimum exposure conditions, signal-to-noise ratios approaching 20–30 dB are not unusual. For such high signal-to-noise ratios and moderate blurring, it is possible to produce image restorations of quite high quality using inverse filtering and/or Wiener filters. The concurrence of moderate blur and a low signal-to-noise ratio constitutes a problem, however, where inverse filters fail and where Wiener filters produce results that are less than desirable. From Figure 8.5(c) it is evident that the inverse filter has emphasized the particular spatial frequency noise associated with the singularity of the OTF at the expense of losing the entire image. In spite of the optimal properties of the Wiener filter [Figure 8.5(d)], restorations by use of the Wiener filter are poor in relation to other methods (see Figure 8.6), the Wiener filter being preferable only to the inverse filter. The use of the Wiener filter to give the "optimal" restoration is part of the "forklore" of image processing, in spite of the preexisting knowledge that the visual system violates the assumptions on which the Wiener filter is based [Sondhi (1972)]. Among the remaining filters (Figure 8.6) the comparative ranking is much more difficult. These filters show clear superiority to the Wiener filter, probably due to the Wiener attempt at suppressing the high-frequency noise, thereby low-pass filtering the image to a greater degree than the eye can tolerate. The parametric Wiener filter result of Figure 8.6(a) demonstrates this visual bias because, for $\gamma = \frac{1}{4}$, the low-pass dominance of the true Wiener filter is less evident. The geometrical mean filter, $\alpha = \frac{1}{2}$, $\gamma = 1$, of Figure 8.6(b) is an attempt to allow the inverse restoration filter to boost the high-frequency portion of the restoration in a

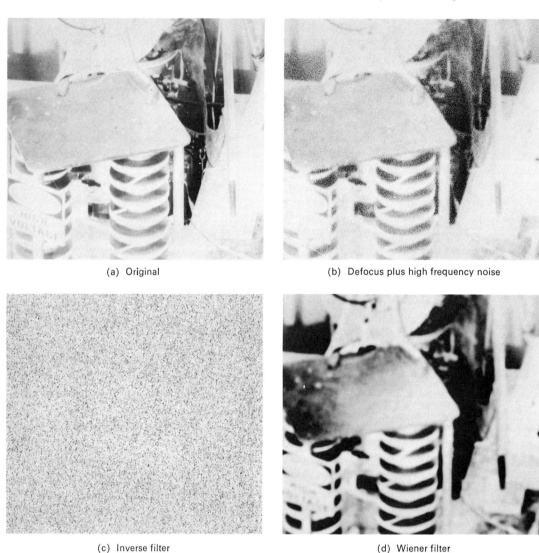

(a) Original   (b) Defocus plus high frequency noise

(c) Inverse filter   (d) Wiener filter

Figure 8.5   Traditional restoration filters.

controlled fashion. The geometrical mean filter of Figure 8.6(c) sets $\gamma = \frac{1}{4}$ and $\alpha = \frac{1}{2}$ thereby further de-emphasizing the effect of the high-frequency noise forcing the filter to roll off too rapidly in spatial frequency. Finally, the constrained least-squares filter with a smooth second difference constraint appears in Figure 8.6(d). It is difficult to rank these filters in any relative way and probably no such ranking should be attempted. Rather, these results are presented as an illustration of the implementation of some of the many filters derived in this section. In subsequent sections the numerical analysis will be examined with respect to aspects of linear algebraic restoration and the endless argument of "best" filters for human visual consumption will be left behind.

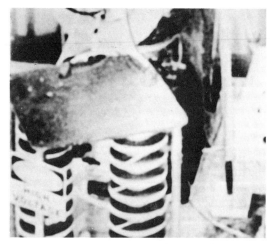

(a) Parametric Wiener filter $\gamma = \frac{1}{4}$

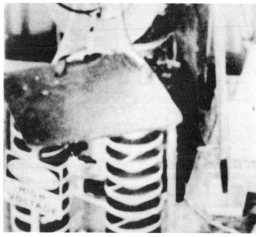

(b) Geometrical mean filter $\alpha = \frac{1}{2}$, $\gamma = 1$

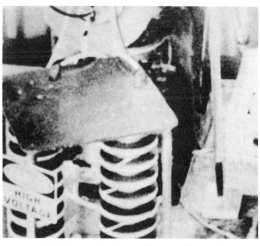

(c) Geometrical mean filter $\alpha = \frac{1}{2}$, $\gamma = \frac{1}{4}$

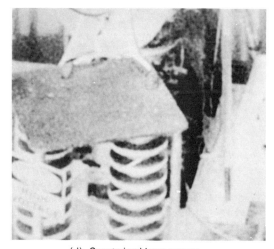

(d) Constrained least squares
[*Q*] = [second difference]

Figure 8.6   Nontraditional restoration filters.

8.2 Properties of [*H*]

Turning now to the numerical means available for removing the degradation introduced by the most general SVPSF blur matrix [*H*], it is realized that some form of matrix inversion must be attempted. Thus, it becomes expedient to investigate as much structure surrounding the PSF matrix as is possible. This structure can be described in terms of the matrix [*H*] or, for the separable case, in terms of the matrices [*A*] and [*B*] where $[H] = [A] \otimes [B]^t$. Much of this structure of the point-spread matrices can be exploited by processing in the eigenspace of the distortion {i.e., in the

SVD of $[H]$ or of $[A]$ and $[B]$}. Toward this direction it was previously noted that $[H]$ is column summable to unity, as is $[A]$, and $[B]$ is row summable to unity. Thus

$$\sum_i^{N^2} h_{ij} = 1 \qquad \forall \, j = 1, \ldots, N^2, \qquad (8.27a)$$

or

$$\sum_i^{N} a_{ij} = 1 \qquad \forall \, j = 1, \ldots, N, \qquad (8.27b)$$

and

$$\sum_j^{N} b_{ij} = 1 \qquad \forall \, i = 1, \ldots, N. \qquad (8.27c)$$

This property guarantees the conservation of light flux throughout the imaging system. In addition, because of the nonnegativity of the h_{ij}, a_{ij}, b_{ij} as well as column or row summability to unity, the $[H]$, $[A]$, and $[B]$ matrices are also known as stochastic matrices [Gantmacher (1959), Bellman (1962)]. This allows us to utilize the theory of stochastic matrices to develop further our knowledge of PSF matrices, the most obvious use of which states that the dominant eigenvalues of $[H]$, $[A]$, and $[B]$ are all, respectively, equal to unity:

$$\lambda_1 = \lambda_{a1} = \lambda_{b1} = 1.0. \qquad (8.28)$$

In addition, it is clear that the eigenvector associated with the dominant eigenvalue of $[B]$ is the unity vector $\mathbf{1} = (1, 1, \ldots, 1)^t$.

Another property of PSF matrices that results from the nonnegative property of the elements of these matrices is that the dominant eigenvectors are themselves componentwise of one sign; i.e., the eigenvector associated with the dominant eigenvalue has no zero crossings. This results from the Perron–Froebenius theorem [Andrews and Patterson (1974)] and implies that often subsequent eigenvectors uniquely exhaust an increasing number of zero crossings. Ekstrom (1974) has observed that often PSF matrices are oscillatory, the definition of which implies that the increasing zero crossing property of the eigenvectors are associated with decreasing eigenvalues [Gantmacher and Krein (1937, 1950)]. Oscillatory matrices occur in linear models of vibration systems in many physical sciences. Unfortunately, it can be shown that the Kronecker (tensor) product of oscillatory matrices is not oscillatory, even though the unique number of zero crossing property does hold (such could be defined as tensor oscillatory but not matrix oscillatory) [Adler (1975)]. Thus, for separable PSF imaging systems, $[H]$ will not be oscillatory if $[A]$ and $[B]$ are, even though the eigenvectors will oscillate but not in accordance with decreasing eigenvalues.

One interesting and quite important aspect of SVPSF matrices becomes quite evident in the eigenspace of such matrices, expressed as a local stability property. By local stability, it is meant that although a PSF matrix may be singular, if it is a SVPSF matrix, it may be singular only in certain spatial regions of the imaging system. By investigating the PSF matrix in its eigenspace (i.e., in its SVD), it is possible to observe this local stability–instability property and to speculate that the inversion of such matrices will themselves have local spatial stability and instability regions. In addition, the SVD of the PSF matrix provides insight into the degrees of freedom of the imaging system through the condition number of the matrix (see Chapter 4). Because of the

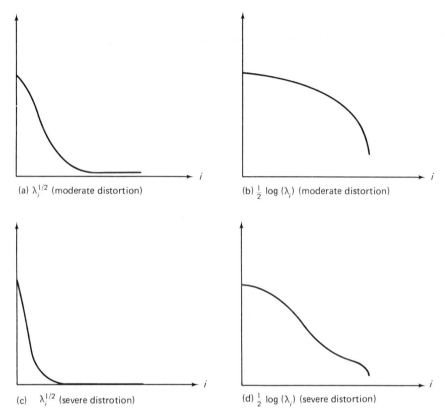

(a) $\lambda_i^{1/2}$ (moderate distortion)

(b) $\frac{1}{2}$ log (λ_i) (moderate distortion)

(c) $\lambda_i^{1/2}$ (severe distrotion)

(d) $\frac{1}{2}$ log (λ_i) (severe distortion)

Figure 8.7   Eigenvalue plots.

importance of the concept of signal processing in the eigenspace (SVD) of the distortion, an exemplary case study will be developed for illustrative purposes.

For computational simplicity, the following imaging model was assumed:

$$[G] = [A][F][A]^t; \tag{8.29}$$

i.e., the row and column distortion was the same although space-variant. Two test cases are developed, euphemistically referred to as *moderate* and *severe* distortion. Figure 8.7 presents the respective eigenvalue plots in which the condition number for the distortion becomes

$$C\{[A_{\text{moderate}}]\} = \frac{\lambda_1^{1/2}}{\lambda_N^{1/2}} = 10^{12}, \tag{8.30a}$$

$$C\{[A_{\text{severe}}]\} = \frac{\lambda_1^{1/2}}{\lambda_N^{1/2}} = 10^{16}. \tag{8.30b}$$

The logarithmic plots serve to illustrate the large dynamic range (and consequent instability) in the distortion matrices. The oscillation in the plots indicates that the eigenvalues at larger indices are not monotonically ordered, although subsequent analysis indicates this occurs far beyond computational stability. In fact, pseudo-inversion of these blurs results in effective ranks of about 110 and 60, respectively, for the moderate and severe cases. Figures 8.8 and 8.9 present selected eigenvectors of $[A]^t[A]^*$ for both distortions such that

$$[A] = [U][\Lambda^{1/2}][V]^t. \tag{8.31}$$

It is clear that the first eigenvector in both distortions are all of one sign (no zero crossings); while as the index increases (decrease in eigenvalue), the aforementioned oscillation property is experienced. When comparing Figure 8.8 with Figure 8.9 it is clear that the eigenvalues drop off in absolute value much more rapidly for the severe distortion case. The center portion of the eigenvectors at the higher indexed eigenvalues play less and less a role. In other words, for low eigenvalues (high number of zero crossings), the eigenvector has no value in the center (of the image) and most of the oscillation occurs toward the ends of the vectors. This is the opposite situation for the high eigenvalues (low number of zero crossings). Thus, one might be led to the conclusion that computational stability (i.e., larger eigenvalues) is associated with the center of the image. Indeed, for this model the SVPSF imaging system was selected to have better focus at the center and increasing distortion toward the edges. Figure 8.10 illustrates this point. Here an array of point sources form the object, and the affect of the moderate and severe distortion becomes immediately obvious in their respectively resulting images. The lossless imaging property preserves the energy under each "hump" in the image associated with a unity energy point source in the object field; the greater the distortion, the lower the image peak and broader the image "hump." One might conjecture from the discussion so far that, due to the local stability of the SVD expansion in the center of the imaging system, greater inversion success will occur on axis than off axis. Indeed this conjecture will be confirmed in Section 8.3.

8.3 Pseudo-Inversion Techniques

The linearization models of imaging systems result in restoration techniques that attempt to invert the imaging process to obtain a better estimate of the object. As mentioned earlier, literal inversion of a linear system (the inverse filter) is always a risky process due to the ill-conditioned nature of the imaging process. Mathematically speaking, if the inverse of a linear process (system) does not exist, then that system is said to be *singular*. There are certain aspects of the original object that are irretrievably lost due to the system singularity. One might argue intuitively that all imaging systems are singular because there is always some aspect of an object that is completely lost in the image, even if it is simply spatial frequencies beyond the diffraction limit. Mathematically, the concept of singularity implies that the inverse of the point-spread-function matrix does not exist; thus

$$\hat{\mathbf{f}} = [H]^{-1}\mathbf{g} \tag{8.32}$$

is not an allowable solution to the restoration task even in the absence of noise. Fortunately, there are filters known as pseudo-inverse and generalized inverses [Rao and Mitra (1971), Albert (1972)], which circumvent the singularity problem associated with

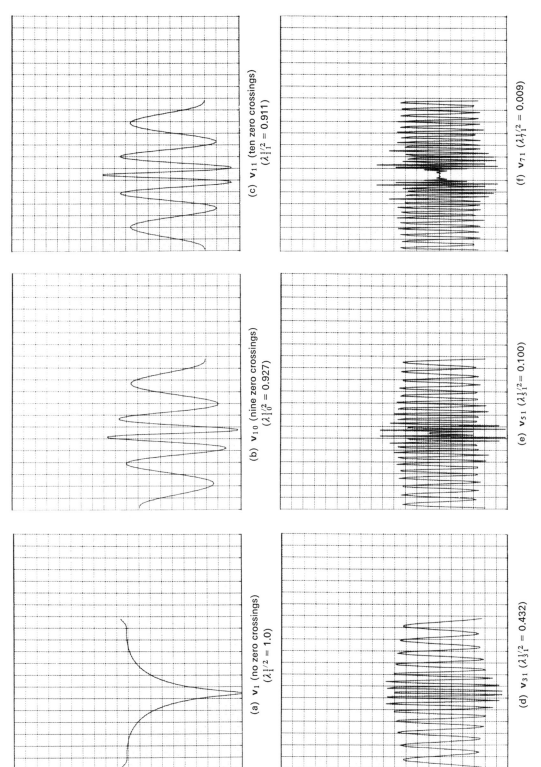

(a) $\mathbf{v}_1$ (no zero crossings) $(\lambda_1^{1/2} = 1.0)$

(b) $\mathbf{v}_{10}$ (nine zero crossings) $(\lambda_{10}^{1/2} = 0.927)$

(c) $\mathbf{v}_{11}$ (ten zero crossings) $(\lambda_{11}^{1/2} = 0.911)$

(d) $\mathbf{v}_{31}$ $(\lambda_{31}^{1/2} = 0.432)$

(e) $\mathbf{v}_{51}$ $(\lambda_{51}^{1/2} = 0.100)$

(f) $\mathbf{v}_{71}$ $(\lambda_{71}^{1/2} = 0.009)$

Figure 8.8 Selected eigenvectors for moderate distortion.

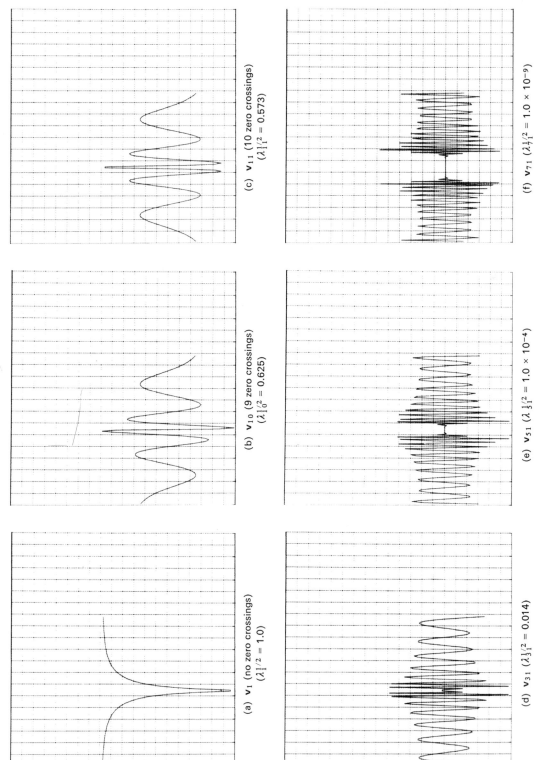

(a) $\mathbf{v}_1$ (no zero crossings)
$(\lambda_1^{1/2} = 1.0)$

(b) $\mathbf{v}_{10}$ (9 zero crossings)
$(\lambda_{10}^{1/2} = 0.625)$

(c) $\mathbf{v}_{11}$ (10 zero crossings)
$(\lambda_{11}^{1/2} = 0.573)$

(d) $\mathbf{v}_{31}$ $(\lambda_{31}^{1/2} = 0.014)$

(e) $\mathbf{v}_{51}$ $(\lambda_{51}^{1/2} = 1.0 \times 10^{-4})$

(f) $\mathbf{v}_{71}$ $(\lambda_{71}^{1/2} = 1.0 \times 10^{-9})$

Figure 8.9 Selected eigenvectors for severe distortion.

166

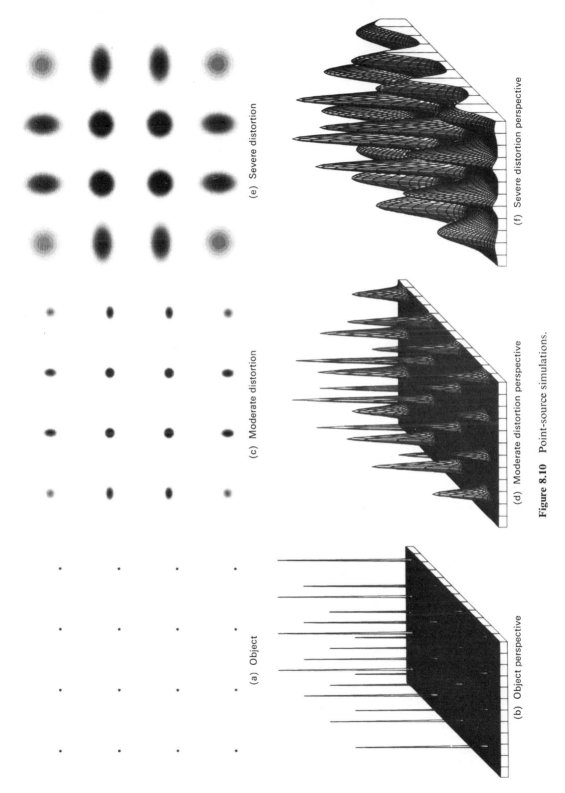

(e) Severe distortion

(c) Moderate distortion

(a) Object

(f) Severe distortion perspective

(d) Moderate distortion perspective

(b) Object perspective

Figure 8.10 Point-source simulations.

nonfull rank PSF matrices. Generally speaking, these filters attempt inversion of the imaging system up to the singularity of that system but avoid the instability of going beyond singularity. Such pseudo-inverse filters have been discussed earlier and result from a minimum norm estimated object $\|\hat{\mathbf{f}}\|^2$ in a least-squares solution of $\|\mathbf{g} - [H]\hat{\mathbf{f}}\|^2$. As indicated above, there are a variety of definitions of such filters, three of which will be reviewed here.

1. Least squares:

$$[H]^+ = \lim_{\gamma \to 0} \{[H]^{*t}[H] + \gamma[I]\}^{-1}[H]^{*t}. \tag{8.33}$$

2. SVD:

$$[H]^+ = [V][\Lambda^{-1/2}]^+[U]^t. \tag{8.34}$$

3. Van Cittert:

$$[H]^+ = \alpha \sum_{k=0}^{\infty} [H]^{*t}(I - \alpha[H][H]^{*t})^k \qquad 0 < \alpha < \frac{2}{\lambda_{\max}}. \tag{8.35}$$

The three definitions above each have their own motivations and potential strong points. The least-squares approach was discussed in an earlier section. The Van Cittert technique uses a power series approximation that requires an infinite summation. The SVD approach is the one that is probably the most illuminating and is discussed below. Specifically, a singular value decomposition of the PSF matrix is

$$[H] = [U][\Lambda^{1/2}][V]^t, \tag{8.36}$$

where the nonzero entries $\lambda_i^{1/2}$ in the diagonal matrix $[\Lambda^{1/2}]$ are the singular values of $[H]$. If $[H]$ is singular, then there will be some $\lambda_i^{1/2}$ that are zero and the traditional inverse of $[H]$ becomes

$$[H]^{-1} = [V][\Lambda^{-1/2}]^t[U]^t = \infty, \tag{8.37}$$

where the entries of the diagonal matrix $[\Lambda^{-1/2}]^t$ are $\lambda_i^{-1/2}$. Reciprocation of zero singular values results in an infinite nonexisting inverse and hence singularity truly means zero or singular eigenvalues. The degree of singularity might be represented by the rank of $[H]$ that is defined to be the number of nonzero singular values. Naturally, if the rank of $[H]$ is full (i.e., N^2), then $[H]$ is nonsingular and its inverse will exist. To eliminate the zero singular value problem, only the nonzero singular values are reciprocated in the pseudo-inverse definition. Equation (8.34) results where $[\Lambda^{-1/2}]^+$ is a diagonal matrix whose nonzero entries are $\lambda_i^{-1/2}$ for all $\lambda_i^{1/2} > 0$ and zero entries are provided for reciprocals associated with those zero singular values. Thus $[H]^+$ becomes a finite matrix but a unique pseudo-inversion is no longer expected, for when the estimated object $\hat{\mathbf{f}}$ becomes

$$\hat{\mathbf{f}} = [H]^+\mathbf{g}, \tag{8.38}$$

it is noted that there might exist a large number of such $\hat{\mathbf{f}}$'s all within the null space of $[H]$ such that when passed through $[H]$ {i.e., $[H]\mathbf{f}$} all equal the image $\mathbf{g}$. Stated in imaging terms, take as an example a badly defocused lens that has zeros in the OTF (a first-order Bessel function divided by its argument, see Chapter 4). There are certain spatial frequencies of the object that never pass through the system (those at the zeros of the OTF) and as such the same image will result from any of an infinite variety of objects whose only difference is the amount of spatial frequency content at the zeros of the OTF. The physical intuitive approach to singularity maps directly into a zero singular value in the SVD of $[H]$.

Pursuing the SVD approach to pseudo-inverse restoration, consider the four cases discussed in Chapter 4. Specifically (referring to Table 4.1),

1. Separable space-invariant point-spread functions (SSIPSF).
    $h(x, y, \xi, \eta) = a(x - \xi)b(y - \eta),$
    $[G] = [A][F][B].$
    $[A]$ and $[B]$ are Toeplitz.
2. Separable space-variant point-spread functions (SSVPSF).
    $h(x, y, \xi, \eta) = a(x, \xi)\mathbf{b}(y, \eta),$
    $[G] = [A][F][B].$
    $[A]$ and $[B]$ are arbitrary.
3. Nonseparable space-invariant point-spread functions (NSIPSF).
    $h(x, y, \xi, \eta) = h(x - \xi, y - \eta),$
    $\mathbf{g} = [H]\mathbf{f}.$
    $[H]$ is block Toeplitz, $[H_{BT}]$.
4. Nonseparable space-variant point-spread functions (NSVSPF).
    $h(x, y, \xi, \eta) = H(x, y, \xi, \eta),$
    $\mathbf{g} = [H]\mathbf{f}.$
    $[H]$ is arbitrary.

The first case, that of SSIPSF, allows a circularization of the matrix approach such that the Toeplitz convolution matrices become circulants. Thus, if the problem is circularized such that the blur matrices become circulants, equivalent to implying that $[F]$ and $[G]$ are periodically repeated throughout the plane, then the Fourier matrix diagonalizes the blur matrices. This implies circular convolution and

$$[A] = [\mathfrak{F}][\Lambda_a^{1/2}][\mathfrak{F}], \tag{8.39}$$

$$[B] = [\mathfrak{F}][\Lambda_b^{1/2}][\mathfrak{F}]. \tag{8.40}$$

Inserting into the imaging equation yields

$$[G] = [\mathfrak{F}][\Lambda_a^{1/2}][\mathfrak{F}][F][\mathfrak{F}][\Lambda_b^{1/2}][\mathfrak{F}]. \tag{8.41}$$

Since $[\mathfrak{F}]$ is unitary and the $[\Lambda]$ matrices are diagonal, the object is

$$[F] = [\mathfrak{F}]^*[\Lambda_a^{-1/2}][\mathfrak{F}]^*[G][\mathfrak{F}]^*[\Lambda_b^{-1/2}][\mathfrak{F}]^*. \tag{8.42}$$

Here * implies complex conjugation. The center portion of this equation, however, is simply the two-dimensional Fourier transform of the image $[G]$ weighted by the inverse Fourier coefficients of the blur matrix. Thus

$$[F] = [\mathfrak{F}]^*[\alpha][\mathfrak{F}]^*, \tag{8.43}$$

where

$$\alpha_{ij} = \lambda_{ai}^{-1/2}\lambda_{bj}^{-1/2}\mathbf{u}_i^t[G]\mathbf{u}_j \tag{8.44}$$

and $\mathbf{u}_i$ is the ith column of the Fourier matrix making $\mathbf{u}_i^t[G]\mathbf{u}_j$ equal to the ijth Fourier coefficient of the image. The matrix $[\alpha]$ can then be interpreted as the inverse filtered

Fourier transform of the image. The object then becomes the two-dimensional transform of [α]. The analysis results in traditional inverse Fourier filtering for removal of
separable space-invariant blur in the context of pseudo-inverse methods.

In the case of SSVPSF systems it might be desirable to obtain a minimum norm
estimate of the object $[\hat{F}]$ by pseudo-inversion of the blur matrices to recover up to
the ranks of the individual blurs. Notationally the pseudo-inverse estimate can be
represented as

$$[\hat{F}] = [A]^+[G][B]^+, \tag{8.45}$$

where $[A]^+$ and $[B]^+$ are the pseudo-inverses of $[A]$ and $[B]$, respectively [Penrose (1956)].
Using the singular value decomposition (SVD) form where

$$[A] = [U_a][\Lambda_a]^{1/2}[V_a]^t \tag{8.46}$$

and

$$[B] = [U_b][\Lambda_b]^{1/2}[V_b]^t, \tag{8.47}$$

then

$$[A]^+ = [V_a][\Lambda_a^{-1/2}]^+[U_a]^t \tag{8.48}$$

and

$$[B]^+ = [V_b][\Lambda_b^{-1/2}]^+[U_b]^t. \tag{8.49}$$

Here, the $[\Lambda_a^{-1/2}]^+$ and $[\Lambda_b^{-1/2}]^+$ matrices are diagonal with entries being reciprocals of
the $[\Lambda_a]^{1/2}$ and $[\Lambda_b]^{1/2}$ nonzero entries. In vector notation

$$[A] = \sum_{i=1}^{R_a} \lambda_{ai}^{1/2} \mathbf{u}_{ai} \mathbf{v}_{ai}^t, \tag{8.50}$$

$$[B] = \sum_{i=1}^{R_b} \lambda_{bi}^{1/2} \mathbf{u}_{bi} \mathbf{v}_{bi}^t, \tag{8.51}$$

and

$$[A]^+ = \sum_{i=1}^{R_a} \lambda_{ai}^{-1/2} \mathbf{v}_{ai} \mathbf{u}_{ai}^t, \tag{8.52}$$

$$[B]^+ = \sum_{i=1}^{R_b} \lambda_{bi}^{-1/2} \mathbf{v}_{bi} \mathbf{u}_{bi}^t, \tag{8.53}$$

and R_a, R_b are the respective ranks of the blur matrices $[A]$ and $[B]$. Using the SVD
expansions and pseudo-inverses described here, the object may be estimated as

$$[\hat{F}] = [V_a][\Lambda_a^{-1/2}]^+[U_a]^t[G][V_b][\Lambda_b^{-1/2}]^+[U_b]^t \tag{8.54}$$

or

$$= [V_a][\alpha][U_b]^t \tag{8.55}$$

or

$$= \sum_i^{R_a} \sum_j^{R_b} \alpha_{ij} \mathbf{v}_{ai} \mathbf{u}_{bj}^t, \tag{8.56}$$

where the matrix [α] is given by

$$[\alpha] = [\Lambda_a^{-1/2}]^+[U_a]^t[G][V_b][\Lambda_b^{-1/2}]^+. \tag{8.57}$$

It is instructive to investigate the ijth entry of [α], which becomes

$$\alpha_{ij} = \lambda_{ai}^{-1/2} \lambda_{bj}^{-1/2} \mathbf{u}_{ai}^t [G] \mathbf{v}_{bj}. \tag{8.58}$$

Note the similarity to the Fourier case for SIPSF's in the previous sections. The $\mathbf{u}_i$ and $\mathbf{v}_j$ vectors are no longer columns of the Fourier matrix, however, but are vectors from the basis system defined by the blur matrices.

For the NSIPSF case our imaging system has a PSF matrix $[H]$ that is of block Toeplitz form. If the individual Toeplitz matrices are circularized to implement circular (rather than full) convolution, however, then $[H]$ becomes block circulant and additional simplifications result (see Appendices A and B). Because $[H]$ is a block circulant matrix, it is diagonalized by a matrix $[\mathcal{F}_{N^2}]$ where

$$[H] = [\mathcal{F}_{N^2}][\Lambda_h][\mathcal{F}_{N^2}], \tag{8.59}$$

$[\Lambda_h]$ is diagonal, and $[\mathcal{F}_{N^2}]$ is block Fourier (i.e., made up of the Kronecker product of two $N \times N$ matrices). Thus

$$[\mathcal{F}_{N^2}] = [\mathcal{F}] \otimes [\mathcal{F}]. \tag{8.60}$$

As a parenthetical comment, the columns or rows of $[\mathcal{F}_{N^2}]$ are generalized Walsh functions [Chrestenson (1955)] and the reader should be aware that $[\mathcal{F}_{N^2}]$ is not a Fourier matrix of size $N^2 \times N^2$ with N^2 roots of unity as entries but is a matrix $N^2 \times N^2$ with N roots of unity as entries. Thus $[\mathcal{F}_{N^2}]$ implies separability (from the equation above) as far as implementation is concerned on a two-variable image. Equivalently $[\mathcal{F}_{N^2}]$ is the stacked version of a two-dimensional Fourier transform matrix. It does not, however, imply separability of the point-spread function. Returning to the restoration problem,

$$\mathbf{g} = [H]\mathbf{f}, \tag{8.61}$$

$$\mathbf{g} = [\mathcal{F}_{N^2}][\Lambda_h][\mathcal{F}_{N^2}]\mathbf{f}; \tag{8.62}$$

but since $[\mathcal{F}_{N^2}]$ is unitary (the Kronecker product of unitary matrices is unitary), then

$$\hat{\mathbf{f}} = [\mathcal{F}_{N^2}]^*[\Lambda_h]^+[\mathcal{F}_{N^2}]^*\mathbf{g}, \tag{8.63}$$

where $[\Lambda_h]^+$ implies a diagonal matrix of entries equal to the reciprocals of the entries in $[\Lambda_h]$ but no division by zero is allowed. The zero entries are replaced by zero. Upon reflection it is seen that the equation above can be implemented on a computer by performing a separable two-dimensional transform on $\mathbf{g}$ (i.e., $[\mathcal{F}_{N^2}]^*\mathbf{g} =$ stacked $([\mathcal{F}]^*[G][\mathcal{F}]^*)$); a point-by-point multiplication by the N^2 entries of $[\Lambda_h]^+$, known as a Hadamard product [Rao and Mitra (1971)]; and a separable two-dimensional transform on the resulting vector $[\Lambda_h]^+[\mathcal{F}_{N^2}]\mathbf{g}$. This, of course, is the typical filtering operation utilized in the vast majority of all Fourier domain image processing filtering algorithms. Thus, two-dimensional Fourier transforming, point-by-point multiplication in the Fourier domain, and inverse transforming is vectorially equivalent to Equation (8.63). Consequently, for nonseparable SIPSF's, implementation of the restoration algorithm can be done separably up to the point-by-point filter multiplication but because this multiplication implies only scalar operations (i.e., no vector sums), the stacked notation is not required in the computer.

In the NSVPSF case, there is very little that can be said about the point-spread-function matrix $h(x, y, \xi, \eta)$ without further analytic knowledge.

One interesting extremal condition for the SVD representation of $[H]$ occurs in the perfect imaging solution. In this case,

$$[H] = [I],$$

and the norm between $[H]$ and $[H_K]$ becomes

$$\|[H] - [H_K]\| = \sum_{i=K+1}^{N^2} \lambda_i$$

but all the eigenvalues of $[H]$ are unity and, consequently,

$$\|[H] - [H_K]\| = N^2 - K.$$

Note that, due to the multiplicity of eigenvalues, there is no unique eigenvector outer product expansion. This, unfortunately, is a very poor approximation as a function of K and indeed, in the perfect imaging limit, SVD does not appear attractive. At the other extreme, $[H]$ is defined by the all-ones matrix to within a scale factor of $(N^2)^{-1}$ as

$$h_{ij} = 1 \; \forall \; ij$$

and

$$\|[H] - [H_1]\| = 0$$

because

$$[H] = \mathbf{1}\mathbf{1}^t.$$

In other words, $[H]$ has rank $r = 1$ and is perfectly represented by one singular value and its associated outer product. Of course, this is equivalent to total lens defocus (i.e., no imaging). It is believed that a type of continuum exists in transversing between these two extreme conditions on $[H]$.

The restoration objective requires the inversion of the $N^2 \times N^2$ matrix $[H]$ to achieve a better estimate of the object $\mathbf{f}$. Thus,

$$\mathbf{f} = [H]^+ \mathbf{g} \tag{8.64}$$

and because

$$[H]^+ = \sum_{i=1}^{R} \lambda_i^{-1/2} \mathbf{v}_i \mathbf{u}_i^t, \tag{8.65}$$

then a form for the object $\mathbf{f}$ is

$$\hat{\mathbf{f}} = [H]^+ \mathbf{g} = \sum_{i=1}^{R} \lambda_i^{-1/2} (\mathbf{u}_i^t \mathbf{g}) \mathbf{v}_i. \tag{8.66}$$

The inner product of $(\mathbf{u}_i^t \mathbf{g})$ is a scalar weighting (along with $\lambda_i^{-1/2}$) on the singular vector $\mathbf{v}_i$ and the kth estimate of $\mathbf{f}$ becomes

$$\hat{\mathbf{f}}_{k+1} = \hat{\mathbf{f}}_k + \lambda_k^{-1/2} (\mathbf{u}_k^t \mathbf{g}) \mathbf{v}_k, \tag{8.67}$$

where a partial summation formulation was used to suggest a convergence to the true object if $[H]$ is truly nonsingular. In addition, the partial computation of $\hat{\mathbf{f}}$ implies that simultaneous computer storage of the entire set of images and point-spread-function matrices is unnecessary.

The partial summation form above suggests a mode of operation for image restoration that is quite luxurious and powerful if affordable. That mode of operation is to place a man interactively in the pseudo-inverse restoration loop to aid in the trunca-

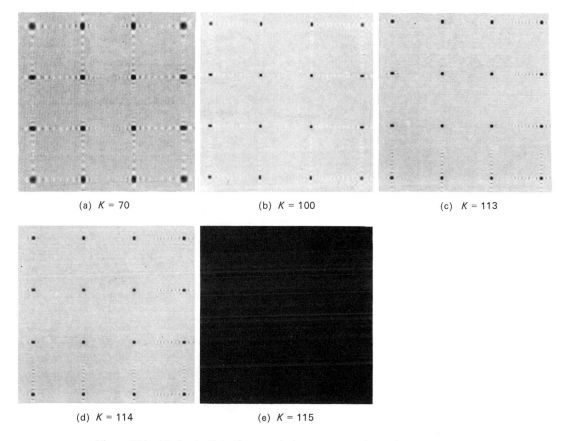

(a) $K = 70$ (b) $K = 100$ (c) $K = 113$

(d) $K = 114$ (e) $K = 115$

Figure 8.11   Moderate distortion pseudo-inverse restoration point sources.

tion of the restoration as the index k approaches singularity. The motivation for such a procedure lies in the computational difficulty in determining the true rank of $[H]$ from its SVD. Specifically, the $\lambda_i^{1/2}$ become quite small (10^{-16}) but not truly zero. Therefore, in forming $[\Lambda^{-1/2}]^+$, very large entities are obtained corresponding to the very small nonzero singular values. Previously it was noted that the stability of the matrix was given by its condition number $\lambda_{max}^{1/2}/\lambda_{min}^{1/2}$ and, for large condition numbers, computational errors will eventually dominate.

To illustrate this point more forcefully, return to our test cases in Section 8.2, Figures 8.7 through 8.10. Pursuing this example a bit further it can be seen, from Figures 8.11 through Figure 8.14, that the pseudo-inverse restoration does tend to go unstable as singularity is approached. Thus, in the SSVPSF formulation,

$$[\hat{F}]_K = [A_K]^+[G][A]_K^{t+} \tag{8.68}$$

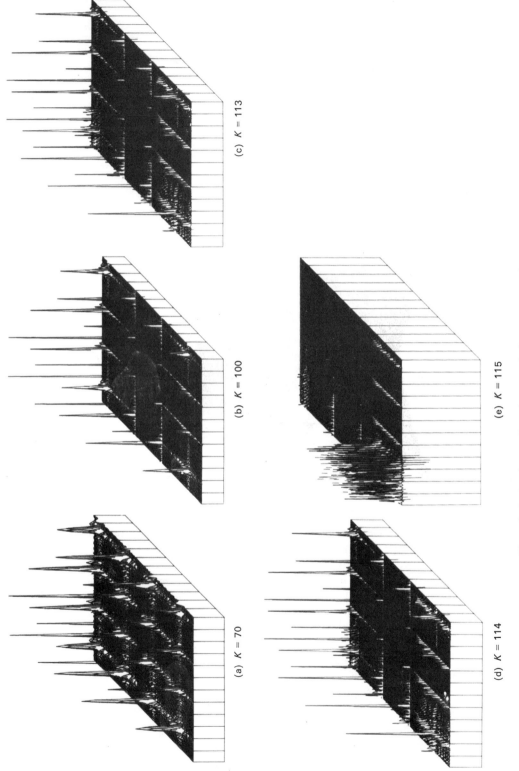

(a) $K = 70$

(b) $K = 100$

(c) $K = 113$

(d) $K = 114$

(e) $K = 115$

Figure 8.12 Moderate distortion pseudo-inverse restoration perspective.

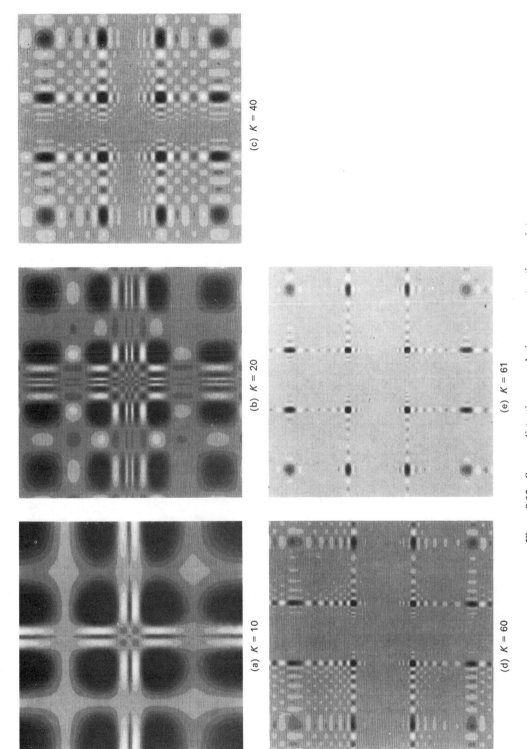

(a) $K = 10$

(b) $K = 20$

(c) $K = 40$

(d) $K = 60$

(e) $K = 61$

Figure 8.13 Severe distortion pseudo-inverse restoration point sources.

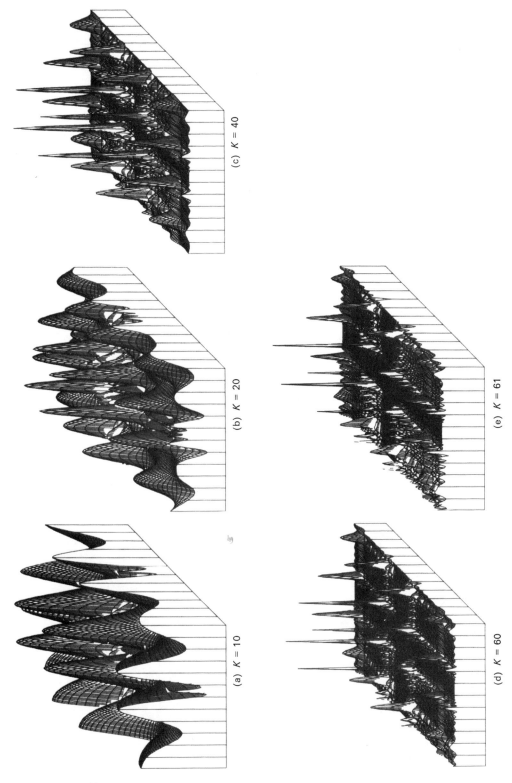

(a) $K = 10$

(b) $K = 20$

(c) $K = 40$

(d) $K = 60$

(e) $K = 61$

Figure 8.14 Severe distortion pseudo-inverse restoration perspective.

and the partial pseudo-inversion formulation allows interactive termination of the restoration process. Adler (1975) has explored a variety of termination criteria but here human intervention provides the criteria. Notice from Figures 8.11 through 8.14 that the local-singularity property of the pseudo-inverse discussed in the previous section becomes quite obvious. Also it would be expected that singularity will occur at about $K = 113$ for the moderate distortion case and at $K = 61$ for the severe distortion case. To illustrate the phenomenon more graphically, a test object was passed through both the moderate and severe distortions resulting in the images of Figures 8.15(a) and 8.17(a), respectively. It is clear from these two blurs that the image is in best focus on the axes (thus the bright cross) and the image is more blurred away from the center. For the moderate distortion case after $K = 40$, the restored object is probably better than the blurred image, while at $K = 100$ a much higher resolution image is available. As singularity is approached, however, it is clear that local ill-conditioning is beginning to dominate and from Figure 8.16 the greater blurred portions of the image are beginning to oscillate (ring). This is due to those eigenvectors, Figure 8.8, that are associated with very small eigenvalues. Notice how the center of the image remains in focus but how, at $K = 113$, the dynamic range of the image is dominated by the oscillation and very little image definition is available. For the severe distortion case, Figure 8.17, the same general phenomena occurs but much earlier in the restoration process. Naturally, this would be expected as more object content has been removed (greater singularity) by the more severe distortion. Notice again from Figure 8.18 the local instability phenomenon and complete singularity at $K = 63$.

The experiments presented above give rise to some interesting computational arguments that are easily demonstrated here. Under the hypothesis that the small singular values are in question due to computational instability but the singular vectors remain orthogonal, a filtering experiment can be hypothesized to extend beyond the computational instability of the pseudo-inverse restoration. Specifically, it is assumed that the computational error in the calculation of the singular values is uncorrelated and independent of a given index; then scalar Wiener filtering theory might be applied to de-emphasize these incorrect singular values. From a filtering viewpoint the traditional pseudo-inverse filter multiplies the singular values of the distortion matrix by $\lambda_i^{-1/2}$ or, equivalently, $\lambda_i^{1/2}/\lambda_i$. In scalar Wiener filtering a white-noise level σ^2 (due to computation error) is assumed; then modification can be implemented by $\lambda_i^{1/2}/(\lambda_i + \sigma^2)$. This operation is very close to the inverse filter for $\lambda_i \gg \sigma^2$ but for small λ_i (i.e., $\lambda_i \ll \sigma^2$) the filter approaches zero. Thus those singular values that are very small do not reciprocate and cause unstable solution. Figures 8.19 and 8.20 serve to illustrate this point. Note that images given by $K = 61$ and $K = 64$ are quite good restorations; whereas without the Wiener modification (Figure 8.18) these images were close to singular. Indeed complete singularity does not occur in the Wiener case until $K = 69$; whereas in the non-Wiener case this occurs at $K = 63$. Obviously the Wiener modification provides a gain and one could envision an interactive system whereby the viewer could participate in the definition of the computational error σ^2 to optimize the resulting restoration. In mathematical justification of the Wiener modification, it could be argued that for the true white-noise case, when $\sigma^2 = \|\mathbf{n}\|^2$, the true Wiener

(a) Blur

(b) $K = 10$

(c) $K = 20$

(d) $K = 40$

(e) $K = 70$

(f) $K = 100$

Figure 8.15 Moderate distortion: pseudo-inverse restoration (coarse tuning).

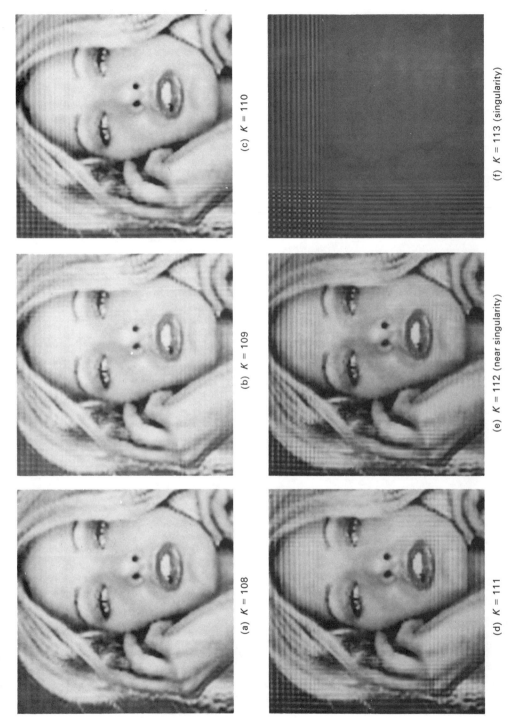

(a) $K = 108$

(b) $K = 109$

(c) $K = 110$

(d) $K = 111$

(e) $K = 112$ (near singularity)

(f) $K = 113$ (singularity)

Figure 8.16 Moderate distortion: pseudo-inverse restoration (fine tuning).

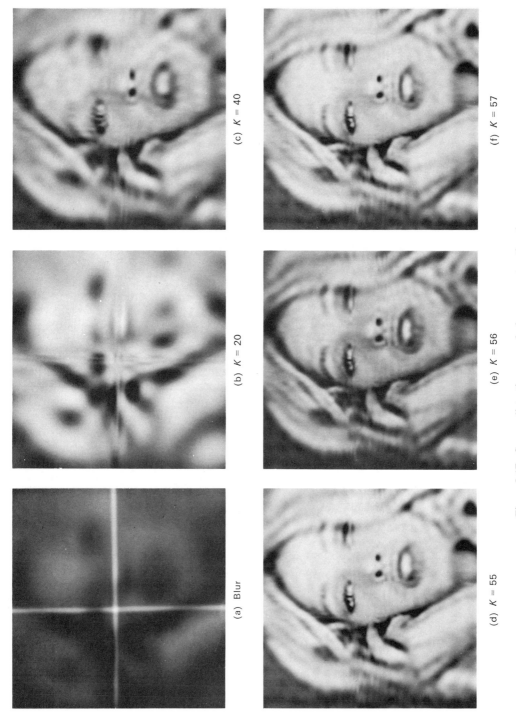

(a) Blur

(b) $K = 20$

(c) $K = 40$

(d) $K = 55$

(e) $K = 56$

(f) $K = 57$

Figure 8.17 Severe distortion: pseudo-inverse restoration (coarse tuning).

180

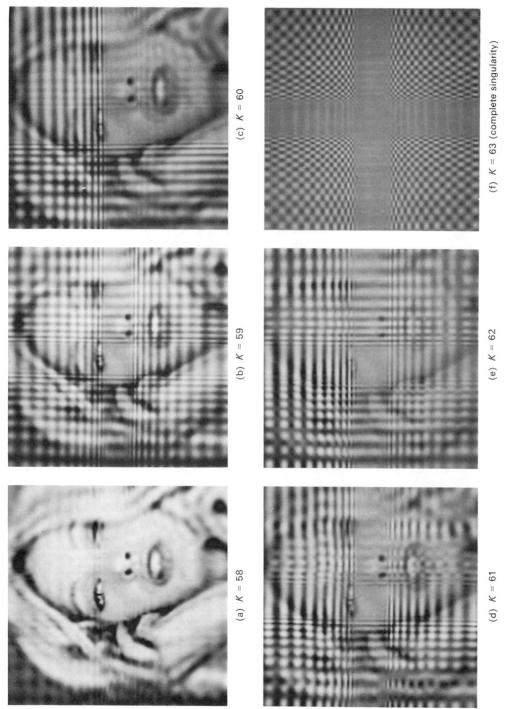

(a) K = 58

(b) K = 59

(c) K = 60

(d) K = 61

(e) K = 62

(f) K = 63 (complete singularity)

Figure 8.18 Severe distortion: pseudo-inverse restoration (fine tuning).

(a) $K = 61$ (b) $K = 62$

(c) $K = 63$ (d) $K = 64$

Figure 8.19   Severe distortion: pseudo-inverse restoration (Wiener case).

filter is implemented in a diagonalized space so that implementation is computationally manageable. (Compare with the Wiener filter of Section 8.1 in nondiagonal space.)

8.4 Continuous-Discrete Model: Least-Squares Technique[2]

This chapter has dealt with linear algebraic restoration methods applied to our discrete–discrete model of imaging systems (see Figure 4.3). Possibly a more realistic

---

[2]This section is mainly due to research by H. S. Hou (1976) in connection with a doctoral dissertation.

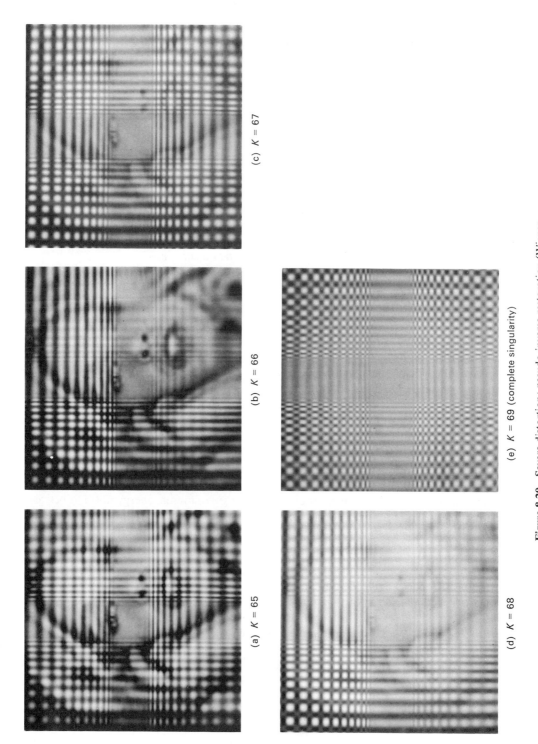

(a) $K = 65$

(b) $K = 66$

(c) $K = 67$

(d) $K = 68$

(e) $K = 69$ (complete singularity)

Figure 8.20 Severe distortion: pseudo-inverse restoration (Wiener case), (continued).

prototype is the continuous–discrete model displayed in Figure 8.21, however, where our object is assumed to be described by continuous variables (ξ, η); whereas our image is sampled as discrete points (i, j). The linear noiseless imaging equation becomes

$$\mathbf{g} = \int \mathbf{h}(\xi) f(\xi) \, d\xi, \tag{8.69}$$

where we have used stacked vector notation and $\mathbf{g}$ and $\mathbf{h}(\xi)$ are vectors $N^2 \times 1$. [Here (ξ) is used as a variable to scan the entire (ξ, η) object plane.]

   In formulating our objective function for minimization (as in Section 8.1) we must keep the following in mind: (1) the trade-off between object resolution and noise smoothing; (2) the feasibility of numerical calculations of very large-size matrices; and (3) the constraints imposed on the equations by a priori knowledge about the object function. For example, we may wish to minimize the estimated noise and the energy in the second derivative (smoothed) of the object. Thus

$$w(f) = \|\mathbf{g} - \hat{\mathbf{g}}\|^2 + \gamma \int [(f''(\xi)]^2 \, d\xi, \tag{8.70}$$

where

$$\hat{\mathbf{g}} = \int \mathbf{h}(\xi) \hat{f}(\xi) \, d\xi \tag{8.71}$$

[i.e., $\hat{\mathbf{g}}$ is the reblurred estimated object and $f''(\xi)$ is the second derivative of the object]. The scalar γ represents the weight the user wishes to place upon the derivation or smoothing energy compared to the noise (numerical or actual) error energy. By virtue of the need to solve this objective function by computational means, we choose a finite-dimensional space in which the object function f is a linear interpolation of the basis functions. Because we are interested in continuity of our object (at least up to some order derivative) and because we must assume some interpolation form of the object between estimate object points, we pick a basis set that is known as *spline functions* [Schoenberg (1965)]. Such functions have the property of continuity at sample points up to a given order derivative as well as providing a minimum energy norm fit between interpolation points. The specific basis functions to be used here are known as cubic *B* splines and our estimated object will then be given by their interpolation equation

$$\hat{f}(\xi) = \sum_i^M d_i s(\xi - \xi_i) = \sum_i^M d_i s_i(\xi), \tag{8.72}$$

where $s_i(\xi)$ is the cubic B spline centered at (ξ_i). Such functions look like truncated Gaussian curves and in fact are pulses, one unit wide, convolved with themselves three times.

   Using the B-spline interpolating coefficients of Equation (8.72) along with the objective function of Equation (8.70), we take partial derivatives with respect to the stacked interpolation coefficients. Thus

$$\frac{\partial w(f)}{\partial c_i} = 0 = -2 \int \mathbf{h}'(\xi) s_i(\xi) \, d\xi \left[\mathbf{g} - \int \mathbf{h}(\xi) \sum_{k=1}^M d_k s_k(\xi') \, d\xi' \right]$$
$$- 2\gamma \int \left[s_i''(\xi) \sum_{k=1}^M d_k s_k''(\xi) \right] d\xi. \tag{8.73}$$

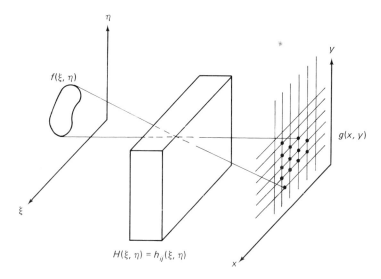

Figure 8.21   Continuous discrete model.

In matrix notation we obtain a solution

$$([H]^t[H] + \gamma[B])\mathbf{d} = [H]^t\mathbf{g}, \tag{8.74}$$

where

$$[H] = \int \mathbf{h}(\xi)\mathbf{s}^t(\xi)\, d\xi, \tag{8.75a}$$

$$\mathbf{d} = (d_1, \ldots, d_m)^t, \tag{8.75b}$$

$$[B] = \int \mathbf{s}''(\xi)\mathbf{s}'''^t(\xi)\, d\xi. \tag{8.75c}$$

Thus we have converted the continuous–discrete model into a linear discrete matrix Equation (8.74). The solution of this equation nominally is given by

$$\mathbf{d} = ([H]^t[H] + \gamma[B])^{-1}[H]^t\mathbf{g}, \tag{8.76}$$

which is surprisingly similar to the results of Section 8.1 except here we use a different interpretation of the $[H]$ matrix.

The continuous–discrete representation above is a proposed method for handling the continuous object model with finite mathematics. The results of Equation (8.76) are unconstrained in the sense that $\hat{f}(\xi, \eta)$ is not guaranteed to be positive or bounded by a finite constant. The solution above is interesting in the sense, however, that if $[B]$ becomes the identity matrix (which it would if we were doing linear interpolation instead of cubic interpolation), we obtain a pseudo-inverse-like restoration. Going in the other direction, i.e., demanding minimum energy in higher-order derivatives of f, causes $[B]$ to become banded wider and wider. Depending on the value of γ and the rank of $[H]^t[H]$, this may cause some stability considerations in the solution of Equation (8.76). These and other extensions are discussed in some detail in Hou (1976) and the interested reader is directed to that reference.

8.5 Conclusions

This chapter has addressed the image restoration task from a purely algebraic viewpoint. It was demonstrated that a large variety of filters (matrices) could be derived using optimization techniques, based on a variety of fidelity criteria, such that the user had a large repertory of restoration filters from which to choose. Illustration of many of these filters was provided and caution was suggested in trying to rank the filters among themselves, as the parameters of human observation are still not easily quantified.

From the linear algebraic approach, the properties of general point-spread-function matrices were developed and pseudo-inversion techniques presented to avoid singularity properties of such PSF. Examples illustrating numerical and local stability of SVD pseudo-inversion methods were developed, indicating a powerful methodology for handling restoration of SVPSF imaging systems.

Finally the very difficult algebraic restoration task of handling the continuous–discrete imaging model was briefly addressed. Here it was suggested that spline functions might be a useful mechanism for providing finite parameters to describe the continuous object f. The continuous–discrete model was then formulated in an optimization fashion indicating directions in which solutions might be obtained.

Chapter 9

Nonlinear Algebraic Restoration

9.0 Introduction

Linear methods of image restoration have accounted for most of the practical applications of restoration to real-world problems. The reason for this is simple: Linear methods are usually capable of being computed in a straightforward and economical fashion. Conversely, nonlinear methods usually require much more elaborate and costly computational procedures, as will be seen in the ensuing discussions in this chapter. In spite of this added difficulty, nonlinear restoration methods cannot be overlooked, for two reasons. First, the capabilities of computers and numerical algorithms are continually increasing. Even conventional linear image processing, of the kind so common today, would have been impossible without the discovery of the fast Fourier transform and fast convolution algorithms. Second, nonlinear methods must be considered for comprehensiveness; many nonlinear problems result from a more concise and accurate description of the image restoration problem than with linear methods.

Nonlinear restoration methods arise in several ways. First, they may come about directly from the image formation and recording system. For example, as described in detail in Chapter 2, common image recording systems, such as photographic film, are inherently nonlinear in response to image incident intensities. The nonlinearities of recording media have been ignored or approximated away in the discussions in previous sections.

A second situation in which nonlinear image restoration may arise is by constraints. For example, it has been explicitly required, as far back as Chapter 2, that an image be formed from always positive radiant energy components. The methods discussed in Chapters 7 and 8 do allow negative components in the restored solution. To produce a positive solution a constraint is required of the form

$$f \geqq 0.$$

Yet the inclusion of such a simple inequality constraint converts the basic linear solutions of the previous chapters into nonlinear problems—the worst kind of nonlinear problems, in fact.

A final way in which a nonlinear image restoration problem can arise is by the way in which the problem is formulated. Formulation of the problem using descriptions—mathematical or probabilistic—that do not simplify to linear forms creates a nonlinear problem in image restoration. Typically such formulations arise from the use of optimization criteria that are more complex than the quadratic or mean-square criteria discussed in previous chapters.

In this chapter a number of nonlinear image restoration problems will be described and the methods proposed for solving them. This chapter is not so rich in practical results as are the previous two chapters, for the simple reason that most of the nonlinear restoration methods are beyond the computational reach of current computers and current numerical algorithms. Consequently, the results of this chapter are more mathematical in nature, showing the formulation of the problem and the currently known methods of solution. It is important to note that the computational problems are of *scale*; virtually all the methods proposed in this chapter can be solved by a suitable combination of analytical and/or numerical algorithms. To be able to solve a mathematically formulated nonlinear restoration problem with 50 unknown variables, however, is of no use in many cases. Digital images will typically consist of 250,000 or more unknown variables. Methods suitable for the small problem are usually meaningless on the much larger problem.

9.1   Positivity Constraints

A constraint that results in considerable complication of the mathematical *solution* of the image restoration problem, even though only a minor modification *of the formulation* of the image restoration problem, is the assumption of positivity.

Reconsider the constrained-least-squares problem formulated in Chapter 8; that is,

$$\text{Minimize}\quad \mathbf{f}^t[Q]\mathbf{f}$$
$$\text{Subject to}\quad (\mathbf{g} - [H]\mathbf{f})^t(\mathbf{g} - [H]\mathbf{f}) = e. \tag{9.1}$$

This is a problem in minimizing a quadratic form subject to an equality constraint. Lagrangian methods are applicable and it is known that the solution can be expressed in a closed form as

$$\hat{\mathbf{f}} = ([H]^t[H] + \gamma[Q])^{-1}[H]^t\mathbf{g}, \tag{9.2}$$

where the parameter γ is determined by iteration. Suppose, however, that the solution to a particular problem was computed and $\hat{\mathbf{f}}$ was found to possess negative values. Since the constrained least-squares problem, as formulated in (9.1), is based on a linear model,

$$\mathbf{g} = [H]\mathbf{f} + \mathbf{n}, \tag{9.3}$$

then negative values in $\hat{\mathbf{f}}$ imply an absurdity: negative intensities of radiant energy in the original object distribution. In a straightforward fashion an extension to the problem of Equation (9.1) can be formulated as

$$\text{Minimize} \quad \mathbf{f}'[Q]\mathbf{f}$$
$$\text{Subject to} \quad (\mathbf{g} - [H]\mathbf{f})'(\mathbf{g} - [H]\mathbf{f}) = e \tag{9.4}$$
$$\text{and} \quad \mathbf{f} \geq 0.$$

The problem posed in Equation (9.4) is not a great complication in formulation over (9.1); but the solution is much worse. The inequality constraint on $\mathbf{f}$ means that Lagrangian methods do not work and there is *no closed form solution*, such as in Equation (9.2), to the positive restoration problem.

As an example of another complication that can be added, consider the following. Often the ill-conditioned nature of a restoration leads to a solution with large values. If the image formation system is an energy–lossless system (which is a good assumption for an image with a moderate amount of blur), however, then the energy in the restored image should be no greater than the energy in the recorded image. Calling this maximum energy E, then we can formulate a problem:

$$\text{Minimize} \quad \mathbf{f}'[Q]\mathbf{f}$$
$$\text{Subject to} \quad (\mathbf{g} - [H]\mathbf{f})'(\mathbf{g} - [H]\mathbf{f}) = e$$
$$\text{and} \quad \mathbf{f} \geq 0 \tag{9.5}$$
$$\text{and} \quad \mathbf{f}'\mathbf{f} \leq E.$$

Again, the solution to (9.5) cannot be obtained as a simple closed form because of the inequality constraints.

Before discussing some aspects of the solution of problems such as Equations (9.4) and (9.5), consider the necessity for a positivity constraint. First, the source of negative values in the solution is the inverse of the point-spread function. Point-spread functions that blur images do so by summing together image points. Heuristically, the inverse to a blur PSF will be a PSF that contains some negative values; as a blur PSF tends to integrate image points, thus the inverse must difference (or differentiate) image points to undo the integration. In a region where the image values of intensity or density are slowly changing, these negative values of the inverse PSF produce no difficulties. In a region with a sharp discontinuity, however, the negative values result in overshoot and undershoot after convolution. Figure 9.1 shows a typical example. Such overshoots and undershoots are often referred to as *superwhites* and *superblacks* or also as *ringing* and sometimes as *Gibbs phenomena* (although the latter is inaccurate). If the undershoots are severe enough, then the resulting values of intensity will go negative. Another source of negative values is noise. Since the negative lobes of an inverse PSF, such as seen in Figure 9.1, accentuate sharp discontinuities, the presence of noise is also accentuated since noise values represent a series of random discontinuities imposed upon the original signal. (This is yet another view of the ill-conditioned nature of image restoration.)

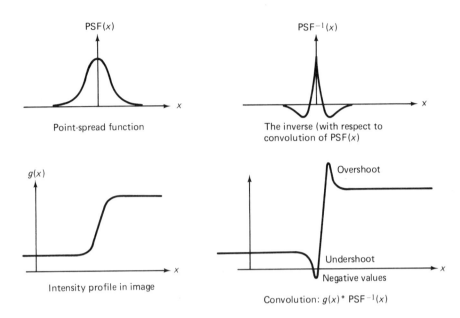

Figure 9.1   Overshoot and undershoot responses.

If an image is basically small variations around a mean intensity (low-contrast assumption), then the undershoots experienced by a restoration process are not likely to go negative; for such images the positivity problem can be dismissed. If the image has a wide dynamic range, however, with sharp discontinuities from low-to-high intensity, negative values are likely to result. A prime example is astronomical imagery, which produces film negatives that are essentially clear with sharp discontinuities of deposited silver where stars or other objects were present.

Another view of the undershoot–overshoot problem is the lack of perfect information. We know that if we deconvolve a profile, such as in Figure 9.1 with the PSF which is the true inverse of the PSF which initially blurred the profile, then there would be no overshoot or undershoot. The fact that such occurs represents cumulative effects of errors in our knowledge: The original PSF is never known with complete accuracy; the true profile is never measured precisely; the inverse PSF is usually infinite in extent but is truncated to a finite size for computational reasons; noise is present; etc. Thus, the negative values can also be viewed as a more fundamental consequence of the inevitable limitations of knowledge, given the framework of problems formulated as in Equation (9.1). Thus it is not so surprising that the introduction of constraints for positivity results in greatly increased complexity in solving the problem.

Solving Equations (9.4) or (9.5) requires methods that optimize the criterion function while continually checking for the violation of a constraint. If a component of $\hat{\mathbf{f}}$ tries to go negative, then the constraint for a lower bound of zero comes into force and is said to be a *binding* constraint. Binding constraints on upper bounds, such as in (9.5), are also possible. [Minimization of problems such as (9.4) or (9.5) is treated by the branch of applied mathematics known as *nonlinear programming*.]

As an illustration of methods for solving nonlinear problems, consider the following simple illustration. Figure 9.2 presents a function of two variables, with a constraint region shown by cross-hatching. The objective is to maximize $W(x_1, x_2)$ within
the constraint region. Obviously the maximum lies on the boundary of a constraint.
We can readily conceive of one way of finding the maximum. We start at an arbitrary
point $\mathbf{x}_0$. Then we compute the value of the gradient at point $\mathbf{x}_0 = (x_{10}, x_{20})$ and
move away from $\mathbf{x}_0$, in the direction of maximum gradient, to a new point $\mathbf{x}_1$. We
compute the gradient at this new point and move again in the maximum gradient
direction and so on, until the gradient goes to zero, at which point the maximum is
achieved since

$$\nabla W(\mathbf{x}) = 0 \tag{9.6}$$

at the maximum point. If the maximum is not unique (there are several local maxima),
then Equation (9.6) is only a necessary condition, and sufficiency must be checked by
searching for greater local maxima. We shall assume here that the optimum point
is unique.

The process above is maximization (minimization) of a function by the technique
of steepest ascent (descent). The general form of the iterative scheme to maximize a
function $f(\mathbf{x})$ by steepest ascent is

$$\mathbf{x}_{k+1} = \mathbf{x}_k + \alpha_k \nabla W(\mathbf{x}_k), \tag{9.7}$$

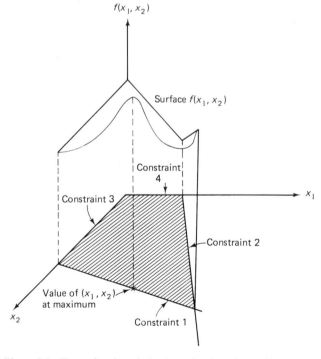

Figure 9.2   Example of optimization of a function subject to constraints.

where α_k is a factor to accelerate convergence [Saaty and Bram (1964)]. The steepest descent minimization is the same, except for a minus sign:

$$\mathbf{x}_{k+1} = \mathbf{x}_k - \alpha_k \nabla W(\mathbf{x}_k). \tag{9.8}$$

From Figure 9.2 the steepest descent or ascent solutions encounter problems when there are boundaries imposed by constraints. For example, there are starting points $\mathbf{x}_0$ in Figure 9.2 that would cause a value of $\mathbf{x}_1$ to be computed which lies outside the regions allowed by the constraints and which does not correspond to the optimum. In Figure 9.2, for example, if the boundary associated with constraint 1 was encountered before the maximum was reached, then movement should take place *along* the boundary in the direction of maximum gradient. This is equivalent to projecting the gradient function onto the boundary and then moving along the boundary as indicated by the gradient function. This is the basis of a method for nonlinear programming known as the *gradient projection* method.

The complete generality of the gradient projection method requires a very detailed discussion using the concepts of linear and nonlinear inequalities and programming [Rosen (1960); Kunzi, Krelle, Oettli (1966)]. Further, the application of the gradient projection method is made difficult by the very large number of variables associated with an image restoration problem; i.e., $N = 500$ yields a nonlinear programming problem with 250,000 variables. It is self-evident that standard computer programs for nonlinear programming by gradient projection, such as would be found in the local computer center, are not likely to be capable of handling such a large number of variables. The computing time requirements will also be large. Solutions of image restoration problems associated with nonlinear programming will have to be done by methods other than direct application of gradient projection. Hopefully, for problems such as seen in Equation (9.4), the constraints can be simple enough to allow the development of a more efficient algorithm.

In concluding this section we mention two other solutions posed for the positive restoration problem. The homomorphic model of Stockham (1972) proposes the processing of a logarithmic transformation of the image, followed by an exponentiation (Chapter 3). Figure 9.3 shows the schematic structure. The logarithm makes impossible the exact restoration of an image since it interposes a nonlinearity in front of the linear restoration processor. The exponentiator guarantees, however, that whatever the restored image it will have no negative values.

MacAdam (1970) formulated a restoration procedure in which upper and lower bounds on the restored intensity and upper and lower bounds on the noise values were imposed as linear inequality constraints. He demonstrated that if the constraints were consistent, they formed a region, in the hyperspace of restored intensity values, wherein the image restoration must lie. Finally, he demonstrated an algorithm for moving from point-to-point within the region allowed by the constraints so as to

Figure 9.3   Stockham's homomorphic processor.

minimize the error in the deconvolution. The algorithm suffers from being complex and probably quite difficult to apply to images with large numbers of samples (Mac-Adam's examples were for digital images of size 32×26). It appears to be an important technique, however; much research in the practical computation and implementation problems appears to be justified but has not been done.

9.2   Bayesian Methods and Sensor Nonlinearities

In Section 9.1 we saw how the imposition of simple constraints—positivity, bounded energy—resulted in the linear solutions of previous models being changed to nonlinear solutions requiring nonlinear programming algorithms. The underlying models of image sensing and recording were linear, however, as the relation between Equations (9.1) and (9.3) indicates. That such an assumption can be unrealistic should be emphasized from the discussion of Chapter 6; Equation (9.3) does not hold in either intensity or film density for high-contrast, high-noise images. It is often assumed that the sensor nonlinearity—be it film or TV—can be removed by a suitable inverse transformation. An inverse transformation is always possible but does *not* yield a model such as (9.3). Recalling the discussion and notation in Chapter 2,

$$g(x, y) = s\{f(x, y) \circledast h(x, y)\} + n(x, y). \tag{9.9}$$

Then

$$s^{-1}\{g(x, y)\} = s^{-1}\{s\{f(x, y) \circledast h(x, y)\} + n(x, y)\}. \tag{9.10}$$

Equation (9.10) cannot be simplified further in the most general case, for, in general, it is *not* true that

$$s^{-1}\{s\{a\} + b\} = a + s^{-1}\{b\}. \tag{9.11}$$

In fact, Equation (9.11) holds only for a linear s, or a linear approximation to s, which is precisely the case not allowed for a high-contrast, high-noise image recorded on a nonlinear medium. Thus, sensor nonlinearity is a problem that has not been treated heretofore, and methods are introduced in this chapter that allow sensor nonlinearity to be handled explicitly.

The method to be employed is that of Bayesian estimation. To estimate a quantity by a Bayesian process requires the value that maximizes the *a posteriori* probability density function. Using the discrete model as formulated in Chapter 7,

$$\mathbf{g} = s\{[H]\mathbf{f}\} + \mathbf{n}, \tag{9.12}$$

where $\mathbf{f}$ is the sampled initial object distribution, $[H]$ is the point-spread-function matrix, $\mathbf{n}$ is the noise, and $\mathbf{g}$ is the sampled image recorded on the image sensor. The function s is the sensor nonlinearity, and the notation $s\{\mathbf{x}\}$ means that every element of the vector $\mathbf{x}$ is transformed by the function s; i.e.,

$$s\{\mathbf{x}\} = \begin{bmatrix} s(x_1) \\ s(x_2) \\ \cdot \\ \cdot \\ \cdot \\ s(x_{N^2}) \end{bmatrix}.$$

The Bayes estimation problem associated with Equation (9.12) is to find the value $\mathbf{f}$ such that

$$\underset{\mathbf{f}}{\text{Maximize}} \quad p(\mathbf{f}|\mathbf{g});$$

from Bayes law we have

$$\underset{\mathbf{f}}{\text{Maximize}} \quad p(\mathbf{f}|\mathbf{g}) = \frac{p(\mathbf{g}|\mathbf{f})p(\mathbf{f})}{p(\mathbf{g})}. \tag{9.13}$$

Equation (9.13) requires that the a priori probability densities on the right-hand side be defined. Recalling the discussion in Chapter 3, choose the multivariate Gaussian process and let

$$p(\mathbf{n}) = K_1 \exp\{-\tfrac{1}{2}\mathbf{n}^t[\phi_n]^{-1}\mathbf{n}\}. \tag{9.14}$$

$$p(\mathbf{f}) = K_2 \exp\{-\tfrac{1}{2}(\mathbf{f} - \hat{\mathbf{f}})^t[\phi_f]^{-1}(\mathbf{f} - \hat{\mathbf{f}})\} \tag{9.15}$$

The mean $\hat{\mathbf{f}}$ and covariance matrix $[\phi_f]$ are assumed to be ensemble statistics (see Chapter 3 concerning the use of mean and covariance as image model properties).

The probability density $p(\mathbf{g})$ is determined by the nonlinear transformation of the random process generated by $[H]\mathbf{f}$, summed with $\mathbf{n}$. The probability $p(\mathbf{g})$ cannot be specified without assuming a specific form for the sensor response function s; however, the maximization of $p(\mathbf{f}|\mathbf{g})$ over the values of $\mathbf{f}$ does not depend on $\mathbf{g}$. The $p(\mathbf{g})$ amounts to a scaling but does not change the value of $\mathbf{f}$ at which the maximum occurs. Therefore, $p(\mathbf{g})$ can be left unspecified and still effect a solution of the maximization problem.

Finally, the conditional a priori density $p(\mathbf{g}|\mathbf{f})$ can be derived. From Equation (9.12), if a value of $\mathbf{f}$ is given and fixed, then the variation in $\mathbf{g}$ is due to the noise $\mathbf{n}$. Thus,

$$p(\mathbf{g}|\mathbf{f}) = K_3 \exp\{-\tfrac{1}{2}(\mathbf{g} - s\{[H]\mathbf{f}\})^t[\phi_n]^{-1}(\mathbf{g} - s\{[H]\mathbf{f}\})\}. \tag{9.16}$$

In Equations (9.14), (9.15), and (9.16) the constant factors K were left unspecified; they are required to make the integrals under the density functions equal one but do not affect the maximization process and can be left as arbitrary constants.

The logarithm of $p(\mathbf{f}|\mathbf{g})$ has the same maximum as $p(\mathbf{f}|\mathbf{g})$. Therefore,

$$\ln p(\mathbf{f}|\mathbf{g}) = -\tfrac{1}{2}(\mathbf{g} - s\{[H]\mathbf{f}\})^t[\phi_n]^{-1}(\mathbf{g} - s\{[H]\mathbf{f}\})$$
$$- \tfrac{1}{2}(\mathbf{f} - \hat{\mathbf{f}})^t[\phi_f]^{-1}(\mathbf{f} - \hat{\mathbf{f}}) + \ln p(\mathbf{g}) + K = W(\mathbf{f}). \tag{9.17}$$

To maximize $W(\mathbf{f})$ in Equation (9.17), recall that the gradient with respect to $\mathbf{f}$, i.e.,

$$\nabla = \begin{bmatrix} \dfrac{\partial}{\partial f_1} \\[6pt] \dfrac{\partial}{\partial f_2} \\[4pt] \cdot \\ \cdot \\ \cdot \\[4pt] \dfrac{\partial}{\partial f_{N^2}} \end{bmatrix}, \tag{9.18}$$

can be computed, equated to zero, and solved to obtain a necessary condition for a minimum. Hence

$$\nabla W(\mathbf{f}) = \nabla \ln p(\mathbf{f}|\mathbf{g})$$
$$= [H]^t[S_b][\phi_n]^{-1}(\mathbf{g} - s\{[H]\mathbf{f}\}) - [\phi_f]^{-1}(\mathbf{f} - \bar{\mathbf{f}}) = 0, \tag{9.19}$$

where $[S_b]$ is a diagonal matrix of partial derivatives

$$[S_b] = \begin{bmatrix} \dfrac{\partial s}{\partial u}\Big|_{u=b_1} & & & & 0 \\ & \dfrac{\partial s}{\partial u}\Big|_{u=b_2} & & & \\ & & \cdot & & \\ & & & \cdot & \\ 0 & & & & \dfrac{\partial s}{\partial u}\Big|_{u=b_{N^2}} \end{bmatrix} \tag{9.20}$$

and

$$b_i = \sum_{j=1}^{N^2} h_{ij} f_j \tag{9.21}$$

is the element obtained from blurring $\mathbf{f}$ with the PSF matrix. The derivation of (9.19) is a straightforward (but tedious) application of the chain rule and partial differentiation.

If there exists a value of $\mathbf{f}$ such that Equation (9.19) is satisfied, then the value is called the *MAP estimate* (for *maximum a posteriori*) and designated by the notation $\hat{\mathbf{f}}_{MAP}$. Assuming $\hat{\mathbf{f}}_{MAP}$ exists, then rearranging (9.19) yields

$$\hat{\mathbf{f}}_{MAP} = \bar{\mathbf{f}} + [\phi_f][H]^t[S_b][\phi_n]^{-1}(\mathbf{g} - s\{[H]\hat{\mathbf{f}}_{MAP}\}). \tag{9.22}$$

This is a nonlinear matrix equation for $\hat{\mathbf{f}}_{MAP}$ and since $\hat{\mathbf{f}}_{MAP}$ appears on both sides, there is a feedback structure as well [Hunt (1975)]. Analogies in the estimation of continuous waveforms have been derived for communication theory problems [Van Trees (1967)].

Associated with the MAP estimate is the *maximum likelihood* (ML) estimate, which is derived by assuming that $p(\mathbf{f}|\mathbf{g}) = p(\mathbf{g}|\mathbf{f})$; i.e., the vector $\mathbf{f}$ is a nonrandom quantity. In this case,

$$\ln p(\mathbf{f}|\mathbf{g}) = [H]^t[S_b][\phi_n]^{-1}(\mathbf{g} - s\{[H]\mathbf{f}\}) = 0. \tag{9.23}$$

This equation is satisfied if

$$\mathbf{g} = s\{[H]\hat{\mathbf{f}}\}, \tag{9.24}$$

which implies

$$\hat{\mathbf{f}}_{ML} = [H]^{-1}s^{-1}(\mathbf{g}). \tag{9.25}$$

Of course, $[H]^{-1}$ need not exist, as the discussion in Chapter 7 indicates. Comparing (9.25) with the comments at the beginning of this section, it is seen that the maximum likelihood estimate requires the inverse transformation of the sensor response. The problems associated with Equation (9.10) and the ill-conditioned nature of $[H]^{-1}$ should be borne in mind. Because of these problems the ML estimate is of limited utility.

As unfamiliar as Equation (9.19) or (9.22) may look, a relationship to previous work can be constructed. If the sensor response is linear, then $[S_b]$ is a diagonal matrix with a single constant (representing slope) on the diagonal elements; it can be chosen as the identity matrix, $[S_b] = [I]$, without loss of generality. In such a case then Equation (9.19) can be rearranged to the same form as the MMSE estimate (the Wiener filter) discussed in Chapter 7, provided $\hat{\mathbf{f}} = \mathbf{0}$. Fourier techniques to solve for the estimate are then applicable. This result is not surprising since it is known in linear systems that MMSE and MAP estimates on Gaussian densities are the same [Van Trees (1967)].

In the case where sensor response is not linear, solving the matrix equations, either (9.19) or (9.22), cannot serially be done in a closed form. Instead, an iterative procedure must be employed.

Maximizing the *a posteriori* density function is equivalent to minimizing the function $W(\mathbf{f})$ shown in Equation (9.17). As discussed in Section 9.1, the steepest descent method can be used to minimize $W(\mathbf{f})$ according to the sequence

$$\mathbf{f}_{k+1} = \mathbf{f}_k - \alpha \nabla W(\mathbf{f}). \tag{9.26}$$

The conditions for convergence of such a process are quite general. For a quadratic function, convergence is always guaranteed; for the sum of two quadratic forms, as in (9.17), the convergence conditions are usually satisfied [Saaty and Bram (1964)] but convergence is not globally guaranteed. Since no constraints have been placed on the solution, such as positivity, then Equation (9.26) can be applied directly, without concern for violation of boundaries imposed by constraints. Of course, the resulting solution is not guaranteed to be positive.

Since (9.26) can be applied to compute the MAP solution, the only question concerns the computation of the gradient function $\nabla W(\mathbf{f})$. The following characteristics of $\nabla W(\mathbf{f})$ as seen in Equation (9.19) are of interest.

1. The form of the matrices $[H]$, $[\phi_n]$, and $[\phi_f]$ is left unspecified in (9.19). Therefore, for general space-variant image formation, with random processes that are not stationary in the covariance statistics, the evaluation of (9.19) requires matrix multiplications and consumes an impossible amount of computer time for any image with a typical number of samples, say a 500×500 image.
2. If the image formation process is space-invariant, then we can replace the general matrix $[H]$ in Equation (9.12) with a block Toeplitz matrix $[H_{\mathrm{BT}}]$. Likewise, if the random process which generates the ensemble from which the image is drawn is a process which is stationary in the covariance statistic, and if the noise is also stationary in covariance, then the matrices $[\phi_f]$ and $[\phi_n]$ can also be replaced by block Toeplitz matrices. All the block Toeplitz matrices can then be approximated by circulant matrices, as used in Chapter 7 and developed in Appendices A and B.
3. Assuming the matrices $[H]$, $[\phi_f]$, and $[\phi_n]$ are approximated by circulants then, except for the nonlinear function s and the diagonal derivative matrix $[S_b]$, all the matrix operations in (9.19) can be computed as convolutions, hence implemented by FFT.

Given the ability to compute the matrix products with FFT operations, the following algorithm can be immediately derived for computing the MAP estimate by the gradient/steepest descent algorithm of (9.26):

1. Set $k = 0$. Construct an initial guess $\mathbf{f}_0$ (e.g., make a Wiener filter estimate for a linear approximation).
2. Compute $[H]\mathbf{f}_k$ by discrete Fourier transforming the PSF, multiplying by the DFT of $\mathbf{f}_k$, and taking the inverse DFT.
3. Using the sensor response function, compute $s\{[H]\mathbf{f}_k\}$ and subtract from the recorded image $\mathbf{g}$ to give $(\mathbf{g} - s\{[H]\mathbf{f}_k\}) = \mathbf{x}_k$.
4. Compute $[\phi_n]^{-1}\mathbf{x}_k$ by DFT's, analogous to step 2. Let $\mathbf{y}_k = [\phi_n]^{-1}\mathbf{x}_k$.
5. Multiply each component of $\mathbf{y}_k$ by the appropriate derivative in $[S_b]$; i.e.,

$$y'_{kj} = \left(\frac{\partial s}{\partial u}\bigg|_{u = \sum_i h_{ji} f_{ki}}\right) y_{kj}.$$

6. Compute $[H]^t[S_b]\mathbf{y}_k$ by DFT's, analogous to step 2.
7. Compute the difference between $\mathbf{f}_k$ and the ensemble mean $\bar{\mathbf{f}}$: $(\mathbf{f} - \bar{\mathbf{f}})$.
8. Compute $[\phi_f]^{-1}(\mathbf{f}_k - \bar{\mathbf{f}})$ by DFT, analogous to step 2.
9. Subtract the result of step 8 from the result of step 6. This quantity is $\nabla W(\mathbf{f})$. Multiply by α_k and subtract from $\mathbf{f}_k$ to generate the next estimate f_{k+1}. Set $k = k + 1$.
10. Repeat steps 2 through 9 until convergence is achieved.

Convergence can be measured by an appropriate measure:

$$\|\mathbf{f}_{k+1} - \mathbf{f}_k\| < \epsilon \tag{9.27}$$

is a criterion for convergence. The construction of the factor α_k can be made by a number of rules [Saaty and Bram (1964)]. The assumption of $\alpha_k = \alpha$ (constant) can be made and an optimum α chosen. Other rules for α based on experimental criteria are also known [Fukunaga (1972)].

Two additional comments are in order to conclude the discussion in this section. First, one advantage of the MAP technique formulated for the nonlinear problem in this section is the known relationship of the MAP estimate to other estimation criteria {e.g., MMSE [Van Trees (1967)]} and the use of error bounds (e.g., Cramer–Rao, Bhattacharyya) to develop performance measures on the estimation process. A general, nonlinear MMSE estimate for the image restoration problem can be conceived; the solution requires the computation of the conditional mean of the *a posteriori* density function, however, and is so difficult for the general case as to make the MAP estimate the practical and desirable alternative.

A second comment can be made concerning the algorithm of steps 1 through 10 above for minimizing the quadratic form through steepest descent computation on the gradient; the reader will notice the similarity in quadratic forms and gradient computation requirements in the algorithm of this section and the nonlinear programming problems discussed in Section 9.1. The use of FFT computations to calculate the gradients associated with space-invariant PSF's in the restoration models of Section 9.1 is established by the discussion of this section. Thus, for space-invariant PSF's it should be possible to develop FFT-based fast algorithms for the nonlinear programming problems discussed in Section 9.1. It should also be possible to combine such positive and bounded restorations with the Bayesian estimates discussed in this section. As the discussion in Section 9.1 indicates, the greatest difficulty in the nonlinear programming problem lies in determining the direction of steepest descent that is consistent with the boundary constraints. The gradient projection algorithm is such a method. It appears possible to formulate an FFT fast-algorithm version of the gradient projection method, to be used for bounded and positive Bayesian restorations of images; the successful formulation of some is one of the problems that the readers are invited to ponder.

9.3   Random-Grain Models

In Chapter 8 an image restoration scheme based upon maximum entropy was discussed. The result was a nonlinear restoration scheme that had the virtue of yielding a positive restoration. The motivation of that section was the demonstration that the linearized approximation to the maximum entropy solution was also interpretable in the light of the least-squares concepts of Chapter 8. In this section the underlying concepts of the maximum entropy model are examined in terms of a random-grain model and the resulting nonlinear restoration equations. The approach is similar to that of Frieden (1971); later extensions were made by Hershel (1971).

The basic model for the discussion in this section is that of the discrete–discrete formulation. Thus, image formation has the model

$$\mathbf{g} = [H]\mathbf{f} + \mathbf{n}.$$

It is assumed that there are N^2 total elements in the discrete representation of the object distribution.

Assume there is a fixed number, say P, of random grains (literally, grains of silver or quanta or radiant energy) that are allocated among the N^2 elements of the object distribution. Thus,

$$\sum_{j=1}^{N^2} f_j = P. \qquad (9.28)$$

Further, assume that the particles are distributed over the N^2 elements in the manner of identical but distinguishable particles, and any particle is equally likely to occupy any of the N^2 elements. (This obviously specifies, in the sense of statistical mechanics, an ensemble of particles governed by Maxwell–Boltzmann statistics; the use of the other assumptions, e.g., identical and indistinguishable particles and Fermi–Dirac statistics, is a reasonable extension that has not yet been explored.)

For noise, let the values n_j be random fluctuations about a positive mean:

$$n_j = N_j - B, \qquad (9.29)$$

where $B > 0$ and $N_j \geqq 0$ is a random variable. Obviously, n_j can be negative or positive. Assume the number of noise grains is also finite,

$$\sum_{j=1}^{N^2} N_j = N_0, \qquad (9.30)$$

and further assume that noise samples behave as identical but distinguishable particles, that any noise sample is equally likely to occur in any of the N^2 elements of the image sample $\mathbf{g}$, and that noise and image are statistically independent.

These assumptions represent what could be called *maximum ignorance* about both the object and noise statistics. Hershel showed that a suitable modification of (9.29), for example, would allow treatment of signal-dependent effects between the noise and the image.

A restoration scheme based upon the following objective can be stated: Find the noise and object grain distributions that are *most likely* to have formed the observed image values;

$$\mathbf{g} = [H]\mathbf{f} + \mathbf{n}. \tag{9.31}$$

Since noise and object grains are equally likely to occur in any of the N^2 sample elements, then the noise and object grain distribution is the one that can be formed from f_j and n_j in the maximum number of ways, given the image formation and recording constraint of Equation (9.31).

From simple combinatorial considerations, the number of ways an object f_1, $f_2, \ldots, f_{N^2}$ can be formed from a fixed number P of distinguishable grains is given by

$$W_f = \frac{P!}{\prod\limits_{j=1}^{N^2} f_j!}. \tag{9.32}$$

Likewise, the number of ways the noise array can be formed is

$$W_n = \frac{N_0!}{\prod\limits_{j=1}^{N^2} n_j!}. \tag{9.33}$$

Since signal and noise are statistically independent, then the maximum number of ways that both object and noise grains may be formed becomes

$$\underset{(\mathbf{f}, \mathbf{n})}{\text{maximize}} \quad W_f W_n \tag{9.34}$$

subject to the constraints on image formation and recording and the bounded particle constraint of (9.28).

Before formulating the complete maximization problem, consider the criterion of (9.34) in a simpler form. As before, the logarithm can be taken without changing the actual location of the maximum. Thus

$$\ln W_f W_n = \ln P! + \ln N_0! - \sum_{j=1}^{N^2} \ln f_j! - \sum_{j=1}^{N^2} \ln n_j!. \tag{9.35}$$

The first two terms are constants and can be neglected in the maximization process. Recall Stirling's approximation to the logarithm of a factorial,

$$\ln k! \cong k \ln k, \tag{9.36}$$

which holds for large n. The optimization problem can then be formulated:

$$\underset{(\mathbf{f}, \mathbf{n})}{\text{maximize}} \quad -\sum_{j=1}^{N^2} f_j \ln f_j - \sum_{j=1}^{N^2} n_j \ln n_j = -\mathbf{f}^t \ln \mathbf{f} - \mathbf{n}^t \ln \mathbf{n}$$

$$\text{subject to} \quad \mathbf{g} = [H]\mathbf{f} + \mathbf{n} \tag{9.37}$$

$$\text{and} \quad \mathbf{1}^t\mathbf{f} = P,$$

where $\mathbf{1}$ is a vector of all ones.

The optimization problem posed in Equation (9.37) has equality constraints and, hence, can be solved by Lagrange multipliers. The image formation constraints require a vector λ plus a scalar μ of Lagrange multipliers. The unconstrained minimization problem, which is equivalent to Equation (9.37), then becomes

$$\text{maximize} \quad -\mathbf{f}^t \ln \mathbf{f} - \mathbf{n}^t \ln \mathbf{n} + \lambda^t([H]\mathbf{f} + \mathbf{n} - \mathbf{g}) + \mu(\mathbf{1}^t\mathbf{f} - P). \quad (9.38)$$
$$(\mathbf{f}, \, \mathbf{n})$$

As before, (9.38) can be maximized by differentiating with respect to $\mathbf{f}, \mathbf{n}, \lambda$, and μ, setting the results equal to zero, and solving the simultaneous equations. Frieden refers to the resulting solution as the *maximum likelihood* estimate of the restored image. Note that the choice of the term *maximum likelihood* by Frieden is *not* consistent with the usage of the term by treatises in statistics, probability, and estimation theory [Van Trees (1967)], where *maximum likelihood* is used in conjunction with the *likelihood function* derived from a parametric description of an underlying probability function.[1]

Before proceeding to derive the restoration equations formally, it is of interest to review similarities between the criterion function of Equation (9.38) and the maximum entropy restoration discussed in Chapter 8. In Chapter 8 a heuristic definition of the quantity was given,

$$\mathbf{f}^t \ln \mathbf{f},$$

as the *entropy* associated with the original object distribution. In this section a maximum entropy criterion results from the use of the Stirling's approximation on a combinatorial criterion. The approximations are well-known in statistical mechanics, of course. Consequently, the maximum entropy restoration derived, and linearized in Chapter 8, can be treated as a particular combinatorial problem of the kind discussed in this section. Equation (9.39) can be derived as the approximation for maximizing the number of ways the object grains can be formed, subject to the constraint of a fixed least-squares residual:

$$\text{Maximize} \quad W_f = \frac{P!}{\prod\limits_{j=1}^{N^2} (f_j!)} \quad (9.39)$$

$$\text{Subject to} \quad (\mathbf{g} - [H]\mathbf{f})^t(\mathbf{g} - [H]\mathbf{f}) = e.$$

The underlying combinatorial nature of the random-grain model is another reason why the term *maximum likelihood* seems an unfortunate choice of terms to describe this method; hence within this work the term *random-grain* model will be used.

Differentiating (9.38) first with respect to $\mathbf{f}$ and then with respect to $\mathbf{n}$ yields

$$-\mathbf{1} - \ln \mathbf{f} + [H]^t\lambda + \mu\mathbf{1} = 0,$$
$$-\mathbf{1} - \ln \mathbf{n} + \lambda = 0.$$

These equations can be rearranged such that the estimates of the restoration are

$$\hat{\mathbf{f}} = \exp{(-\mathbf{1} + [H]^t\lambda + \mu\mathbf{1})}$$
$$\hat{\mathbf{n}} = \exp{(-\mathbf{1} + \lambda)}, \quad (9.40)$$

---

[1]The definition of $n = N - B$ in (9.29) can be substituted in (9.39) and the solution carried out with $N - B$ instead of n. Since (9.29) is a definition chosen for positivity, it can be ignored; the positivity of n is seen in Equation (9.42).

which must be solved along with the simultaneous linear equations (from differentiating with respect to λ and μ):

$$\mathbf{g} = [H]\mathbf{\hat{f}} + \mathbf{n}$$
$$P = \mathbf{1}^t\mathbf{\hat{f}}.$$

(9.41)

Substituting from (9.40) into (9.41) yields

$$\mathbf{g} = [H]\exp{(-\mathbf{1} + [H]^t\lambda + \mu\mathbf{1})} + \exp{(-\mathbf{1} + \lambda)}$$
$$P = \mathbf{1}^t(\exp{(-\mathbf{1} + [H]^t\lambda + \mu\mathbf{1})}).$$

(9.42)

Equation (9.42) constitutes a set of $N^2 + 1$ nonlinear equations in the $N^2 + 1$ un-
knowns λ, μ. Once a solution is obtained to (9.42), then the λ and μ are used in (9.40)
to construct $\mathbf{\hat{f}}$ and $\mathbf{\hat{n}}$. Note that in (9.40) the solution $\mathbf{f}$ is constructed from the exponential operating on linear combinations of the rows of the PSF matrix.[2]

The solution of the equations of (9.42) is not trivial (nonlinear solutions seldom
are in *any* field of endeavor). Frieden originally solved the equations of (9.42) by means
of an Newton–Raphson technique. If a system of nonlinear equations is expressed in
the form

$$t\{\mathbf{x}\} = \mathbf{0},$$

(9.43)

where $\mathbf{t}$ is a vector function with components of the vector $\mathbf{x}$, then the Newton–Raphson iteration to find the solution to (9.43) is given by

$$\mathbf{x}_{k+1} = \mathbf{x}_k - [J(\mathbf{x}_k)]^{-1}t\{\mathbf{x}_k\},$$

(9.44)

where $[J(\mathbf{x}_k)]$ is the Jacobian matrix of partial derivatives,

$$\{[J]\}_{ij} = \frac{\partial t_i}{\partial x_j},$$

evaluated at $\mathbf{x} = \mathbf{x}_k$. Frieden's solution by Newton–Raphson methods was made
possible by the small number of points in the one-dimensional examples chosen to
demonstrate the method. Detailed inspection of (9.44) and (9.42) reveals that for a
realistic digital image, say a 500×500 image, the construction and inversion of the
Jacobian matrix becomes prohibitive. Hence, the application of Frieden's method to
real digital images has not been made, except small images with separable point-spread
functions.

The discussion in Section 9.2, concerning the MAP estimate by minimization of
a quadratic form, pointed out the use of steepest descent gradient techniques to compute the minimum. Such techniques are also applicable to the general case posed by
Frieden's method. Let Equation (9.38) be written in terms of an objective function
W, which it is desired to maximize:

$$\begin{array}{c} \text{Maximize} \\ (\mathbf{f}, \mathbf{n}, \lambda, \mu) \end{array} \quad W(\mathbf{f}, \mathbf{n}, \lambda, \mu) = \mathbf{f}^t \ln \mathbf{f} - \mathbf{n}^t \ln \mathbf{n}$$
$$+ \lambda^t([H]\mathbf{f} + \mathbf{n} - \mathbf{g}) + \mu(\mathbf{1}^t\mathbf{f} - P).$$

(9.45)

Formulation of a steepest ascent (gradient) scheme, in the form of Equation (9.26),
is direct. There are more variables to solve for than in (9.26), of course. Letting the
vector $\mathbf{x}$ denote the collection of variables,

---

[2]Note that the exponential guarantees that (9.40) is also a positive restoration.

$$\mathbf{x} = \begin{bmatrix} \mathbf{f} \\ \mathbf{n} \\ \lambda \\ \mu \end{bmatrix},$$

Maximizing W by the iteration,

$$\mathbf{x}_{k+1} = \mathbf{x}_k + \boldsymbol{\alpha}_k \nabla W(\mathbf{x}_k), \tag{9.46}$$

where the sign of the gradient term is positive because a maximum is desired [cf. with (9.26)]. In the case where the PSF matrix [H] arises from a space-invariant point-spread function, then the gradients can be computed by FFT operations, which results in an implementation of Frieden's method by an algorithm which is within the capability of current digital computers.

Likewise, if the maximum entropy model of Chapter 8 is reexamined, then it may be solved, without recourse to linearization, by the use of FFT computations to generate gradients in an iterative scheme of the form of (9.46).

Hershel's work is an extension of the basic method of Frieden and generates the restoration in a form analogous to Equation (9.42). Hershel also extensively analyzed the relation between various linear approximations to Equation (9.42) and the nonlinear equations themselves and treated a number of special cases for images and PSF's. The general solution of equations such as (9.42) was proposed as a problem in successive approximations by Hershel, who formulated the solution to (9.42) by a linear approximation in Taylor series and then computed a series of linear estimates. The convergence of the processes such as (9.26) and/or (9.46) to the solution can be demonstrated under quite general assumptions [Saaty and Bram (1964)] and makes the solution by gradient methods appear even more attractive, except for the slow convergence typical with gradient methods.

This section is closed with a comment on a general perspective for viewing the methods of this section and the previous one. In Sections 9.2 and 9.3, the solution of certain nonlinear image restoration problems was emphasized by directly solving an associated optimization problem. The approach is the direct product of viewing image restoration in the framework of a problem lacking a unique solution and thereby requiring an optimization criterion for selecting among the many candidate solutions. Further, the direct solution approach has been seen to provide fast computation algorithms, for space-invariant PSF's, by using the FFT to compute the necessary gradient iteration steps. This emphasis on direct solution and FFT gradient computations is new and discussed here for the first time. It seems logical to expect, however, that the optimization framework for image restoration will become widespread. Likewise it is expected that even more complex nonlinear image restoration schemes may be solved in the future by the use of fast algorithms to solve directly an image restoration/optimization problem by means of FFT computations to carry out iterative gradient procedures. The fruition of such methods may well be by hybrid/optical digital devices to carry out such restorations, with optical processors to perform the required spatial filtering operations and digital computers to control the iteration process.

9.4 Optimal Recursive Processing

The application of recursive estimation methods are discussed in this section. A problem that could be legitimately described as a *degenerate* image restoration problem, inasmuch as the PSF will be assumed to be a Dirac function, will be discussed. Given the discrete–discrete model

$$g = f + n, \tag{9.47}$$

in terms of the actual sampled image matrices,

$$g(x, y) = f(x, y) + n(x, y), \tag{9.48}$$

$$g(x, y) = s\{f(x, y)\} + n(x, y). \tag{9.49}$$

The estimation of f is the classical problem of *smoothing*.

One of the most significant developments in filtering theory in recent years has been the theory of Kalman and Bucy [Van Trees (1967)], which demonstrated the computation of optimal filters for state estimation and smoothing in a recursive form. The extension of these methods to two dimensions is possible, and preliminary work has been reported by Nahi (1972) and Habibi (1972). The approach in this section will follow that taken by Habibi.

It is desired to estimate $f(x + 1, y + 1)$ as a function of its immediate upper left neighbors and the value of the recorded image at those points. Thus, the estimate will be computed recursively in the form

$$f(x + 1, y + 1) = a_1 f(x + 1, y) + a_2 f(x, y + 1)$$
$$+ a_3 f(x, y) + a_4 g(x, y). \tag{9.50}$$

Obviously, the problem is to find the coefficients a_i for some set of reasonable assumptions about the statistics of the image $g(x, y)$ and the initial object distribution $f(x, y)$. Because of the obvious difficulties with the nonlinearity in transforming the statistics of f, consider first the linear model in (9.4). It will be assumed that the statistics of f are generated by a horizontally separable Markov process, with parameters ρ_x and ρ_y specifying the horizontal and vertical correlation, respectively (*cf.* the discussion in Chapter 3). The object f is assumed generated from

$$f(x + 1, y + 1) = \rho_x f(x + 1, y) + \rho_y f(x, y + 1) - \rho_x \rho_y f(x, y)$$
$$+ \sqrt{(1 - \rho_x^2)(1 - \rho_y)^2} u(x, y), \tag{9.51}$$

where the u's are uncorrelated random variables with the same variance as the picture elements. The demonstration of (9.51) is by factorization of the spectral density [Habibi (1972)]. Equations (9.50) and (9.51) constitute the model of the image and its additive noise.

It is well-known [Nahi (1965)] that the principle of orthogonality of the estimation error determines the minimum mean-square-error estimate. Thus, an estimate is sought such that

$$E\{[\hat{f}(x + 1, y + 1) - f(x + 1, y + 1)]g(x, y)\} = 0. \tag{9.52}$$

By substituting for f from (9.51) and for $\hat{f}$ from (9.50) it is possible to show that

$$
\begin{aligned}
a_1 &= \rho_x, \\
a_2 &= \rho_y, \\
a_3 &= [\rho_x \rho_y + a_4],
\end{aligned}
\tag{9.53}
$$

leaving only a_4 to be specified [Habibi (1972)]. By similar manipulations it is possible to specify a_4 by the relation

$$
a_4 = \frac{\rho_x \phi_{10} + \rho_y \phi_{01} - \rho_x \rho_y \phi_{00}}{\phi_{00} + \sigma_n^2},
\tag{9.54}
$$

where σ_n^2 is the noise variance and

$$
[\phi] = \mathcal{E}\{(\mathbf{f} - \hat{\mathbf{f}})(\mathbf{f} - \hat{\mathbf{f}})'\}
\tag{9.55}
$$

is the error covariance matrix.

Readers familiar with the Kalman filter will recognize the relations between the one- and two-dimensional Kalman filters, including the orthogonality principle and the importance of the error covariance matrix in computing the recursive estimate. Indeed, just as in the one-dimensional case, it is possible to show for the recursive two-dimensional estimator that the error covariance matrix can be evaluated by a recursive computation [see Habibi (1972) for details]. The recursive evaluation requires attention to boundary effects at the edge of the image but can be shown to behave well under reasonable approximations.

No further discussion will be given for the actual formalism of deriving the recursive estimators that can be derived for more general two-dimensional autoregressive random processes. The interest in the remaining discussion is in nonlinear effects that can be associated with the estimate of (9.50).

The difficulty with the process derived above is not in the linear estimate (9.50) but with the assumed statistical model for the image (9.51). Recalling the discussion in Chapter 3, it is seen that (9.51) encompasses all the degrees of freedom of the image into just two parameters, the horizontal and vertical correlations ρ_x and ρ_y. Demonstrations of the process of (9.50) on real images show disappointing results [see Habibi (1972)]. It is tempting to surmise that part of the disappointment in such results is due to the risky nature of the assumption that two parameters, ρ_x and ρ_y, can embody the features of interest in a typical image. A better assumption would be that there are different regions in an image where different correlation coefficients would apply.

For example, consider the image in Figure 9.4. It is obvious that the grass field, in which the mother and child are sitting, has greatly different horizontal and vertical correlations than the tree-covered hillside in the background. Likewise, the uniform sides of the apartment building in the background are so featureless as to possess almost no rectangular correlation at all. One can carry out a similar exercise on virtually any picture that comes to hand.

Given the difference in statistics in different regions of the image, the natural thought is to develop a method based upon (9.50) in which the horizontal and vertical correlation statistics change with position in the image. The recursive process of Equations (9.50) and (9.53) through (9.55) can be started anywhere, provided the boundary

Figure 9.4   Picture of woman and child in field.

conditions are specified. Thus, the boundary conditions could be specified at natural segments in the image where the correlation parameters change from one set to another. The result is an estimation process that is *linear* within segments with constant correlation parameters but is *nonlinear* over the whole image because of the switching from one set of correlation parameters to another across different image segments.

This concept of switching statistics is simple to state but difficult to implement. For example, how should the image segments, and the corresponding change in statistics, be implemented? By actually estimating the statistics as the image is processed or by examining the image prior to processing and developing segments from the examination? If the latter choice is made, then should the examination be made by a human observer, who interprets the segments according to features of interest? Or should an automatic method of picture segmentation be used? This course may prove to be an even more difficult problem because it requires substantial progress in image pattern recognition; methods of automatic picture segmentation using syntactical and/or statistical procedures are far from being failure-proof [Kanal (1974)].

The difficulties of implementing a recursive estimate that switches its correlation statistics, as the image demands, are so great that not much has been done in actually processing images according to such schemes, the exception being the results achieved by Nahi and Habibi (1973).

From a more general viewpoint, the recursive methods discussed in this chapter are intriguing. First, much less is known about the structure and design of two-dimensional Kalman filters. Second, certain properties of images (e.g., positivity) present additional difficulties in Kalman filter design, which usually are based upon zero-mean Gaussian statistics. Third, the Kalman filter, in its most general form, is a space-varying filter and thus offers the potential of treating problems where space-variant PSF's are involved. By the time the state of two-dimensional Kalman filter processing of images is as completely developed as Fourier processing techniques, we may find the Kalman filter to be an even more powerful tool. The computational speed of the Kalman filter [examine the small number of add and multiply operations in (9.51) and (9.53) through (9.55)] has the potential of making it the most attractive of all processing schemes, provided the problems and uncertainties discussed in this section can be resolved. It is for such reasons that this section has briefly introduced the reader to optimal recursive processing.

9.5 Nonlinear Eigenspace Computations[3]

This chapter has concentrated on general algorithms that the authors feel might be applicable to image restoration under nonlinear conditions. Needless to say many of the nonlinear (as well as linear) programming methods put forth will be computationally cumbersome for images of any respectable size. One possible means of reducing such computations is by processing in the eigenspace of the distortion. This means that all nonlinear programming will be implemented in the SVD space of the PSF matrix, allowing the nonlinear programming variables to be decoupled from one another, thereby intuitively minimizing the crosstalk effect of variable adjustment in constrained restoration.

To pursue this point further, consider the bounded restoration problem whereby the restored object $\hat{\mathbf{f}}$ is constrained to be componentwise within finite energy bounds; i.e.,

$$f_i \geqq 0 \qquad (i = 1, \ldots, N^2) \tag{9.56}$$

$$f_i \leqq A \qquad (i = 1, \ldots, N^2). \tag{9.57}$$

[3]This section is mainly due to the work of Adler (1976) in research connected with a doctoral dissertation.

Using the noise-free linear imaging model, the objective function can be reformulated to find $\hat{\mathbf{f}}$ that minimizes

$$W(\mathbf{f}) = \|\mathbf{g} - [H]\mathbf{f}\|^2 \tag{9.58}$$

subject to $\mathbf{f}$ being componentwise bounded as in Equations (9.56) and (9.57). Pursuing the minimization in the SVD space, it may be shown that

$$W(\mathbf{f}) = \|\mathbf{g} - [U][\Lambda][V]^t\mathbf{f}\|^2 \tag{9.59a}$$

or

$$W(\mathbf{f}) = \|\mathbf{g}\|^2 - 2\mathbf{g}^t[U][\Lambda][V]^t\mathbf{f} + \|[U][\Lambda][V]^t\mathbf{f}\|^2 \tag{9.59b}$$

and in summation notation

$$W(\mathbf{f}) = \|\mathbf{g}\|^2 - 2\sum_{i=1}^{N^2} \lambda_i(\mathbf{g}^t\mathbf{u}_i)(\mathbf{v}_i^t\mathbf{f}) + \sum_{i=1}^{N^2} \lambda_i^2(\mathbf{v}_i^t\mathbf{f})^2. \tag{9.59c}$$

Here the terms in parentheses are themselves scalars. Since $(\mathbf{v}_i^t\mathbf{f})$ is unknown, then it can be represented by the variable α_i. Consequently the objective function becomes

$$W(\mathbf{f}) = \|\mathbf{g}\|^2 - 2\sum_{i=1}^{N^2} \lambda_i\alpha_i(\mathbf{g}^t\mathbf{u}_i) + \sum_{i=1}^{N^2} (\lambda_i\alpha_i)^2. \tag{9.59d}$$

The result is a quadratic programming problem in the variables α_i. By examining the form of the objective function in Equation (9.59d), it is seen that the variable α_i always exists with λ_i, the singular values of the PSF matrix. Thus, intuitively optimization is really an adjustment (filter) of the singular values subject to a bounded restoration constraint. Taking partial derivatives with respect to α_i and setting equal to zero, a gradient algorithm can be used in a nonlinear programming environment [Fiacco and McCormick (1968)] for optimization. Thus

$$\frac{\partial W(\mathbf{f})}{\partial \alpha_i} = 0 = -2\lambda_i(\mathbf{g}^t\mathbf{u}_i) + 2\lambda_i^2\alpha_i \quad (i = 1, \ldots, N^2), \tag{9.60}$$

and for the unconstrained problem

$$\alpha_i = \lambda_i^{-1}(\mathbf{u}_i^t\mathbf{g}). \tag{9.61}$$

It is noted that this is just the pseudo-inverse solution (if reciprocation of zero singular values is avoided). Therefore a lower bound to the constrained minimization problem is the pseudo-inverse solution.

Intuitively, the algorithm can be described using variables α_i that are decoupled (in the SVD space) for nonlinear optimization. Computational implementation becomes quite appealing for two reasons. First, in actuality it is unnecessary to use all $N^2\alpha_i$ variables due to the singularity of the PSF matrix as well as an aide in computational speed by allowing only those α_i near i close to singularity to be variable. In addition a good initial condition for the nonlinear programming algorithm is $\alpha_i = \lambda_i^{-1}$. Second, the constraint conditions need not be N^2 in number but may be a very small subset of that. Specifically if a large number of pixels go out of range in an iterative restoration environment (as in Section 8.3) due to nearing singularity, then only a small number of these pixels are needed as constraints. Adjustment of one or two α_i

variables will usually compensate for all out-of-range pixels. In the eigenspace of the distortion, where the α_i variables are being adjusted, a single variable affects the entire N^2 point restored object.

The algorithm described in this section has been implemented on imagery with the following results. The reconstructed picture was always a good picture; i.e., a mathematically correct but visually worthless result was never computed. The values for α_i were always close to λ_i^{-1} and in all cases $0 < \alpha_i < 2\lambda_i^{-1}$. The minimum value of the constrained problem has a lower bound, namely the minimum value of the unconstrained problem (i.e., the pseudo-inverse). In cases where there were few constrained points, the minimum value was very close to its lower bound. While these results are still somewhat preliminary, they are encouraging.

APPENDICES

Appendix A

Space-Invariant Point-Spread-Function Matrices

Systems characterized by space-invariant point-spread functions will be considered. When sampled and structured as linear systems of equations, the resulting matrix properties make possible a very elegant analysis. To provide a complete understanding of these properties in two-dimensional entities, it is initially desirable to derive the corresponding properties in one dimension.

The one-dimensional convolution is given by

$$g(x) = \int_{-\infty}^{\infty} h(x - \xi)f(\xi)\,d\xi. \tag{A.1}$$

It will be assumed that the original object distribution and the point-spread function are of finite extent. Without loss of generality, it can also be assumed that the object f and h are both zero for $\xi < 0$. Thus, Equation (A.1) becomes, under these assumptions,

$$g(x) = \int_{0}^{x_{max}} h(x - \xi)f(\xi)\,d\xi. \tag{A.2}$$

We sample Equation (A.2) to arrive at a discrete approximation [Ralston (1965)]:

$$g(x) = \sum_{\xi=0}^{N-1} h(x - \xi)f(\xi), \qquad (\text{for } x = 0, 1, 2, \ldots, M + N - 2). \tag{A.3}$$

211

Using Figure A.1, it is simple to show (A.3) as a matrix equation. By inspection,

$$
\begin{bmatrix}
g(0) \\
g(1) \\
\cdot \\
\cdot \\
\cdot \\
g(j) \\
\cdot \\
\cdot \\
\cdot \\
g(M+N-2)
\end{bmatrix}
$$

$$
=
\begin{bmatrix}
h(0) & & & & & & \\
h(1) & h(0) & & & & & \\
\cdot & \cdot & & \cdot & & & 0 \\
\cdot & & \cdot & & \cdot & & \\
\cdot & & & \cdot & & \cdot & \\
h(M-1) & & & \cdot & h(1) & & h(0) \\
& \cdot & & & \cdot & & \\
0 & & \cdot & & & \cdot & \\
& & & \cdot & h(M-1) & \cdot & & h(M-2) \\
& & & & & \cdot & & h(M-1)
\end{bmatrix}
\begin{bmatrix}
f(0) \\
f(1) \\
\cdot \\
\cdot \\
\cdot \\
f(N-1)
\end{bmatrix}
\tag{A.4}
$$

or in matrix vector form

$$\mathbf{g} = [H]\mathbf{f}, \tag{A.5}$$

where $\mathbf{f}$ is an $N \times 1$ vector, $\mathbf{g}$ is an $M + N - 1$ vector, and the matrix $[H]$ is of size $(M + N - 1) \times N$.

The development of Equation (A.4) is based upon finite sizes for the sequences $\mathbf{f}$ and $\mathbf{h}$. It is not always realistic, however, that the sequence $\mathbf{f}$ attributed to the original object distribution be finite. In many cases the scene is of far greater physical extent than the area capable of being imaged and recorded. For example, if a picture is blurred by motion of a camera, the image recorded on film is just a section out of a blurred image of the object field that could have been seen with a wide-angle lens.

In Figure A.2, a sequence $\mathbf{g}$, consisting of digital samples from a section of a large blurred function, is shown. The first $M - 1$ samples of $\mathbf{g}$ are affected by values of $\mathbf{f}$ that lie outside the interval from which the segment of $\mathbf{g}$ was cut. The shading indicates samples of $\mathbf{g}$ that are affected by the shaded samples of $\mathbf{f}$. A total of P samples are in the segment $\mathbf{g}$. As before, M is the number of samples in the PSF. The $P + M - 1$ samples from the sequence $\mathbf{f}$ are involved in the convolution with the PSF to form the sequence $\mathbf{g}$. As before, the process can be formulated in a set of linear equations. Calling the first point of $\mathbf{g}$ as the zero point, it is seen that

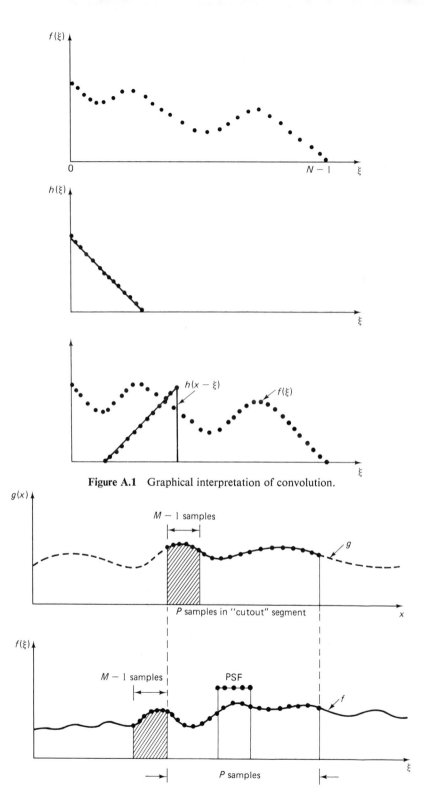

Figure A.1 Graphical interpretation of convolution.

Figure A.2 Relations between f and g when g is a segment cut out from a larger sequence.

$$
\begin{bmatrix} g(0) \\ g(1) \\ \cdot \\ \cdot \\ \cdot \\ g(P-1) \end{bmatrix}
$$

$$
= \begin{bmatrix} h(M-1) & h(M-2) & \cdots & h(1) & h(0) & & \\ & h(M-1) & \cdot & \cdot & \cdot & h(1) & h(0) & 0 \\ & & \cdot & & & & \cdot \\ 0 & & & \cdot & & & & \cdot \\ & & & h(M-1) & \cdot & \cdot & \cdot & h(1) & h(0) \end{bmatrix}
\begin{bmatrix} f(-M+1) \\ f(-M+2) \\ \cdot \\ \cdot \\ f(-1) \\ f(0) \\ f(1) \\ \cdot \\ \cdot \\ \cdot \\ f(P-1) \end{bmatrix}
\quad \text{(A.6)}
$$

Equation (A.6) is expressible in a vector-matrix form:

$$\mathbf{g}_s = [H_s]\mathbf{f}_s, \tag{A.7}$$

where the subscript s indicates a *segment* from a large sequence.

Consider the relationship between Equations (A.4) and (A.6). First, recognize that the matrix $[H_s]$ can be partitioned such that the first $M-1$ columns are separate. This gives

$$
\begin{bmatrix} g(0) \\ g(1) \\ \cdot \\ \cdot \\ g(P-1) \end{bmatrix}
=
\begin{bmatrix} h(0) & & & & \\ h(1) & h(0) & & & \\ & \cdot & & & 0 \\ & & \cdot & & \\ h(M-1) & \cdots & & h(0) & \\ 0 & \cdot & & & \cdot \\ & & h(M-1) & \cdots & h(1) & h(0) \end{bmatrix}
\begin{bmatrix} f(0) \\ f(1) \\ \cdot \\ \cdot \\ f(P-1) \end{bmatrix}
$$

$$
+
\begin{bmatrix} h(M-1) & \cdot & \cdot & \cdot & h(2) & h(1) \\ & h(M-1) & \cdot & \cdot & \cdot & h(1) \\ & & \cdot & & & \\ 0 & & & \cdot & & \\ & & & & h(M-1) \end{bmatrix}
\begin{bmatrix} f(-M+1) \\ f(-M+2) \\ \cdot \\ \cdot \\ f(-1) \end{bmatrix},
\quad \text{(A.8)}
$$

which can be written as

$$\mathbf{g}_s = [H_T]\mathbf{f}_1 + [H_1]\mathbf{f}_2, \tag{A.9}$$

where $[H_T]$ is a $P \times P$ matrix, $\mathbf{f}_1$ is a $P \times 1$ vector, $[H_1]$ is a $P \times (M-1)$ matrix, and $\mathbf{f}_2$ is an $(M-1) \times 1$ vector. To relate (A.8), which is a rewritten form of (A.6), to

(A.4), let the vector $\mathbf{f}_2 = \mathbf{0}$; i.e., elements $f(-M+1), f(-M+2), \ldots, f(-1)$ are all equal to zero. Then

$$\mathbf{g}_s = [H_T]\mathbf{f}_1. \tag{A.10}$$

Now in (A.10), we choose P to be equal to $M+N-1$. Then if the last $M-1$ elements of $\mathbf{f}_1$ are equal to zero,

$$\mathbf{g}_s = [H \mid H_2]\begin{bmatrix} \mathbf{f} \\ \mathbf{0} \end{bmatrix}, \tag{A.11}$$

where partition $[H_2]$ consists of the last $M-1$ columns of H_T and is of size $P \times (M-1)$, partition $[H]$ is the same matrix $[H]$ as in (A.4), and $\mathbf{f}$ is the same vector as in (A.4).

Equation (A.11) shows that the finite extent problem in (A.4) is just a special case of the more general segment problem of Equation (A.6).

Examine the $P \times P$ matrix $[H_T]$ in (A.9):

$$[H_T] = \begin{bmatrix} h(0) & & & & & \\ h(1) & h(0) & & & & \\ \vdots & & \ddots & & \mathbf{0} & \\ \vdots & \ddots & & \ddots & & \\ h(M-1) & \cdots & & h(1) & h(0) & \\ \vdots & & \ddots & & & \ddots \\ \mathbf{0} & & \ddots & & & \ddots \\ & & & h(M-1) & \cdots & h(0) \end{bmatrix} \tag{A.12}$$

Since $[H_T]$ is a square matrix and satisfies the property that

$$[H_T]_{jk} = [H_T]_{mn} \qquad \text{if } j - k = m - n,$$

then $[H_T]$ is a Toeplitz matrix or finite Toeplitz form.

A matrix that has useful properties and is closely related to $[H_T]$ is the *circulant*. A circulant matrix demonstrates the property that each row is a circular right shift of the row above it.

The first row is a circular right shift of the last. A circulant can be constructed from $[H_T]$ by the simple addition of elements to the portions of $[H_T]$ that are zeros. The circulant $[H_c]$ constructed from $[H_T]$ is

$$[H_c] = \begin{bmatrix} h(0) & h(M-1) & \cdot & \cdot & \cdot & h(1) \\ h(1) & h(0) & h(M-1) & \cdot & \cdot & h(2) \\ \vdots & \ddots & & \mathbf{0} & & \vdots \\ \vdots & & \ddots & & & \vdots \\ h(M-1) & & & h(0) & & \cdot \\ \vdots & \ddots & & & \ddots & \\ \mathbf{0} & & \ddots & & & \ddots \\ & h(M-1) & \cdot & & \cdot & h(0) \end{bmatrix} \cdot \tag{A.13}$$

It may be noted that the first row can be created by a circular (end-around) right shift of the last row. The second row is a circular right shift of the first row, and so on.

Consider now the two-dimensional convolution

$$g(x, y) = \int_{-\infty}^{\infty} \int_{-\infty}^{\infty} h(x - \xi, y - \eta) f(\xi, \eta) \, d\xi \, d\eta. \tag{A.14}$$

Sampling this equation for a discrete approximation,

$$g(x, y) = \sum_{\xi=0}^{M-1} \sum_{\eta=0}^{N-1} h(x - \xi, y - \eta) f(\xi, \eta), \tag{A.15}$$

where it was further assumed that f is from a matrix of size $M \times N$, h is a matrix of size $J \times K$, and g is therefore of size $(M + J - 1) \times (N + K - 1)$.

The convolution process from Figure A.3 and Equation (A.15) aligns rows of the PSF matrix with the image matrix and forms the sums of products. A lexicographic ordering of the image matrix creates a vector $\mathbf{f}$ by stacking the rows of $\mathbf{f}$ into a column:

$$\mathbf{f} = \begin{bmatrix} f(0, 0) \\ f(0, 1) \\ \cdot \\ \cdot \\ \cdot \\ f(0, N - 1) \\ f(1, 0) \\ \cdot \\ \cdot \\ \cdot \\ f(M - 1, N - 1) \end{bmatrix} . \tag{A.16}$$

From inspection of (A.15) and Figure A.3, explicit equations can be written for the elements of lexicographically ordered vector $\mathbf{g}$. Thus

$$\begin{bmatrix} g(0, 0) \\ g(0, 1) \\ \cdot \\ \cdot \\ \cdot \\ g(0, K + N - 1) \end{bmatrix}$$

$$= \begin{bmatrix} h(0, 0) & & & & & \\ h(0, 1) & h(0, 0) & & & \mathbf{0} & \\ \cdot & \cdot & \cdot & & & \\ \cdot & & \cdot & & & \\ h(0, K-1) & \cdots & h(0, 0) & & & \\ & \cdot & & \cdot & & \\ & & \cdot & & \cdot & \\ & & & \cdot & & h(0, 0) \\ \mathbf{0} & & & & \cdot & \cdot \\ & & & & & h(0, K-1) \end{bmatrix} \begin{bmatrix} f(0, 0) \\ f(0, 1) \\ \cdot \\ \cdot \\ \cdot \\ f(0, N - 1) \end{bmatrix}, \tag{A.17}$$

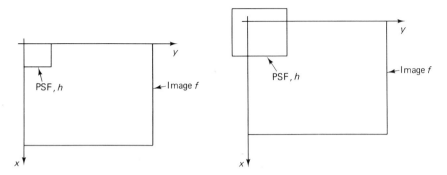

Figure A.3   Matrix convolution in sampled images.

which describes the first partition of **g** in terms of the first partition of **f** and the first row of the PSF matrix. The matrix is of size $(M + N - 1) \times N$. Likewise, the first row of the PSF matrix slides by the second, third, etc., rows of **f**. A generalization of (A.17) follows:

$$
\begin{bmatrix} \mathbf{g}_0 \\ \mathbf{g}_1 \\ \mathbf{g}_2 \\ \cdot \\ \cdot \\ \cdot \\ \mathbf{g}_{J+M-1} \end{bmatrix}
=
\begin{bmatrix}
[H_0] & & & & & \\
[H_1] & [H_0] & & & \mathbf{0} & \\
\cdot & \cdot & \cdot & & & \\
\cdot & & \cdot & & & \\
[H_{J-1}] & \cdots & [H_0] & & & \\
\cdot & & \cdot & & & \\
& & & [H_0] & & \\
& \mathbf{0} & & \cdot & & \\
& & & \cdot & & \\
& & & [H_{J-1}] & &
\end{bmatrix}
\begin{bmatrix} \mathbf{f}_0 \\ \mathbf{f}_1 \\ \cdot \\ \cdot \\ \mathbf{f}_{M-1} \end{bmatrix},
\qquad (A.18)
$$

where the rows of the lexicographic orderings, stacked as columns, are subscripted:

$$
\mathbf{g}_j = \begin{bmatrix} g(j, 0) \\ g(j, 1) \\ \cdot \\ \cdot \\ \cdot \\ g(j, K + N - 1) \end{bmatrix}; \qquad \mathbf{f}_k = \begin{bmatrix} f(k, 0) \\ f(k, 1) \\ \cdot \\ \cdot \\ \cdot \\ f(k, N - 1) \end{bmatrix}. \qquad (A.19)
$$

The matrices $[H_j]$ in (A.18) are each of size $(K + N - 1) \times N$, and each is formed from the jth row of the PSF matrix h according to

$$[H_j] = \begin{bmatrix} h(j,0) & & & & & \\ h(j,1) & h(j,0) & & & & 0 \\ \cdot & \cdot & & & & \\ \cdot & & \cdot & & & \\ \cdot & & & \cdot & & \\ h(j,K-1) & \cdots & h(j,0) & & & \\ & \cdot & & \cdot & & \cdot \\ & & & & h(j,0) & \\ & & & & & \cdot \\ 0 & & & \cdot & & \cdot \\ & & & & & h(j,K-1) \end{bmatrix} \qquad (A.20)$$

Finally, (A.18) can be written in the form

$$\mathbf{g} = [H_B]\mathbf{f}, \qquad (A.21)$$

where $[H_B]$ is a matrix of size $(J + M - 1)(K + N - 1) \times MN$, termed herein as a *block-matrix* generalization of (A.4).

The two-dimensional generalization of Equation (A.6) is direct. As seen in Figure A.4, a segment may be extracted from a larger two-dimensional scene. By analogy to Figure A.2, the shaded area in **f** represents values that contribute to the segment **g**, and the shaded areas in **g** are the corresponding values affected.

The reader may note that the shaded areas in Figure A.4 border only the upper left edges of the rectangular segments **f** and **g**. The same is true in Figure A.2. This is due to the assumption that places the point-spread function such that it is convenient since it allows the lower limits of the sums in Equation (A.15) to be zero. The resultant output of the convolution at (x, y) is affected only by values of **f** to the left and/or above the values x, y. A real image formation system is not likely to behave in this fashion since the PSF is centered about the origin in typical optical analysis [Goodman (1968)]. The difference between an origin-centered PSF and the assumption used above is trivial, it constitutes only a shift of the image **g**. Digital filters that are not causal, i.e., possess origin-centered impulse responses, can be computed at the expense (usually trivial) of having the output shifted and delayed.

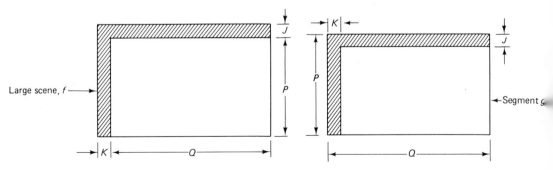

Figure A.4   Two-dimensional analog to Figure A.2.

Generalizing by inspection of Figure A.4, the one-dimensional results yield

$$
\begin{bmatrix} \mathbf{g}_0 \\ \mathbf{g}_1 \\ \cdot \\ \cdot \\ \cdot \\ \mathbf{g}_{P-1} \end{bmatrix} = \begin{bmatrix} [H'_{J-1}] & [H'_{J-2}] & \cdots & [H'_0] & & \\ & [H'_{J-1}] & \cdot & \cdot & \cdot & [H'_0] & 0 \\ & & \cdot & & & & \cdot \\ 0 & & & \cdot & & & \cdot \\ & & & & [H'_{J-1}] & \cdots & [H'_0] \end{bmatrix} \begin{bmatrix} \mathbf{f}'_{J+1} \\ \cdot \\ \cdot \\ \cdot \\ \mathbf{f}'_1 \\ \mathbf{f}'_0 \\ \cdot \\ \cdot \\ \cdot \\ \mathbf{f}'_{P-1} \end{bmatrix},
\tag{A.22}
$$

where each $[H'_j]$ matrix is of size $Q \times (Q + K - 1)$ with the same general form as in (A.6). Each row partition in $\mathbf{g}$ is of length Q with P partitions for a total length of PQ for vector $\mathbf{g}$. There are $P + J - 1$ partitions in $\mathbf{f}$, but each partition is of length $Q + K - 1$. In vector-matrix form,

$$
\mathbf{g}_s = [H'_{BS}]\mathbf{f}'_s.
\tag{A.23}
$$

The block segment matrix $[H'_{BS}]$ is of size $PQ \times [(P + J - 1)(Q + K - 1)]$.

It is obvious that (A.22), (A.23) can be partitioned into equations of the form of (A.8), (A.10). The final form of the partitioning is not so simple as in one dimension. The two-dimensional structure means that the partition must operate within each of the $[H'_j]$ partitions in (A.22) as well as between them. A bit of reflection shows that the partition can be written

$$
\begin{bmatrix} \mathbf{g}_0 \\ \mathbf{g}_1 \\ \cdot \\ \cdot \\ \cdot \\ \mathbf{g}_{P-1} \end{bmatrix} = \begin{bmatrix} [H_0] & & & & \\ [H_1] & [H_0] & & & \\ \cdot & & & 0 & \\ \cdot & & & & \\ [H_{J-1}] & & \cdot & & \\ \cdot & & & \cdot & \\ 0 & & & & \cdot \\ & [H_{J-1}] & \cdots & [H_0] \end{bmatrix} \begin{bmatrix} \mathbf{f}_0 \\ \mathbf{f}_1 \\ \cdot \\ \cdot \\ \cdot \\ \mathbf{f}_{P-1} \end{bmatrix}
$$

$$
+ \begin{bmatrix} [H'_{J-1}] & \cdots & [H'_1] & [H''_0] & & \\ \cdot & & & & 0 & \\ \cdot & & & & & \\ & [H'_{J-1}] & [H''_{J-2}] & \cdots & [H''_0] & \\ \cdot & & & & & \cdot \\ 0 & & & \cdot & & \cdot \\ & & [H''_{J-1}] & \cdots & [H''_0] \end{bmatrix} \begin{bmatrix} \mathbf{f}'_{-J+1} \\ \cdot \\ \cdot \\ \cdot \\ \mathbf{f}'_{-1} \\ \mathbf{f}''_0 \\ \cdot \\ \cdot \\ \mathbf{f}''_{P-1} \end{bmatrix}
\tag{A.24}
$$

The symbolism is used to show the details of the partition structure. In Equation (A.22) the original partitions were identified with one prime. Thus, the rows $\mathbf{f}'_{-J+1} \dots \mathbf{f}'_{-1}$ are carried along with their associated PSF matrices. The partitions without primes have been grouped in the first term. Thus, in the first term, vector $\mathbf{g}$ is still length PQ, having P partitions of length Q, vector $\mathbf{f}$ of length PQ in (A.24), having P partitions of length Q. Thus the matrix in the first term is composed of P^2 partitions, each of size $Q \times Q$, and a typical partition $[H_j]$ has the form

$$
[H_j] =
\begin{bmatrix}
h(j,0) & & & & & \\
h(j,1) & h(j,0) & & & & 0 \\
\vdots & & \ddots & & & \\
\vdots & & & \ddots & & \\
h(j,K-1) & \cdots & & \cdots & h(j,0) & \\
\vdots & & \ddots & & & \ddots \\
0 & & \ddots & & & \ddots \\
& h(j,K-1) & \cdots & \cdots & & h(j,0)
\end{bmatrix}
\qquad (A.25)
$$

$$
(\text{for } j = 0, 1, 2, \ldots, J-1).
$$

Finally, in (A.24), the partition symbols carrying double primes are used to represent elements partitioned away from the single prime partitions in Equation (A.22) to form the partitions without primes in Equation (A.24). Thus, each matrix $[H_j'']$ is of size $Q \times (K-1)$ since $K-1$ elements are partitioned away from the $\mathbf{f}_j'$ partitions in (A.22). Likewise, the $\mathbf{f}_j''$ partitions in (A.24) are each of length $K-1$.

In vector-matrix form we have

$$
\mathbf{g}_s = [H_{BT}]\mathbf{f}_1 + [H_1]\mathbf{f}_2, \qquad (A.26)
$$

where $[H_{BT}]$ is a *block Toeplitz* matrix of size $PQ \times PQ$, $\mathbf{f}_1$ is a vector of length PQ, $\mathbf{f}_2$ is a vector of length $(J-1)(Q+K-1) + (K-1)P$ and $[H_1]$ is of size $PQ \times [(J-1)(Q+K-1) + (K-1)P]$.

The structure of $[H_{BT}]$ is of interest in that it is a matrix of partitions, arranged in Toeplitz fashion. In addition, each partition is a Toeplitz matrix. As with the one-dimensional case there is a matrix closely related to $[H_{BT}]$. Define the two-dimensional *block circulant* matrix to be

$$
[H_{BC}] =
\begin{bmatrix}
[H_0^c] & [H_{J-1}^c] & \cdot & \cdot & \cdot & [H_1^c] \\
[H_1^c] & [H_0^c] & [H_{J-1}^c] & \cdots & & [H_2^c] \\
\vdots & \ddots & & \ddots & & \vdots \\
[H_{J-1}^c] & & [H_0^c] & & 0 & \vdots \\
\vdots & & & \ddots & & \vdots \\
0 & \ddots & & & \ddots & \\
& [H_{J-1}^c] & \cdot & \cdot & \cdot & [H_0^c]
\end{bmatrix},
\qquad (A.27)
$$

where each partition in $[H_{BC}]$ is also a circulant; i.e.,

$$[H_j^c] = \begin{bmatrix} h(j,0) & h(j,K-1) & \cdot & \cdot & \cdot & h(j,1) \\ h(j,1) & h(j,0) & h(j,K-1) & \cdots & & h(j,2) \\ \cdot & \cdot & \cdot & & & \cdot \\ \cdot & \cdot & \cdot & & & \cdot \\ \cdot & \cdot & \cdot & & & \cdot \\ h(j,K-1) & \cdots & h(j,0) & & 0 & \cdot \\ \cdot & & \cdot & & & \\ 0 & & \cdot & & & \\ & & h(j,K-1) & \cdot & \cdot & \cdot & h(j,0) \end{bmatrix} \qquad \text{(A.28)}$$

As in the one-dimensional case, the block circulant is structurally close to the original block Toeplitz matrix, and the differences are only in the addition of elements in the rows to complete the cyclic shift structure.

The primary difference between the matrix $[H_{BC}]$ and $[H_{BT}]$ is that they differ only by elements added to produce a cyclic structure in the rows. The matrix size is $PQ \times PQ$ with the elements of the point-spread function embedded in both. It is possible for P and Q to become larger with J and K remaining fixed. Since J and K determine the number of elements added to the upper right corner of $[H_{BT}]$ to make a circulant [see Equations (A.27) and (A.28)], then increasing P and Q does not affect the number of terms added to the upper right but does increase the number of PSF elements around the main diagonal. As P and Q increase, the PSF elements must be placed on the main diagonal to carry out the convolution of the fixed-size point-spread function with the larger image. The number of upper right terms of $[H_{BC}]$ decreases in proportion to the main diagonal terms as P and Q increase. One imagines that in the limit the two matrices resemble each other. Using the Euclidean norm,

$$\|[A]\| = \left(\sum_{k=0}^{N-1} \sum_{j=0}^{N-1} [a_{jk}] \right)^{1/2}, \qquad \text{(A.29)}$$

then it is possible to show that

$$\lim_{P,Q \to \infty} \|[H_{BT}] - [H_{BC}]\| = 0, \qquad \text{(A.30)}$$

and the matrices $[H_{BT}]$ and $[H_{BC}]$ are said to be *asymptotically equivalent* in the sense of the *Euclidean norm* [Gray (1971)]. Asymptotic equivalence will be signified as

$$[H_{BT}] \sim [H_{BC}]. \qquad \text{(A.31)}$$

It can be shown that if

$$[H_{BT}] \sim [H_{BC}],$$

then it is also true that

$$[H_{BT}]^{-1} \sim [H_{BC}]^{-1}, \qquad \text{(A.32)}$$

provided both inverses exist. It may be possible to replace computations requiring $[H_{BT}]^{-1}$ with computation using $[H_{BC}]^{-1}$. Since limiting behavior is involved, then larger matrices will improve the approximation [Gray (1971)].

Substituting into (A.26) from (A.32),

$$[H_{BC}]^{-1}\mathbf{g}_s \cong \mathbf{f}_1 + [H_{BC}]^{-1}[H_1]\mathbf{f}_2, \tag{A.33}$$

which may be taken as an approximate restoration, corrupted by an additional term. From discussions of ill-conditioned behavior in Chapter 8 it should be expected that if $[H_{BC}]^{-1}$ exists, then the ill-condition properties could obscure $\mathbf{f}_1$. In reality only a portion of $\mathbf{f}_1$ is obscured. To see why, return to the one-dimensional case and examine Equation (A.9):

$$\mathbf{g}_s = [H_T]\mathbf{f}_1 + [H_1]\mathbf{f}_2. \tag{A.34}$$

Multiplying both sides by $[H_T]^{-1}$,

$$\mathbf{g}_s = \mathbf{f}_1 + [H_T]^{-1}[H_1]\mathbf{f}_2. \tag{A.35}$$

Now in (A.9) the vector $\mathbf{f}_2$ was of length $(M-1) \times 1$, and $[H_1]$ was of size $P \times (M-1)$. But as shown in (A.8), $[H_1]$ was all zero entries past row number $M-1$. Thus the product $[H_1]\mathbf{f}_2$ is a vector of length P with zeros for rows $M, M+1, \ldots,$ $P-1$. The second term of (A.35) is

$$[H_T]^{-1} = \left[\frac{\mathbf{f}_3}{\mathbf{0}}\right],$$

where $\mathbf{f}_3$ is the nonzero result of the product $[H_1]\mathbf{f}_2$. Since the matrix $[H_T]$ is a lower triangular matrix, then the inverse $[H_T]^{-1}$ is also lower triangular. Further, $[H_T]$ has a band structure, i.e., nonzero entries in a region of the diagonal, with zeros in the upper right, lower left regions. Although $[H_T]^{-1}$ is not a true band matrix, i.e., it has nonzero entries in the lower left corner, the magnitude of the lower left entries falls off rapidly; hence it is possible to approximate $[H_T]^{-1}$ by another band matrix. If $[H_T]^{-1}$ is a band matrix, and the width of the band is R points, then only the first $M + R - 2$ points of $\mathbf{f}_1$ are corrupted by the errors associated with cutting a segment from a larger set of data. The segment effects are then localized and do *not* extend over the whole solution. If the vector is such that $P \gg M$, then typically $P \gg (M + R - 2)$ also, and only a small number of data points are affected in deconvolving a segment.

Examination of Equations (A.24) and (A.26) shows that similar behavior holds in the two-dimensional case but is made more complicated by the two-dimensional partition structure. Again, only a border (shaded in Figure A.4) is affected by the restoration of a segment. If the original PSF matrix was size $J \times K$, and the inverse PSF is truncated to $R \times S$, then the border has dimensions $R + J - 2$ and $S + J - 2$. Again, assume $P \gg J$ and $Q \gg K$, so that $P \gg (R + J - 2)$ and $Q \gg (S + K - 2)$. Thus, only a relatively small number of border elements are affected in restoring the image.

Note again that the discussions use a PSF that is zero for indices less than zero and is *not* centered at the origin or coordinates. The use of an origin-centered PSF would not change the results but would introduce only effects associated with a phase shift; e.g., the shaded borders in Figure A.4 would appear on all sides. The convention above was used to simplify the analysis.

Appendix B

Circulants and
Fourier Computations

Let $[C]$ be a circulant:

$$[C] = \begin{bmatrix} c(0) & c(N-1) & c(N-2) & \cdots & c(1) \\ c(1) & c(0) & c(N-1) & \cdots & c(2) \\ \vdots & & & \cdot & \vdots \\ & & & & \cdot \\ c(N-1) & \cdot & \cdot & \cdot & c(0) \end{bmatrix}, \quad \text{(B.1)}$$

where $[C]$ is $N \times N$, formed by cyclic shifts of the sequence $c(0), c(1), \ldots, c(N-1)$. Let $w(k)$ be the N roots of unity; i.e.,

$$\left| \exp\left(\frac{2\pi i k}{N}\right) \right| = 1 \quad \text{(for } k = 0, 1, 2, \ldots, N-1\text{).} \quad \text{(B.2)}$$

Define the eigenvectors of $[C]$ to be $\lambda(k)$, and let

$$\lambda(k) = \sum_{j=0}^{N-1} c(-j) \exp\left(\frac{i2\pi}{N} kj\right)$$

$$= \sum_{j=0}^{N-1} c(j) \exp\left(-\frac{i2\pi}{N} kj\right) \quad \text{(for } k = 0, 1, 2, \ldots, N-1\text{).} \quad \text{(B.3)}$$

The properties of circulant matrices can be summarized [Hunt (1971)].

1. The complete collection of eigenvectors of a circulant are obtained from the unitary transform matrix $[\mathcal{F}]$ (discrete Fourier transform).
2. The eigenvalues of a circulant are computed by Equation (B.3), which is the discrete Fourier transform (DFT) of the cyclic sequence $c(j)$ that makes up the circulant $[C]$.

The application of the diagonal property to convolution problems such as described in Appendix A is straightforward. Recalling Equation (A.9),

$$\mathbf{g}_s = [H_T]\mathbf{f}_1 + [H_1]\mathbf{f}_2, \tag{A.9}$$

it was shown that this equation was sufficiently general to encompass (A.4) in which the second term is zero. Using (A.9) with the second term equal to zero,

$$\mathbf{g}_s = [H_T]\mathbf{f}_1; \tag{B.4}$$

then using the circulant approximation,

$$\mathbf{g}_s \cong [H_c]\mathbf{f}_1. \tag{B.5}$$

Represent the circulant $[H_c]$ in its diagonal form:

$$[H_c] = [\mathfrak{F}][\Lambda_h][\mathfrak{F}]^{-1}; \tag{B.6}$$

substituting into (B.5) yields

$$[\mathfrak{F}]^{-1}\mathbf{g}_s \cong [\Lambda_h][\mathfrak{F}]^{-1}\mathbf{f}_1. \tag{B.7}$$

The products $[\mathfrak{F}]^{-1}\mathbf{f}_1$ and $[\mathfrak{F}]^{-1}\mathbf{g}_s$ are equivalent to computing DFT's of the vectors $\mathbf{f}_1$ and $\mathbf{g}_s$. Denoting these transforms by subscripted letters,

$$\mathbf{g}_{s\mathfrak{F}} = [\Lambda_h]\mathbf{f}_{1\mathfrak{F}}. \tag{B.8}$$

The relevance of (B.8) is summarized as

1. The relation between $\mathbf{g}_s$ and $\mathbf{f}_1$ is *explicitly diagonal in the eigenspace of the point-spread function*. This property was seen for other transformations, such as the singular value decomposition in Chapter 8.
2. Computationally, the matrix operations in (B.4) are not required. Computing the DFT's of $\mathbf{f}_1$ and the PSF sequence, multiplication to obtain $\mathbf{g}_{\mathfrak{F}}$ and inverse is the basis of high-speed convolution by fast Fourier transform [Rader and Gold (1969)].
3. The circulant approximation of the original Toeplitz matrix makes the restoration computable by the fast transform algorithm since

$$\mathbf{f}_{1\mathfrak{F}} \cong [\Lambda_h]^{-1}\mathbf{g}_{s\mathfrak{F}}, \tag{B.9}$$

assuming $[\Lambda_h]^{-1}$ exists.

Completely analogous operations apply to the diagonalization of block-circulant matrices by the two-dimensional DFT. See Hunt (1973) for specific details.

References

ADAMS, J. AND E. BARRETT, private communications (1970).

ADLER, M. (1975), USCIPI Report No. 620, Department of Computer Science, University of Southern California, Los Angeles, California (September).

AHMED, N., T. NATARAYAN, AND K. R. ROO (1974), "Discrete Cosine Transform," *IEEE Transactions on Computers*, vol. C-23, no. 1, pp. 90–93.

AITCHISON, J. AND J. A. C. BROWN (1957), *The Lognormal Distribution*, Cambridge University Press, New York, New York.

ALBERT, A. (1972), *Regression and the Moore–Penrose Pseudoinverse*, Academic Press, New York, New York.

ANDREWS, H. C. (1970), *Computer Techniques in Image Processing*, Academic Press, New York, New York.

ANDREWS, H. C. (1972), "Digital Computers and Image Processing," *Endeavour*, vol. XXXI, no. 113, pp. 88–94 (May).

ANDREWS, H. C. (1972), "*N* Topics in Search of an Editorial: Heuristics, Superresolution and Bibliography," *IEEE Proc.*, vol. 60, no. 7, pp. 891–894 (July).

ANDREWS, H. C. (1974), "Digital Image Restoration: A Survey," *Computer*, vol. 7, no. 5, pp. 36–45 (May).

ANDREWS, H. C. (1974), "Digital Fourier Transforms as Means for Scanner Evaluation," *Applied Optics*, vol. 13, no. 1, pp. 146–149 (January).

ANDREWS, H. C. AND C. L. PATTERSON (1974), "Outer Product Expansions and their Uses in Digital Image Processing," *American Math Monthly*, vol. 82, no. 1, pp. 1–13 (January).

ANDREWS, H. C., A. G. TESCHER, AND R. P. KRUGER (1972), "Image Processing by Digital Computers," *IEEE Spectrum*, pp. 20–32 (July).

APOSTOL, T. M. (1958), *Mathematical Analysis*, Addison-Wesley, Reading, Massachusetts.

ARNOLD, B. A., B. E. BJARNGARD, AND J. C. KLOPPING (1973), "A Modified Pinhole Camera Method for Investigation of X-Ray Tube Focal Spots," *Phy. Med. Biol.*, vol. 18, no. 4, pp. 540–549.

BELLMAN, R. (1960), *Introduction to Matrix Analysis* (2nd ed., 1970), McGraw-Hill Book Co., New York, New York.

BIBERMAN, L. M. (ed.) (1973), *Perception of Displayed Information*, Plenum Press, New York, New York.

BIBERMAN, L. M. AND S. NUDELMAN (1971), *Photoelectronic Imaging Devices*, Plenum Press, New York, New York.

BOAS, P. AND R. KAC (1945), *Duke Math Journal*, vol. 13, p. 189.

BOGERT, B., M. HEALY, AND J. TUKEY (1963), "The Quefrency Alanysis of Time Series for Echoes," *Proc. Symp. on Time Series Analysis*, M. Rosenblatt (ed.), John Wiley & Sons, New York, New York, Chapter 15, pp. 209–243.

CAMPBELL, F. W. AND R. W. GUBISCH (1966), "Optical Quality of the Human Eye." *J. Physiol. London*, vol. 186, p. 558.

CANNON, T. M. (1974), "Digital Image Deblurring by Nonlinear Homomorphic Filtering," Ph.D. thesis, Computer Science Department, University of Utah, Salt Lake City, Utah.

CASASENT, D. P. (1975), "Optical Digital Radar Signal Processing," International Optical Computing Conference, Washington, D.C., April 23, 1975.

CHRESTENSON, H. E. (1955), "A Class of Generalized Walsh Functions," *Pacific J. Math.*, vol. 5, pp. 17–31.

COLAS–BAUDELAIRE, P., (1973), "Digital-Picture-Processing and Psychophysics, A Study of Brightness Perception," report UTEC-Csc-74-025, Computer Science, University of Utah, Salt Lake City, Utah (March).

COLE, E. R. (1973), "The Removal of Unknown Image Blurs by Homomorphic Filtering," Ph.D. thesis, Department of Electrical Engineering, University of Utah, Salt Lake City, Utah.

Computer (1974), special issue on "Digital Picture Processing," vol. 7, no. 6 (May).

COMTAL Corp. (1974), Proprietary Product Line Information, Pasadena, California.

DAVENPORT, W. B. AND W. L. ROOT (1958), *An Introduction to the Theory of Random Signals and Noise*, McGraw-Hill Book Co., New York, New York.

EKLUNDH, J. O. (1972), "A Fast Computer Method for Matrix Transposing," *IEEE Trans. Comp.*, vol. C-21, pp. 801–803 (July).

EKSTROM, M. P. (1971), "Numerical Restoration of Random Images," report UCRL-51129 LLL, Livermore, California.

EKSTROM, M. P. (1973), "A Numerical Algorithm for Identifying Spread Functions of Shift-Invariant Imaging Systems," *IEEE Trans. Comp.*, vol. C-22, no. 4, pp. 322–328.

EKSTROM, M. P. (1974), "Numerical Image Restoration by the Method of Singular-Value Decomposition," *Proc. Seventh Hawaii International Conference on Systems Science*, Honolulu, Hawaii, pp. 13–15 (January).

FALCONER, D. G. (1970), "Image Enhancement and Film-Grain Noise," *Optica Acta*, vol. 17, pp. 693–705.

FIACCO, A. V. AND G. P. MCCORMICK (1968), *Nonlinear Programming: Sequential Unconstrained Minimization Techniques*, John Wiley & Sons, New York, New York.

FRANKS, L. E. (1969), *Signal Theory*, Prentice-Hall, Englewood Cliffs, New Jersey.

FRIEDEN, B. R. (1971), "Restoring with Maximum Likelihood," technical report 67, University of Arizona, Tucson, Arizona (February).

FRIEDEN, B. R. (1972), "Restoring with Maximum Likelihood and Maximum Entropy," *JOSA*, vol. 62, no. 4, pp. 511–518 (April).

FUKUNAGA, K. (1972), *An Introduction to Statistical Pattern Recognition*, Academic Press, New York, New York.

GANTMACHER, F. R. (1959), *The Theory of Matrices*, vol. II, Chelsea Publishing Company, New York, New York.

GANTMACHER, F. R. AND M. G. KREIN (1937), "Sur les Matrices Oscillatoires et Completement Non-Negatives," *Compositive Math*, vol. 4, pp. 445–476.

GANTMACHER, F. R. AND M. G. KREIN (1950), *Oscillation Matrices and Kernels and Small Vibrations of Dynamical Systems*, 2nd ed., Moscow: Gostekhizdat.

GOLD, B. AND C. M. RADER (1969), *Digital Processing of Signals*, McGraw-Hill Book Co., New York, New York.

GOLUB, G. H. AND C. REINSCH (1970), "Singular Value Decomposition and Least Squares Solutions," *Numer. Math*, vol. 14, pp. 403–420.

GOODMAN, J. W. (1968), *Introduction to Fourier Optics*, McGraw-Hill Book Co., New York, New York.

GRAHAM, C. H. (ed.) (1965), *Vision and Visual Perception*, John Wiley & Sons, New York, New York.

GRAY, R. M. (1971), "Toeplitz and Circulant Matrices: A Review," report SU-SEL-71-032, Stanford University, California.

GRAYBILL, F. A. (1969), *Introduction to Matrices with Applications in Statistics*, Wadsworth Publishing Co., Belmont, California.

HABIBI, A. (1972), "Two-Dimension Bayesian Estimate of Images," *IEEE Proc.*, vol. 60, pp. 878–883.

HABIBI, A. (1975), "A Note on the Performance of Memoryless Quantizers," *Proceedings of NTC 175*, pp. 38–16 (December).

HABIBI, A. AND G. S. ROBINSON (1974), "A survey of digital picture coding," *IEEE Computer*, vol. 7, no. 5, pp. 22–34.

HABIBI, A. AND P. A. WINTZ (1971), "Image Coding by Linear Transformation and Block Quantization," *IEEE Trans. Communication Technology*, vol. COM-19, no. 1, pp. 50–63.

HALL, E. L. (1974), "Almost Uniform Distributions for Computer Image Enhancement," *IEEE Trans. Computers*, vol. C-23, no. 2, pp. 207–208 (February).

HALL, E. L., *et al.* (1971), "A Survey of Preprocessing and Feature Extraction for Radiographic Images," *IEEE Trans. Computers*, vol. C-20, no. 9, pp. 1032–1045 (September).

HARALICK, R. M. AND K. SHANMUGAM (1974), "Comparative Study of a Discrete Linear Basis for Image Data Compression," *IEEE Trans. Systems, Man, and Cybernetics*, vol. SMC-4, no. 1, pp. 16–28.

HARMAN, W. W. (1963), *Principles of the Statistical Theory of Communications*, McGraw-Hill Book Co., New York, New York.

HARMUTH, H. F. (1972), *Transmission of Information by Orthogonal Functions* (2nd ed.), Springer–Verlag, New York, New York.

HELLSTROM, C. W. (1967), "Image Restoration by the Method of Least Squares," *J. Opt. Soc. Amer.*, vol. 57, pp. 297–303.

HERSHEL, R. S. (1971), "Unified Approach to Restoring Degraded Images in the Presence of Noise," technical report 71, Optical Sciences Center, University of Arizona, Tucson, Arizona (December).

HOU, H. S. (1976), Ph.D. dissertation, Department of Electrical Engineering, University of Southern California, Los Angeles, California.

HUANG, T. S. (1966), "Some Notes on Film-Grain-Noise," Appendix 14, *Restoration of Atmospherically Degraded Images*, NSF Summer Study Report, Woods Hole, Massachusetts, pp. 105–109.

HUANG, T. S. (ed.) (1972), *Picture Bandwidth Compression*, Gordon & Breach, New York, New York.

HUANG, T. S., W. F. SCHRIEBER, AND O. J. TRETIAK (1971), "Image Processing," *Proc. IEEE*, vol. 59, no. 11, pp. 1586–1609.

HUNT, B. R. (1971), "Block-Mode Digital Filtering of Pictures," *Math. Biosci.*, vol. 11, pp. 343–354.

HUNT, B. R. (1971), "A Matrix Theory Proof of the Discrete Convolution Theorem" *IEEE Trans.*, vol. AU-19, pp. 285–288.

HUNT, B. R. (1972), "A Theorem on the Difficulty of Numerical Deconvolution," *IEEE Trans.*, vol. AU-20, pp. 94–95.

HUNT, B. R. (1972), "Data Structures and Computational Organization in Digital Image Enhancement," *Proc. IEEE*, vol. 60, pp. 884–887.

HUNT, B. R. (1973), "The Application of Constrained Least Squares Estimation to Image Restoration by Digital Computer," *IEEE Trans. Computers*, vol. C-22, no. 9, pp. 805–812 (September).

HUNT, B. R. (1975), "Digital Image Processing," *IEEE Proc.*, vol. 63, pp. 693–708 (April).

HUNT, B. R. AND J. BREEDLOVE (1975), "Scan and Display Consideration in Processing Images by Digital Computer," *IEEE Trans. Computers,* vol. C-24, pp. 848–853 (August).

HUNT, B. R. AND H. B. DEMUTH (1974), "ORNL Fuel Element Analysis," Group C-8 report, Los Alamos Scientific Laboratory, Los Alamos, New Mexico.

HUNT, B. R., D. H. JANNEY, AND R. K. ZEIGLER (1970), "Introduction to Restoration and Enhancement of Radiographic Images," report no. LA 4305, Los Alamos Scientific Lab, Los Alamos, New Mexico.

HUNT, B..R. AND H. J. TRUSSELL (1973), "Recent Data on Image Enhancement Programs," *Proc. IEEE*, vol. 61, p. 466.

IEEE Proceedings (1972), special issue on "Digital Picture Processing," vol. 60, no. 7 (July).

Information International, Inc. (1974), Proprietary Product Line Information on the FR-80 Microfilm Graphics System, Los Angeles, California.

JAIN, A. (1973), "Geodesics in Schrodinger's Color Theory," *JOSA*, vol. 63, no. 8, p. 934 (August).

JENKINS, G. M. AND D. G. WATTS (1968), *Spectral Analysis and its Applications*, Holden-Day, San Francisco, California.

JOHNSON, N. L. AND S. KOTZ (1972), *Distributions in Statistics: Continuous Multivariate Distributions*, John Wiley & Sons, New York, New York.

JOHNSON, N. L. AND F. C. LEONE (1964), *Statistics and Experimental Design*, John Wiley & Sons, New York, New York.

KANAL, L. N. (1974), "Patterns in Pattern Recognition, 1968–1974," *IEEE Trans. Info. Theory*, vol. IT-20, no. 6, pp. 697–722.

KRUGER, R. P., W. B. THOMPSON, AND A. F. TURNER (1974), "Computer Diagnosis of Pneumoconiosis," *IEEE Trans. Systems, Man, and Cybernetics*, vol. SMC-4, no. 1, pp. 40–49 (January).

KRUSOS, G. A. (1974), "Restoration of Radiologic Images by Optical Spatial Filtering," *Optical Engineering*, vol. 13, no. 3, pp. 208–218.

KUNZI, H. P., W. KRELLA, AND W. OETTLI (1966), *Nonlinear Programming*, Blaisdell, Waltham, Massachusetts.

LANCASTER, P. (1969), *Theory of Matrices*, Academic Press, New York, New York.

LANDAN, H. J. AND H. O. POLLAK (1961), "Prolate Spheroidal Wave Functions, Fourier Analysis and Uncertainty—II," *BSTJ*, vol. 40, pp. 65–84 (January).

LARSON, R. V. (1971), "Polypagos User's Manual," Aerospace report no. TR-0172 (2311)-1, The Aerospace Corporation, El Segundo, California (October).

LEGRAND, Y. (1968), *Light, Color, and Vision*, Barnes and Noble, New York, New York.

LEPAGE, W. R. (1961), *Complex Variables and the Laplace Transform for Engineers*, McGraw-Hill Book Co., New York, New York.

LEVINE, L. (1964), *Methods for Solving Engineering Problems Using Analog Computers*, McGraw-Hill Book Co., New York, New York.

LINDGREN, B. W. (1960), *Statistical Theory*, McMillan Company, New York, New York.

LUKOSZ, W. (1962), "Transfer of Nonnegative Signals through Linear Filters," *Optical Acta*, vol. 9, pp. 335–364.

MACADAM, D. P. (1970), "Digital Image Restoration by Constrained Deconvolution," *JOSA*, vol. 60, pp. 1617–1627.

MANDEL, L. (1959), "Fluctuations of Photon Beams, the Distribution of the Photoelectrons," *Proc. Phys. Soc. of London*, vol. 74, pp. 233–243.

MAX, J. (1960), "Quantizing for Minimum Distortion," *IRE Trans. on Information Theory*, vol. IT-6, pp. 7–12.

McCORMICK, E. J. (1964), *Human Factors Engineering*, McGraw-Hill Book Co., New York, New York.

McGLAMERY, B. L. (1967), "Restoration of Turbulence Degraded Images," *JOSA*, vol. 57, no. 3, pp. 293–297 (March).

MEES, C. E. K. (1954), *The Theory of the Photographic Process*, McMillan Company, New York, New York.

MERSERAU, R. AND D. DUDGEON (1975), "Two-Dimensional Digital Filter," Proc. IEEE, vol. 63, pp. 610–623 (April).

MOORE, E. H. (1920), "On the Reciprocal of the General Algebraic Matrix (abstract)," *Bull. Amer. Math. Soc.*, vol. 26, pp. 394–395.

NAHI, N. E. (1965), *Estimation Theory and Applications*, John Wiley & Sons, New York, New York.

NAHI, N. E. (1972), "Role of Recursive Estimation in Statistical Image Enhancement," *IEEE Proc.*, vol. 60, pp. 872–877.

NAHI, N. E. (1973), "Nonlinear Adaptive Recursive Image Enhancement," USCEE report 459, University of Southern California, Los Angeles, California, p. 70 (September).

O'HANDLEY, D. A. AND W. B. GREEN (1972), "Recent Developments in Digital Image Processing at the Image Laboratory at the Jet Propulsion Laboratory," *IEEE Proc.*, vol. 60, no. 7, pp. 821–828 (July).

OPPENHEIM, A. V., R. W. SCHAFER, AND T. G. STOCKHAM, JR. (1968), "Nonlinear Filtering of Multiplied and Convolved Signals," *Proc. IEEE*, vol. 56, pp. 1264–1291 (August).

PANTER, P. F. AND W. DITE (1951), "Quantization Distortion in Pulse Count Modulation with Nonuniform Spacing of Levels," *Proc. IRE*, vol. 39, no. 1, pp. 44–48.

PAPOULIS, A. (1965), *Probability, Random Variables, and Stochastic Processes*, McGraw-Hill Book Co., New York, New York.

PEARL, J., H. C. ANDREWS, AND W. K. PRATT (1972), "Performance Measures for Transform Data Coding," *IEEE Trans. Comm. Tech.*, vol. COM-20, no. 3, pp. 411–415 (June).

PENROSE, R. (1955), "A Generalized Inverse for Matrices," *Proc. Cambridge Philos. Soc.*, vol. 51, pp. 406–413.

PENROSE, R. (1956), "On Best Approximate Solutions of Linear Matrix Equations," *Proc. Cambridge Philos. Soc.*, vol. 52, pp. 17–19.

PHILLIPS, D. L. (1962), "A Technique for the Numerical Solution of Certain Integral Equations of the First Kind," *JACM*, vol. 9, pp. 97–101.

POLYAK, S. (1957), *The Vertebrate Visual System*, University of Chicago Press, Chicago, Illinois.

PRATT, W. K. (1971), "Spatial Transform Coding of Color Images," *IEEE Trans. on Comm. Tech.*, vol. COM-19, no. 6, pp. 980–992.

PRATT, W. K., W. H. CHEN, AND L. R. WELCH (1974), "Slant Transform Image Coding," *IEEE Trans. Communications*, vol. COM-22, no. 8, pp. 1075–1093 (August).

PRATT, W. K., J. KANE, AND H. C. ANDREWS (1969), "Hadamard Transform Image Coding," *Proc. IEEE.*, vol. 57, no. 1, pp. 58–68 (January).

RALSTON, A. (1965), *A First Course in Numerical Analysis*, McGraw-Hill Book Co., New York, New York.

RAO, C. R. AND S. K. MITRA (1971), *Generalized Inverse of Matrices and Its Applications*, John Wiley & Sons, New York, New York.

RAY, W. D. AND E. M. DRIVER (1970), "Further Decomposition of the Karhunen–Loeve Series Representation of a Stationary Random Process," *IEEE Trans. Infor. Theory*, vol. IT-16, no. 6, pp. 663–668.

RINO, C. L. (1970), "The Inversion of Covariance Matrices by Finite Fourier Transforms," *IEEE Trans. Infor. Theory*, vol. IT-16, pp. 230–232.

ROBBINS, G. M. (1970), "Image Restoration for a Class of Linear Spatially-Variant Degradations," *Pattern Recognition*, vol. 2, no. 2, pp. 91–105.

ROBBINS, G. M. AND T. S. HUANG (1972), "Inverse Filtering for Linear Shift-Variant Imaging Systems," *Proc. IEEE.*, vol. 60, no. 7, pp. 862–872 (July).

ROSEN, J. B. (1960), "The Gradient Projection Method," *J. SIAM*, vol. 8, pp. 181–217.

ROSENFELD, A. (1969), *Picture Processing by Computer*, Academic Press, New York, New York.

SAATY, T. L. AND J. BRAM (1964), *Nonlinear Mathematics*, McGraw-Hill Book Co., New York, New York.

SAKRISON, D. J. AND V. R. ALGAZI (1971), "Comparison of Line-by-Line and Two-Dimensional Encoding of Random Images," *IEEE Trans. Infor. Theory*, vol. IT-17, no. 4, pp. 386–398 (July).

SAWCHUK, A. A. (1972), "Space-Variant Image Motion Degradations and Restoration," *Proc. IEEE*, vol. 60, no. 7, pp. 854–861 (July).

SAWCHUK, A. A. (1973), "Space-Variant System Analysis of Image Motion," *JOSA*, vol. 63, no. 9, pp. 1052–1063 (September).

SAWCHUK, A. A. (1974), "Space-Variant Image Restoration by Coordinate Transformation," *JOSA*, vol. 64, no. 2, pp. 138–144 (February).

SCHOENBERG, I. J. (1965), "On Monospline of Least Square Derivation and Best Quadrature Formulae," *J. SIAM Numer. Anal.*, Ser. B, vol. 2, pp. 144–170.

SHEPPARD, J. J., JR. (1969), "Pseudocolor as a Means of Image Enhancement," *Am. J. Optom., Arch. Am. Acad. Optom.*, vol. 46, pp. 735–754.

SLEPIAN, D. AND H. O. POLLAK (1961), "Prolate Spheroidal Wave Functions, Fourier Analysis and Uncertainty—I," *BSTJ*, vol. 40, pp. 43–62 (January).

SONDHI, M. M. (1972), "Image Restoration: The Removal of Spatially Invariant Degradations," *IEEE Proc.*, vol. 60, no. 7, pp. 842–852 (July).

STOCKHAM, T. G., JR. (1972), "Image Processing in the Context of a Visual Model," *IEEE. Proc.*, vol. 60, pp. 828–841.

STOCKHAM, T. G., JR. (1973), private communications.

STOCKHAM, T., R. INGEBRETSEN, AND T. M. CANNON (1975), "Blind Deconvolution by Digital Signal Processing," *IEEE Proc.*, vol. 63, pp. 679–692 (April).

TATIAN, B. (1965), "Method for Obtaining the Transfer Function from the Edge Response Function," *JOSA*, vol. 55, pp. 1014–1019 (August).

TESCHER, A. G. AND H. C. ANDREWS (1972), "Data Compression and Enhancement of Sampled Images," *Applied Optics*, vol. 11, no. 4, pp. 919–925 (April).

THOMAS, J. B. (1969), *An Introduction to Statistical Communication Theory*, John Wiley & Sons, New York, New York.

THOMPSON, W. S. (1975), "The Role of Texture in Computerized Scene Analysis," Ph.D. dissertation, University of Southern California, Los Angeles, California.

TOMNOVEC, F. M. AND R. L. MATHER (1957), "Experimental Gamma-Ray Collimator Sensitivity Patterns," *J. Appl. Phys.*, vol. 28, pp. 1208–1211 (October).

TUKEY, J. W. (1971), *Exploratory Data Analysis*, vol. 3, Addison-Wesley (limited preliminary edition), Reading, Massachusetts.

TWOGOOD, R. E. AND M. P. EKSTROM (1976), "An Extension of Eklundh's Matrix Transposition Algorithm and Its Application in Digital Image Processing" (to be published), *IEEE Trans. Comp.*

VAN BLADEL, J. (1964), *Electromagnetic Fields*, McGraw-Hill Book Co., New York, New York.

VAN NESS, F. L., M. A. BOUMAN (1967), "Spatial Modulation Transfer in the Human Eye," *J. Opt. Soc. Am.*, vol. 57, p. 401.

VAN TREES, H. L. (1967), *Detection, Estimation, and Modulation Theory*, Vol. I, John Wiley & Sons, New York, New York.

VOLTERRA, V. (1959), *Theory of Functions and of Integral and Intego-Differential Equations*, Dover Press, New York, New York.

WALKUP, J. F. AND R. F. CHOENS (1974), "Image Processing in Signal-Dependent Noise," *Optical Engineering*, vol. 13, pp. 258–266.

WALLIS, R. (1975), Ph.D. dissertation, Department of Electrical Engineering, University of Southern California, Los Angeles, California.

WEBSTER, M. (1968), *Webster's New Collegiate Dictionary*, G&C Merriam Company, Springfield, Massachusetts.

WECKSUNG, G. W. AND K. CAMPBELL (1974), "Digital Image Processing at EG & G," *Computer*, vol. 7, no. 5, pp. 63–71 (May).

WIENER, N. (1942), *Extrapolation, Interpolation, and Smoothing of Stationary Time Series*, MIT Press, Cambridge, Massachusetts.

WILLIAMS, C. S. AND O. A. BECKLUND (1972), *Optics: A Short Course for Scientists and Engineers*, John Wiley & Sons—Interscience, New York, New York.

WINTZ, P. A. (1972), "Transform Picture Coding," *Proc. IEEE*, vol. 60, no. 7, pp. 809–820.

Author Index

Subject Index